Beatrice

BY *Lynn McDonald*

HARRIET MARTINEAU

Marie-Jeanne Roland

Catharine Macaul

JANE ADDAMS

Germaine
de Staël

Mary Astell

The WOMEN
FOUNDERS
of the SOCIAL
SCIENCES

Florence

Harriet Taylor Mill

Nightingale

FLORA TRISTAN

Marie le Jars de Gournay

MARY WOLLSTONECRA

There are no incoherent facts

There is an order in the march of Nature

Moral faculties shew general Laws: & immoral ones the
Same -

In crimes, as we have seen, the numbers are reproduced
with amazing regularity.

Even murders, which seem the result of 'vows' without
motive: are yet uniform & regular, year by year:
even as to the instruments employed.

The "Prison's Budget" is paid with more regularity
than the Treasury's.

We can number beforehand how many poisonings,
how many forgeries, just as we number beforehand

Births & Deaths

In this sense, 'Society prepares: the Criminal only
executes' Crime.

In every Social state, that is. Certain crimes result
from its organization.

This is no discouragement: but the reverse -
Men can be improved by improving their Institutions.
& all that influences their being -

Same causes: Same effects.   Alter the causes.

Man can govern by Laws Moral, as he does by Laws
Physical.

For mankind can discover the Laws & govern by
their means.

Facsimile page from Florence Nightingale's commentary on Quetelet
Nightingale Papers: Add. Mss. 45842:f187. By permission of The British Library

Beatrice Web

BY *Lynn McDonald*

HARRIET MARTINEAU

Catharine Macaul

arie-Jeanne Roland

for Diane

JANE ADDAMS

Germaine
de Staël

from

The
WOMEN

FOUNDERS

Mary Astell

of the
SOCIAL

SCIENCES

Florence

Harriet Taylor Mill

Nightingale

Lynn
June, 1994

FLORA TRISTAN

Marie le Jars de Gournay

MARY WOLLSTONECRA

CARLETON UNIVERSITY PRESS
Ottawa, Canada
1994

Canadian Cataloguing in Publication Data

McDonald, Lynn, 1940-
  Women founders of the social sciences

(Carleton women's experience series)
Includes bibliographical references and index.
ISBN 0-88629-218-2 (bound).–
ISBN 0-88629-219-0 (pbk.)

1. Women social scientists–History. 2. Social sciences–History.
3. Social sciences–Methodology–History. I. Title. II. Series.

H57.M33 1994   300'.92'2   C93-090451-6

Carleton University Press   Distributed in Canada by:
160 Paterson Hall, 1125 Colonel By Dr. Oxford University Press Canada
Ottawa K1S 5B6 Canada   70 Wynford Dr., Don Mills, ON M3C IJ9
(613)788-3740   (416)441-2941

Cover Design: Victory Design, Ottawa
Back cover photo of author by Robert Stanley Adams
Interior: Xpressive Designs, Ottawa. Typeset using: Century Oldstyle,
                                    Gill Sans & Nuptial Script

Acknowledgements

Carleton University Press gratefully acknowledges the support extended to its publishing programme by the Canada Council and the Ontario Arts Council.

The Press would also like to thank the Department of Communications, Government of Canada, and the Government of Ontario through the Ministry of Culture, Tourism and Recreation, for their assistance.

This book has been published with the help of a grant from the Social Science Federation of Canada, using funds provided by the Social Sciences and Humanities Research Council of Canada.

Every effort has been made by the publisher to contact owners of the copyright materials reproduced in this volume. The publisher would welcome information to rectify any omission.

Dedicated to
Madeleine Parent

Table of Contents

Illustrations

Preface

Women's contributions are so commonly undervalued that, when I began to research the early origins of the social sciences, I felt sure there must be many more women of notable achievement than were acknowledged in the usual histories of the subject. I set out to look for them, and succeeded well beyond my, in retrospect, all too modest expectations. I included the major women contributors in the *Early Origins of the Social Sciences*, published by McGill-Queen's University Press earlier this year. Much more space was needed to do the women justice, and to include a number of very interesting, if less significant, contributors as well. Hence this book.

Paradoxically, at the same time as my work of recovery was going on, the very enterprise of empirical social science in which these women were engaged was under attack — in the name of feminism no less. It seemed that these women founders might be recovered only to be rejected, in principle, for their choice of empiricism as a model, for their belief in the Enlightenment ideal of knowledge for application. For me, a long-time feminist and activist — with much experience in using sociological skills and methods in research for many causes — this rankled.

I have come to understand the attack on empiricism as a reaction to much bad work, some, but not all, the product of male bias. The risk now was the proverbial one of throwing out the baby with the bath water. I am convinced that much of the "feminist critique" of methodology is based on a false premise: that the social sciences have been developed by and for men. That the standard texts and university and college courses on the subject deal almost exclusively with male theorists and examples fosters this erroneous impression. Even the more substantial two-volume histories have not managed to find space for women contributors.

Whatever their bad press now, the social sciences have an honourable history as the methodology of the underdog, the choice of radicals, reformers, and even revolutionaries, the methodology through which everyone, regardless of rank or gender, can fight back against established authority, conventional wisdom, and oppressive customs. I believe that when women discover the considerable contribution their older sisters have made, over several centuries, they will be more likely to see the social sciences as useful means to advance their own causes.

The exercise of recovery was not easy, for there was so much to unlearn. It often took me a long time simply to believe what I was reading, to give full value to the original observations, insights, theories, propositions, and practical research examples provided by these women. I would frequently tell myself that what the woman had said reminded me of work by some other, prominent, male theorist, only to realize that her work predated his by years, even decades.

Thus I gradually recognized Harriet Martineau, Florence Nightingale, and Beatrice Webb as major founders of the social sciences. The Enlightenment for women did indeed begin in the eighteenth century, with contributions as early as Emilie du Châtelet, and on through Mme de Staël in France. Mary Wortley Montagu, Catharine Macaulay, and Mary Wollstonecraft in Britain were all significant contributors. There were women political theorists from the seventeenth century on, quite contrary to the complaints of today's women political scientists that there are no women classical theorists to teach.

Many people assisted in the research process with encouragment, provocative questions, and helpful tips on sources. Several departments of sociology invited me to give colloquia, and gave useful feedback in the ensuing discussions. I especially thank faculty members and graduate students at Simon Fraser University, McGill University, the University of Toronto, University of Waterloo, Brock University, and the graduate seminar at my own University of Guelph.

Deborah Gorham gave excellent advice early on, both on substance and organization. A number of people gave help and advice, notably Diane Marshall, Paul Marshall, Jean McKenzie Leiper, Bruce Curtis, Alex Mann, and Ron Lambert. I owe a special debt of thanks to Thelma McCormack, now retired from the Department of Sociology at York University and the York Centre for Feminist Research. She not only read and commented on several drafts of the work, but gave enormously valuable advice at various stages from the initial conceptualization on. I had the benefit, as I did for the *Early Origins*, of the excellent copy editing services of Frances Rooney. Jennie Strickland of Carleton University Press handled the manuscript with exemplary good sense and judgment. Obviously the faults in the final product are my own responsibility, not any of the above.

The *Women Founders* is dedicated to a woman activist who exemplifies the best tradition described in this book. Madeleine Parent is well known for her years of work as a union organizer, beginning in Duplessis' Quebec, and as a feminist, notably with the National Action Committee on the Status of Women. Less known is the fact of her own university background in sociology, which she has so ably used in briefs, memoranda, and speeches on issues of social justice as diverse as equal pay for work of equal value, aboriginal women, human rights, peace, disarmament, and the environment.

Lynn McDonald
University of Guelph, Ontario
Canada, 1993

Author's Note

To facilitate the referencing of large numbers of works I have adopted a hybrid system. The author's name and the title are given in full for the first reference, either in the text or a foot-note. Subsequent page references to the same work are given in parentheses in the text, without an *ibid*. Abbreviated titles are normally used for references after the full title has been given.

When, in a paragraph, there are several citations from the same page the reference is placed at the last one. (This avoids the frequent use of *loc. cit.*)

In the bibliography, recommended references at the end of the biographies, and in footnotes giving secondary sources, the works are listed in order of their importance/relevance to the topic.

Every effort has been made to give original dates of publication in the text or the biography. The original date of publication is shown also in square brackets in the bibliography. To make it easier for contemporary readers to find early works I use or otherwise refer to reprints and the more available later editions.

Chapter 1

THE WOMEN FOUNDERS
OF THE
SOCIAL SCIENCES

omen have played a major role in the development of the social sciences, from the formulation of their most basic methodological assumptions, techniques, and key theoretical concepts to the pioneering use of the methodology in actual research. Women as well have been prominent in the defence of all of the above from attack. Women's contributions have been greater in number, more important in quality, and considerably more distinctive than is commonly realized. Traditional textbooks on the history of the social sciences or on the "founding fathers" of sociology typically include only male contributors, at best acknowledging a peripheral role for women. Courses on "classical social theory" continue to treat only the contributions of men, in some cases acknowledging the recent arrival of women's studies. Feminist political theorists complain that they must confine their teaching to the works of "dead men," in effect declaring that there are no women theorists to teach. Students in the social sciences must be forgiven if they conclude that women have been absent from the development of their discipline until the recent emergence of the women's movement.

No less important, the prominent participation of some of these early women in the struggle for women's rights is also little known. Yet the movement for equality rights and for empirical methodology was closely linked for several centuries. Women, and some men, found in the new methodology of empiricism a useful instrument for the cause. The environment was not a subject of concern in this early period, yet it is another little known fact that some of the founders of social science methodology were pioneers also in a more respectful understanding of the environment and espousal of environmental ethics.

The substantial, distinctive role women have played in all these developments is the subject matter of this book. The importance of women's contributions was a major discovery of the research I did for *The Early Origins of the Social Sciences* (1994). That book gives the women founders their rightful place, to my knowledge for the first time in a treatment of the origins and development of the social sciences. These women are still, however, a minority among many other, male, contributors. Here the object is to focus on the women, to give detailed analysis of their work, provide biographical background and historical context, and show the links, including active collaboration, among them. How these women contributors used the methodology of the social sciences for their various causes is also described. The influence of their perspective as women on their approach to social, political, and environmental theory is shown as well.

Contrary to the feminist critique of the social sciences, that empiricism necessarily supports the powers-that-be, advocates of women's equality for three hundred years used empiricism to expose bias and prejudice and argue for equality. At the beginning of the seventeenth century Marie de Gournay, as well as editing Montaigne's *Essays*, wrote some of the earliest arguments for women's equality. In the late seventeenth century Mary Astell was both a Lockean empiricist and the author of a powerful denunciation of injustice to women. *A Serious Proposal to the Ladies* argues for both and shows their connection. In eighteenth-century Britain, Mary Wortley Montagu, Catharine Macaulay, and Mary Hays similarly were advocates for both their sex and empiricist methodology. Mary Wollstonecraft is now acknowledged as a feminist, but her commitment to empiricism has been ignored. In France the next generation of supporters of empiricism were advocates of political liberty generally, not only for their sex. Still, Marie-Jeanne Roland and Germaine de Staël deserve their place as early social scientists and political theorists.

Among the nineteenth century theorists Harriet Martineau is known as the translator of Comte more than for her own methodology. She has been rediscovered for her work on women's issues while she is still largely ignored as a founder of the discipline of sociology. Similarly Harriet Taylor Mill is increasingly recognized for her analysis of women's situation but not yet for her methodological contribution. Flora Tristan, apart from being a radical feminist and union organizer, was a careful observer and reporter of social data. Frances Wright was no less radical in her politics, as well as being an advocate for empiricism and an observer of American society. Florence Nightingale remains "the lady with the lamp," her work as a "passionate statistician" goes undiscussed. Beatrice Webb is sometimes listed with her husband among the founders of sociology, although she was the methodologist of the two and deserves treatment in her own name. While Jane Addams's role as a peace activist and originator of the settlement house movement has been recognized, her pioneering work in quantitative methods has been largely forgotten. How the early origins of women's studies relates to these developments will be shown, especially with the work of Charlotte Perkins Gilman and Matilda Joslyn Gage.

The Women Founders of the Social Sciences is an attempt to do justice to all these women. Their contribution to the methodology of the social sciences, and to the evolution of social and political theory, will be recounted. Their political commitments, especially to the women's movement — at whatever stage it then was — will be related. Some attention will be paid also to men advocates of women's equality for purposes of comparison. Thus we will consider Condorcet with de Staël in France, Francis Hutcheson and John Millar with the eighteenth-century British women, and John Stuart Mill with Harriet Taylor Mill, Harriet Martineau, and Florence Nightingale. Along with the major women contributors we will look also at a larger group of women who played ancillary roles as translators and editors, promoters of ideas, revisers of drafts, salon hostesses, and correspondents with leading writers. Marie de Gournay was Montaigne's editor, Sophie de Grouchy the translator of Adam Smith and editor of her late husband, Condorcet's, work. The princess who corresponded with Descartes deserves some note, but I do not include the queens, Christina of Sweden and Catherine of Russia, who merely *commissioned* research. Mary Booth aroused her husband's interest in poverty and assisted him in the years of research on *Life and Labour of the People in London*, to which her contributions ranged from providing ideas and organization to editing every page of the final work. Marianne Weber wrote the first biography of her husband, Max Weber, edited the first volume of his *Economy and Society*, and herself wrote on women's history and participation in science.

The Women Founders of the Social Sciences will set out the contributions these women made to methodology, including underlying assumptions, notions of probability and hypothesis, and specific methods of data collection and analysis. As well it will show where women contributed to the evolution of key concepts used in the social sciences, notably on such fundamentals as individual liberty, social cohesion, stratification, law, and morality. That women have contributed to political theory since the seventeenth century will be documented with examples. *The Women Founders* will describe pioneering examples of the use of empirical methods in social reform, especially on issues of access to education, political rights, and health promotion. This book is not a history of women's studies, but it will highlight some early contributions to that field as well as relate its emergence in the late nineteenth century.

The Feminist Attack on Empiricism

These numerous, distinctive contributions by women fly in the face of the contemporary "feminist" critique of the social sciences. Let us now examine that critique, both its healthy and well-founded elements, and the extreme case it makes: that the methodology of the social sciences is so fundamentally flawed that it must be repudiated as "malestream methodology." This critique can be seen as part of the re-examination of all social institutions prompted by the re-emergence of the women's movement in the 1960s.

Modern feminists have subjected universities, professional and research organizations, actual research methods, terms, and the very assumptions of long-accepted methodology to well-deserved scrutiny. They have exposed and denounced sexist bias in virtually every academic discipline. Common practices such as the use of male-only samples with results generalized to all humanity were documented. Bias in the phrasing of survey questions was demonstrated. The assigning of higher value to male traits compared to female was shown.[1] The sheer absence of women in history was not only decried but new books appeared on women in classical Greece, the Middle Ages, and on

---

[1] For wide-ranging critiques in the social sciences see Pamela Abbott and Claire Wallace, *An Introduction to Sociology: Feminist Perspectives*; Sandra Harding, *Feminism and Methodology*; Sandra Harding and Merrill B. Hintikka, *Discovering Reality*; Jessie Bernard, *The Female World*; Winnifred Tomm and Gordon Hamilton, *Gender Bias in Scholarship*; R.A. Sydie, *Natural Women, Cultured Men*; Jill McCalla Vickers, *Taking Sex Into Account*; Angela R. Miles and Geraldine Finn, *Feminism in Canada* and *Feminism from Pressure to Politics*; Carole Pateman and Elizabeth Gross, *Feminist Challenges*; Eloise C. Snyder, *The Study of Women*; Michele A. Paludi and Gertrude A. Steuernagel, *Foundations for a Feminist Restructuring of the Academic Disciplines*; Elizabeth Langland and Walter Gove, *A Feminist Perspective in the Academy*; Helen Roberts, *Doing Feminist Research*; Janet Siltanen and Michelle Stanworth, *Women and the Public Sphere*; Liz Stanley, *Feminist Praxis*; Julia A. Sherman and Evelyn Torton Beck, *Prism of Sex*; Ann Garry and Marilyn Pearssall, *Women, Knowledge, and Reality*; Arlene Tigar McLaren, *Gender and Society*; Kate Campbell, *Critical Feminism*; Mary Margaret Fonow and Judith A Cook, *Beyond Methodology*; Center For Twentieth Century Studies, *Feminist Studies/Critical Studies*.

through revolutions, war, and periods of reform and liberation. Economists with varying commitments to Marxism and classical economic thought described how women's work was defined out of economics. Similar critiques and similar efforts at redress went on in philosophy,[2] literature, theology, and the fine arts. Women natural scientists examined the biases of their own disciplines,[3] and historians of science worked to recover lost or undervalued earlier scientists.[4]

All these disciplines badly needed both criticism and new work. The social sciences and other subjects will be better for both. Yet along with all this overdue analysis also came a repudiation of basic elements of empirical social science. Empiricism was said in and of itself to promote patriarchy. The use of empirical methods in research was said to be destructive of women's values, necessarily resulting in exploitation and control of the subject. Feminists joined many radical men in criticizing empirical methods as inherently supportive of the status quo. Sometimes the villain was quantification, sometimes value neutrality, and sometimes any attempt at objectivity.

Bowles and Klein in their introduction to *Theories of Women's Studies* explained:

> Many feminist social scientists are actively hostile toward quantitative research because they believe that human behavior cannot be measured and that those who measure wish also to control.[5]

Maria Mies, in an article in the same collection, affirmed that "the quantitative survey method is itself not free from androcentric bias."[6] She

---

[2] Andrea Nye, *Feminist Theory and the Philosophies of Man*; Jean Grimshaw, *Philosophy and Feminist Thinking*; Genevieve Lloyd, *The Man of Reason*; Martha Lee Osborne, *Woman in Western Thought*; Carol Gilligan, *In a Different Voice*; Lorraine Code, *Feminist Perspectives*; Jane Duran, *Toward a Feminist Epistemology*; Prudence Allen, *The Concept of Woman*; Diana H. Coole, *Women in Political Theory*; Nancy J. Holland, *Is Women's Philosophy Possible?*; Ellen Kennedy and Susan Mendus, *Women in Western Political Philosophy*; Nancy J. Hirschmann, *Rethinking Obligation*.

[3] See especially Evelyn Fox Keller, *Reflections on Gender and Science*; Sandra Harding, *The Science Question in Feminism*; Margaret Benston, "Feminism and the Critique of Scientific Method," in Miles and Finn, *Feminism from Pressure to Politics*; Ruth Bleier, *Feminist Approaches to Science*; Ursula Franklin, Hannah Gay and Angela Miles, *Women in Science and Technology*; Londa Schiebinger, *The Mind Has No Sex?*; Ruth Herschberger, *Adam's Rib*.

[4] Margaret Alic, *Hypatia's Heritage*; Margaret W. Rossiter, *Women Scientists in America*; Londa Schiebinger, *The Mind Has No Sex?*; Phina G. Abir-Am and Dorinda Outram, *Uneasy Careers and Intimate Lives*.

[5] Gloria Bowles and Renate Duelli Klein, *Theories of Women's Studies*, 20.

[6] Maria Mies, "Towards a Methodology for Feminist Research," in Bowles and Klein, *Theories*, 118.

considered that *"there is a contradiction between the prevalent theories of social science and methodology and the political aims of the women's movement"* (120; any emphasis in quotations appears in the original). The methodology she condemned was value-free, neutral, uninvolved, hierarchical, and nonreciprocal between research subject and research object. Further, "Max Weber's famous principle of separating science and politics (praxis) is not in the interests of women's liberation" (124). Mies warned of the dire consequences of continuing to use empiricism:

> If women's studies uses these old methodologies, they will again
> be turned into an instrument of repression. New wine should not
> be poured into old bottles. (120)

Instead, "the postulate of *value free research*, of neutrality and indifference towards the research objects, has to be replaced by *conscious partiality*" (122).

For Mary Daly in *Beyond God the Father*, method was a false god serving higher powers. "The tyranny of methodolatry hinders new discoveries ... Under patriarchy Method has wiped out women's questions so totally that even women have not been able to hear and formulate our own questions to meet our own experience." This occurred because the very survival of the social and cultural institutions of patriarchy depended on "the classification of disruptive and disturbing information as nondata" (11-12).

Jane Flax declared that "the desire to know is inextricably intermeshed with the desire to dominate. Nature is posited as pure otherness, which must be conquered to be possessed and transformed into useful objects."[7] Flax's postmodernism rejects such prevalent beliefs of the Enlightenment as the search for laws of nature and the use of scientific methods for objective and reliable knowledge.[8]

Linda Nicholson, in her introduction to *Feminism/Postmodernism*, argued that feminists "had to counter" the norm of objectivity to gain legitimacy for their theories (3). Feminist scholars responded by challenging the notion itself, not only that claims put forward as universal "have invariably been valid only for men of a particular culture, class, and race. They have further alleged that even the ideals which have given backing to these claims, such as 'objectivity' and 'reason' have

---

[7] Jane Flax, "Political Philosophy and the Patriarchal Unconscious: a Psychoanalytic Perspective on Epistemology and Metaphysics," in Harding and Hintikka, *Discovering Reality*, 260.

[8] Jane Flax, "Postmodernism and Gender Relations in Feminist Theory," 624. See also her *Thinking Fragments*.

reflected the values of masculinity at a particular point in history" (5).

Sherry Gorelick, in introducing her "'Giving Voice,' Giving Vision," similarly derided the "pretence of a value-free science and the presumptions of 'objectivity'."

> Feminist methodology grows out of an important qualitative leap in
> the feminist critique of the social sciences: the leap from a critique
> of the invisibility of women in the social sciences both as objects of
> study and as social scientists to the critique of the method and
> purpose of social science itself. (1)

The power structure maintained the dominant methodologies in place, relegating alternatives to the periphery.

In *Is Women's Philosophy Possible?* Nancy Holland unequivocally rejected conventional empiricism, asserting: "The problem with British empiricism, then, is not just that it reflects male thinking, but that it reflects atomistic, empiricist male thinking" (17). Male bias influences even the conception of what constitutes a human person.

For some critics of empiricism, phenomenology provides an acceptable way out. Dorothy Smith argued for a "sociology for women," although she did not propose an "immediate and radical transformation of the subject matter and methods of the discipline nor the junking of everything that has gone before."[9] What, precisely, should be junked and what kept she did not say. She advocated direct experience of the everyday world as the problematic. Yet with these other critics she held that sociology was "part of the ruling apparatus."[10] It had, to a significant extent, done the "classifying, organizing, mapping, and extending the relations of the institutional forms of ruling." The "one true story" is nothing more than a partial perspective claiming generality on the basis of "social privilege and power." Against this hegemony "postmodernists have celebrated and theorized the overthrow of the transcendental subject, replacing it with a recognition of multiple alternative narratives, none of which can claim a privileged status over others" (121).

In "Phenomenological Sociology Reconsidered," Louise Levesque-Lopman saw promise in phenomenology "to overcome the shortcomings of positivist, objectivist attempts to measure and count all aspects of 'human' behavior" (1). It was a characteristic of "male culture" to insist that all forms of experience be studied objectively, as fact or

---

[9] Dorothy E. Smith, "Women's Perspective as a Radical Critique of Sociology," in Harding, *Feminism and Methodology*, 91.
[10] Dorothy E. Smith, *The Everyday World as Problematic*, 109.

institution which exists independent of personal experience. "This positivist ideal of scientifically valid knowledge is insufficient for understanding women's and men's experience" (3). Phenomenologists/ ethnomethodologists reject "the metaphysical assumptions of empirical sociology — that there is a real social and cultural world capable of being objectively studied by scientific methods."[11] They would correct the "established, narrow (male-oriented) perspective that presently exists in sociology" (12).

A number of feminists have fought back, arguing for a "feminist empiricism" that will employ the methods of social science to work for women and equality. This has not convinced ethnomethodologists, phenomenologists, and postmodernists. Mary Hawkesworth, for example, retorted:

> Feminist empiricism is committed to untenable beliefs about the
> nature of knowledge and process of knowing that render it unable
> to explain the persistence of sexist bias within the established
> disciplines.[12]

While warning that the post-modernist alternative reinforces the status quo, Hawkesworth yet found much in it to commend. She lauded it for counselling abandoning truth as a "hegemonic and, hence, destructive illusion" (554). Ignoring all the constructive scepticism of the empiricist tradition she condemned empiricism for its "futile quest for an authoritative truth." Feminist postmodernism rejected "the very possibility of *a* truth about reality" (536). Knowledge was the result of invention, not discovery. This is not to disagree with her observation that "prejudice, faulty inference, overgeneralization, omission, distortion, and unwarranted conclusions" abound in "authoritative texts" about women.[13] Rita Mae Kelly et al., similarly argue that the "reality depicted in disciplinary models does not always reflect the reality lived and perceived by females."[14] The cognitive reality of the models, not that of the subject, is reflected. "Objectification of social reality" increases the probability that existing institutions, such as the patriarchal family, will appear to be natural, permanent social structures (19). A "masculine gender bias" is inherent in "positivistic epistemology" (13).

[11] Louise Levesque-Lopman, *Claiming Reality*, 14.
[12] Mary Hawkesworth, "Knowers, Knowing, Known: Feminist Theory and Claims of Truth," 553.
[13] Mary Hawkesworth, "Feminist Epistemology: A Survey of the Field," 116.
[14] Rita Mae Kelly, "Liberal Positivistic Epistemology," 13.

In *Feminist Thought and the Structure of Knowledge* Mary McCanney Gergen held that feminist perspectives have been introduced into the mainstream disciplines to some extent, but lamented that "many so-called feminist social scientists continue to practise their sciences in forms that violate the precepts of an enlightened feminist perspective." New methods are required to support "feminist metatheories."

> We must reject many of the traditional methods of economics, psychology, political science, and sociology, for example, as violations of our feminist beliefs.[15]

For Gergen the shortcomings of empiricism again include objectivity and even the independence of the scientist relative to subject matter:

> An empiricist theory of science holds that the only way to establish valid knowledge is through scientific procedure. Thus, all other claims to knowledge are by definition inferior.

Further, "the researcher is assumed to be more knowledgable and competent than the subject" (93).

Ruth Hubbard, in the same work, also called for feminists to challenge the particular definition of objectivity on which scientific method rests:

> A feminist science would have to start by acknowledging our values and our subjectivity as human observers with particular personal and social backgrounds and with inevitable interests.[16]

Feminist and other empirical methodologists for centuries have indeed acknowledged the power of interests and values, but with the hope of countering their impact so as not to unduly prejudice results.

The goal of objectivity is routinely misrepresented in these critiques. Linda Nicholson in *Feminism/Postmodernism* is typical:

> While the meaning of this norm varies within the academy, one popular interpretation is that of inquiry immune to the nonacademic influences of politics or values. (3)

Yet none of the methodologists included in this study, and none I encountered in the research for my much larger *Early Origins of the Social Sciences*, remotely meets this description. Most empiricist methodologists went to some trouble to stress the difficulties, urging that we do what we can to avoid bias, never suggesting that anyone

---

[15] Mary McCanney Gergen, "Toward a Feminist Metatheory and Methodology in the Social Sciences," in Gergen, *Feminist Thought and the Structure of Knowledge*, 88.

[16] Ruth Hubbard, "Some Thoughts on the Masculinity of Knowledge," in Gergen, *Feminist Thought*, 9.

would totally succeed.

For Rhoda Kesler Unger the "positivist empiricist model ... restricts analysis to a few clearly observable units of behavior."[17] Over the centuries empiricists have keenly felt the limits of their methods, but were cheered by the prospect of collecting at least some data on the real social world. Criticizing empiricists for narrowing their research to avoid imposing their values, Unger advocates a value-imbued social science. But what if the values are patriarchal or fascist or both?

Liz Stanley and Sue Wise in *Breaking Out: Feminist Consciousness and Feminist Research*, called for "experience and feeling" to be at the heart of feminist research.

As feminists, we should not be involved in traditional male academic

routines for disguising our own feelings and involvements. (50)

Stanley and Wise rejected both "positivism" and "naturalism" in favour of ethnomethodology, which attempts "to use the personal in ways which are in sympathy with feminism" (150). Positivist methods are "objectionable, sexist even," not only in terms of quantification and statistics, but also in terms of specific assumptions made about the researcher/researched relation and the very nature of reality (159).

Barbara DuBois similarly rejected such a core element of empiricism as the separation of the observer from the observed, the knower from the known. "To polarize the subjective and the objective falsifies experience and reality, and the possibility of knowing them."[18] Consequently, "feminism withdraws consent from the patriarchal construction of reality." The task of science should not be the examination of reality: "our science-making, rooted in, animated by and expressive of our values, empowered by community, is *passionate scholarship*" (112).

Four panelists at a session at the 1991 meetings of the Canadian Sociology and Anthropology Association all attacked empiricism, objectivity, and quantification in the name of "feminist methodology." The thesis was that such practices constitute male methodology and should be rejected as a matter of feminist commitment. The speakers asserted that qualitative and quantitative methods are mutually exclusive. Qualitative work was the method of feminism, and could not be engaged in by anyone who did quantitative research. These opinions were not universally accepted by the audience, but it is noteworthy that there was no one to speak for empiricism on the program.

[17] Rhoda Kesler Unger, "Through the Looking Glass: No Wonderland Yet!" 10.
[18] Barbara DuBois, "Passionate Scholarship," in Bowles and Klein, *Theories*, 111.

Feminist sociologist Thelma McCormack has aptly summed up the feminist attack:

> The myth persists and recurs over and over again so that anyone who does any kind of quantitative research is called a positivist and accused of abetting patriarchy.[19]

"Positivist" in turn has become a vague code word meaning bourgeois at best, patriarchal at worst. Papers become talk about talk: "No research can be done, for inevitably the doing of research is compromising" (21). McCormack argues instead for use of a broad range of methods, quantitative, qualitative, comparative, longitudinal, laboratory, field, experimental, surveys, case histories, group studies, participant observation, and interviews (25). A feminist methodology would not be radically different from other methodologies in the social sciences, which have a tradition of studying stratification and disadvantaged groups.

> If I had to choose between male subjectivity and male objectivity with all its limitations, I would infinitely prefer the latter if only because it was more accountable and vulnerable to the criticism of bias. (27)

Margrit Eichler offers a way to avoid sexism, focus on women, and bring feminist perspectives to bear without losing the strengths and knowledge of the discipline. She does this by analyzing and precisely naming the problem, as indicated by the title of her much-cited 1986 essay: "The Relationship between Sexist, Nonsexist, Woman-Centred, and Feminist Research."

Janet Radcliffe Richards is another welcome exception to feminist opposition to empiricism, in this case so bold as to use the title of a plea for empiricism in chemistry by a male natural scientist, Robert Boyle. *The Sceptical Feminist* argues for all the skills of science and logic to be used for the cause:

> It is essential that *in addition* to their concern for individuals and their experiences feminists must learn the logic and science that have been the traditional preserve of men. To resist them is to cling to the very deprivation of which women complain, and try to move into liberation loaded with the heaviest chains of their oppression. (31)

Women need to know the nature of the world they are dealing with to proceed with their own program of change (62).

---

[19] Thelma McCormack, "Feminism and the New Crisis in Methodology," in Winnie Tomm, *Effects of Feminist Approaches*, 20.

Shulamit Reinharz, in *Feminist Methods in Social Research,* argued for use of a wide range of methods. She showed how feminist scholars have, in fact, used a multiplicity of methods, including innovative quantitative methods, participant observation and other non-distancing techniques. She concluded that "feminism is a perspective, not a method" (241).

Joyce McCarl Nielsen came to a different conclusion in *Feminist Research Methods.* She also showed how feminists have used and adapted social science methods, but affirmed the existence of "an identifiable feminist approach to research that is grounded in both an older positivist empirical tradition and in a newer postempirical one" (1). This would seem to be having it both ways. On the one hand it would be "archaic to endorse a return to nonempirical inquiry," and so "the element of empiricism" was needed to "guard against the use of superstition or personal bias" as a basis for knowledge (31). Yet she identified herself with the "postempiricist researchers" (27) and clearly defined postempiricism as "an alternative to scientific methods for studying the social and cultural world" (32).

Other feminists have sought to reform empiricism rather than to eliminate it. Sandra Harding, in her *Feminism and Methodology,* negatively answers her own question, "Is There a Feminist Method?" However much I concur, I must object to her dismissal of the project of recovering lost women theorists and her utter contempt for writers prior to 1967. Writing in 1987 she faulted work done before the "breakthrough" of the preceding two decades, when women were still "under pressure" to make their research conform to what men thought about social life.

> We should not expect their research projects to produce the kinds
> of powerful analyses that can emerge when women's and men's
> thinking is part of a broad social revolution. (3)

Yet the women, and some men, to be discussed shortly made powerful breakthroughs two centuries before the period she praises as exemplary!

To me one of the most objectionable features of the recent feminist critique of empiricism is the assumption/assertion that no one before ever even raised the salient critical questions. It would seem that postmodernists were the first to discuss the situatedness of knowledge and limits to generalization. Thus Flax has feminist theorists entering into and echoing postmodernist discourses "as we have begun to deconstruct notions of reason, knowledge, or the self and to reveal the effects of the gender arrangements that lay beneath their neutral and univer-salizing facades."[20] Her footnote gives four examples, dating between 1983 and 1985.

The chapters to follow will show that these questions were raised hundreds of years before postmodernism was ever thought of; indeed they predate the modern period. The sceptics of ancient Greece raised similar questions and there have been revivals of that sceptical prob-ing from time to time ever since. Montaigne's revival of ancient scep-ticism, in the sixteenth century, was key to the emergence of modern empiricism. Many thinkers who raised these issues chose to remain in the tradition of empiricism, unlike the postmodernists. The notion that they did so uncritically, with no awareness of context, bias, and limits to generalization is simply false.

The association between modernity and general laws is another instance of ignoring the work of earlier periods. The search for general laws and the close relationship between the social and natural sciences are also, like scepticism, products of ancient Greek thinking. Since they well predate modernity the argument that they ought to and inevitably will decline with modernity loses some force.

The Ecological Feminist Critique

Ecological feminists joined in the attack on scientific method, linking it with both the domination of nature and subjugation of women.[21] The discussion often implied, if it did not expressly state, that to oppose the oppression of women and degradation of the environment, we must reject scientific method. These ecofeminists prefer an older, vitalist, organic model of nature to the mechanical conceptions of Western science. Carolyn Merchant's influential *Death of Nature* described the unhappy results of acceptance of the mechanical philosophy. It could then func-tion "as a subtle sanction for the exploitation and manipulation of nature and its resources" (103). Mechanical philosophy took over the concept of the manipulation of nature from the magical tradition, in the course divesting it of life and vital action. This "removal of animistic, organic

[20] Jane Flax, "Postmodernism and Gender Relations in Feminist Theory," in Nicholson, *Feminism/Postmodernism*, 42.

[21] As well as the sources quoted here see Judith Plant, *Healing the Wounds*; Irene Diamond and Gloria Feman Orenstein, *Reweaving the World*; Léonie Caldecott and Stephanie Leland, *Reclaim the Earth*; Françoise d'Eaubonne, *Féminisme ou la mort*. For a good critical account of ecofeminism see Janet Biehl, *Finding Our Way*.

assumptions about the cosmos constituted the death of nature — the most far-reaching effect of the Scientific Revolution" (193).

To Vandana Shiva, in *Staying Alive*, "the scientific revolution in Europe transformed nature from *terra mater* into a machine and a source of raw material; with this transformation it removed all ethical and cognitive constraints against its violation and exploitation" (xvii). Andrée Collard, in *Rape of the Wild*, was straightforward: "In patriarchy, nature, animals and women are objectified, hunted, invaded, colonised, owned, consumed and forced to yield and produce (or not)" (1). Ynestra King saw the opposition to nature in Western industrial civilization as reinforcing the subjugation of women. "In the process of building Western industrial civilization, nature became something to be dominated, made to serve the needs of men. She was stripped of her magical powers and properties as these beliefs were relegated to the trashbin of superstition.[22] Susan Griffin in *Woman and Nature* regretted the separation of thought and feeling (117). "Patriarchal thought" is rejected for its claims to objectivity/separation from feeling. Griffin best discovered her own insights by going "underneath logic ... writing associatively, and thus enlisting my intuition or uncivilized self instead" (xv).

Yet the historical record examined in the main body of this work shows quite different associations. The organic, vitalist models some modern feminists propose as better alternatives also turn out to be rigidly hierarchical.[23] Some of the most vigorous protestors against the subjugation of women were supporters of both scientific method and greater sensitivity to the whole creation. In fact, in past centuries few methodologists of either sex paid much attention to environmental concerns. We will carefully look at those who did in the light of the ecological feminist critique.

Parameters

The Women Founders of the Social Sciences examines the early modern period to the beginning of the twentieth century. The book begins with Marie de Gournay in the late sixteenth century, omitting the interesting, if largely anecdotal, material increasingly becoming available on women in the ancient world, medieval, and early Renaissance. We end with women, like Beatrice Webb and Jane Addams, who began their

---

[22] Ynestra King, "Toward an Ecological Feminism," in Joan Rothschild, *Machina ex Dea*, 120.

[23] This is discussed at much greater length, with material on both men and women theorists, in my *Early Origins of the Social Sciences*.

scholarly work before the end of the nineteenth century and continued it after 1900. Women who began to publish only after the turn of
the century are not included. Since the research depends on written
sources I have not attempted to include women who contributed to the
development of knowledge in societies with purely oral traditions.

The Women Founders is not a history of the social sciences but an
attempt to fill in the gaps of existing histories. It does not deal with
all of women's intellectual achievements but only those by women
who helped develop the social sciences. It covers the natural sciences,
arts, philosophy, or literature only in so far as women contributors
to the social sciences also wrote in these other fields. In fact, since
many of the women founders did so, there is some discussion of this
other work to complete the picture of each woman's oeuvre. Because
of the times in which these women lived, the contribution of women
to the development of universities and professional organizations in
the social sciences is not included. The Women Founders is not a
history of the status of women but, since so many of the theorists
were concerned with women's place in society, will touch on issues
of status as they arise.

The Women Founders of the Social Sciences will not attempt to deal
with language in any comprehensive way, but will report early criti-
cisms of sexist language and attempts at inclusivity. Thus the eighteenth-century emergence of such terms as "humankind" and sex-
neutral expressions for God will be described. J.S. Mill's discussion of
the lack of a generic pronoun in English captures the problem for the
whole period considered here: "The pronoun he is the only one available to express all human being, none having been invented to serve
the purpose of designating them generally ... This is more than a defect
in language, tending to prolong the almost universal habit of thinking
and speaking of one-half the human species as the whole."[24]

Most of the women founders discussed here were British or French,
as were most of the founding "fathers" of the social sciences. The interaction between the two countries was significant for both sexes.
Throughout this history we see British writers who were unabashedly
francophile, fluent in French, and much involved in French social issues.
The French Revolution was pivotal for a number of them, moving them
to write defences and suggesting possibilities for social reform. The
French, too, were significantly influenced by the British, attracted by

[24] J.S. Mill, System of Logic, Collected Works, 8: 837.

freer British social institutions and the new philosophy of Bacon, Locke, and Newton.

American involvement began in the eighteenth century with Macaulay's trip to the United States and correspondence with George Washington. The nineteenth century brought more connection, beginning with de Staël's correspondence with Thomas Jefferson. Harriet Martineau's work as a methodologist was prompted by her trip to the United States. She remained in touch with American abolitionists and suffragists and was a source for both. Jane Addams's English visits were key both for her founding of the first settlement house in the United States and the early research she and her co-workers did from it. Hull House itself promoted intellectual exchanges, welcoming such notables as Peter Kropotkin and Beatrice and Sidney Webb. *The Women Founders* ends with the work of two American women prominent in the early development of women's studies, Frances Perkins Gilman and Matilda Joslyn Gage.

Empiricism and Equality Rights

The following chapters present a succession of women committed both to the empiricism of their day and the emancipation of women. Some were thorough and consistent in their advocacy of women's equality, while others were more qualified and cautious. Yet for each empiricism was a means to the realization of her goals. To change a society you had first to understand it. Thus women sought, as did men reformers, liberals, radicals, and revolutionaries, to explain what was wrong and what could be done differently. The term "social science" was itself first used in the French Revolution, if not by Condorcet by one of his reform-minded colleagues. "Social science" was needed to ground the "social art," the new institutions which were needed to establish a better society. Germaine de Staël wrote about the "political science" that was needed to found a liberal, republican social order.

Any feminist who wishes to argue that the empirical social sciences imply a "male method," that objectivity is a trap, that recourse to the established methods of gathering data limits one to supporting the status quo, will find no help from the women discussed here. Rather these methodologists contributed to the very framework of empiricism from its terms and underlying assumptions to advice on the practicalities of how to do research. Their research provides examples of actual empirical work: hypothesis development, data collection, and interpretation. When empiricism was the underdog methodology, condemned by the authorities of church, state, and university, these

women spoke out in its defence. Most of them also shared in the emancipation movement as it then was, variously for educational opportunities for women, the vote, the right to control property, enter the
professions, and to divorce. Some even recognized the need for
women's studies and argued the lack of balance in their field because
of the exclusion of women. The women founders included in this study
were chosen for their *methodological* contribution: the definition of
empiricism, elucidation of terms and concepts, and pioneering examples of research. It simply happens that most, but not all, were also
advocates for women's rights. Any definition of feminism or a women's
agenda will itself have to be considered in historical context, for what
seems tame and uncontroversial now (like education for women and
the vote) was dangerously radical earlier. The point is that in each
period there were advocates for women's most urgent concerns, and
women methodologists were prominent among them in every age.

The right to education and admittance to the life of reason was *the*
quest for centuries. Only in the late eighteenth century did a claim emerge
for political representation and full access to occupations and professions.
By the mid-nineteenth century there were comprehensive demands for
political, legal, religious, and economic reform, along with new concerns
over violence against women and the double sexual standard.

Another misconception to be exploded: a number of these women
did both historical research *and* mainstream sociology. For them, as I
would argue more generally, the focus on great events and their expli-
cation, often called interpretive or *verstehende* sociology, was not an
alternative approach to the search for general laws or regularities.
Catharine Macaulay was noted for her histories. Mary Wollstonecraft,
Germaine de Staël, and Harriet Martineau all wrote conventional histories. Yet all of those women were proponents of general explanation
in the conventional understanding of sociology. De Staël was even hard
line in her advocacy of number crunching. Instead of treating interpretive or hermeneutic sociology as an alternative methodology, and
rejecting empiricism, I will treat it here as a component, differing in
emphasis or focus but not in fundamental assumptions from mainstream sociology. Max Weber himself argued for the integration of
interpretive and causal explanation. His opening definitions in *Economy and Society* treat interpretive sociology as a part of "empirical sociology."[25] His own historical studies were laced with causal chains, as
were those of his feminist wife, Marianne Weber.

[25] Max Weber, *Economy and Society*, 1: 3.

These writers of history made concerted efforts to include women, to identify them, describe them, and assess their roles in society. Mary Hays went one further in *Female Biography* by treating only women, to make up for past omissions. By and large these writers strove to incorporate women into what was generally a man's world. Along the way they raised questions about male values and male bias, short of upsetting the system. That step was taken most decisively by the American Matilda Joslyn Gage in the late nineteenth century.

I will not here follow those who prefer the term "herstory" to the usual "history," not only because "theirstory" would be more accurate. The word from which "history" is derived is simply the Greek word for the facts, *istoria*. Thus Francis Bacon planned "histories" of the air, clouds, and rainbows and Aristotle wrote a *History of Animals*. John Locke claimed that he was applying the "historical, plain method" in his *Essay concerning Human Understanding*, meaning that he based his conclusions on observation rather than tradition or authority (1: 27).

The terms "empirical" and "empiricism" come from the Greek word for experience, *empeiria*, and for centuries carried no pejorative baggage with them whatsoever. The empirical school of medicine in Alexandria taught medical practice based strictly on observed results, that is without reference to underlying theory. Florence Nightingale occasionally used the term in that limited sense. "Empirical" has since evolved so that it now implies a basis in experience, a basis which does not exclude any attempt at general explanation. Throughout the period under consideration speculation and recourse to authority have been the opposites of empiricism. Karl Marx used the term "empirical," always favourably, in opposition to "mystification and speculation."[26] The young Beatrice Potter became a "pure empiricist" in 1887, throwing off "the comfortable doctrines" of laissez-faire liberalism.[27] Her empiricism next took her to socialism. Only more recently has empiricism, for some, come to infer mindless quantification or slavish adaptation of physical science models.

In recent years the terms "positive" and "positivism" have come into even greater ill repute. Strictly speaking their meaning is about the same as "empirical" and "empiricism." A positive law simply means a law that has actually been passed, as opposed to a speculated "natural law" or a "law of nature" like gravity. The seventeenth-century feminist

---

[26] Karl Marx and Friedrich Engels, *The German Ideology*, 13.
[27] Beatrice Webb, *My Apprenticeship*, 464.

François Poullain stated that he would establish the principle of equality between the sexes by "positive" arguments, after demolishing the "proofs" of women's inferiority offered by experts.[28] From Saint-Simon around 1820 through to Max Weber in 1920 "positive" arguments simply referred to those based on experience of the real world. Again the opposition was, for Saint-Simon, the "presumed facts of conjectures."[29] Marx used the term positive interchangeably with empirical. So did John Stuart Mill and other mainstream methodologists. Weber, in his Vienna lectures on Marx's economic interpretation of history, called his analysis a "positive critique," because it was based on historical facts, although his conclusion regarding Marx's thesis was negative.[30] Where the term "positive" appears it should be understood in this simple sense, without any imputation of modelling on natural science or entailing any particular kind or level of quantification.

Empiricism as it is used here refers to the attempt at explanation of social phenomena, the search for regularities and, as much as possible, the search for causal relations that determine them. More explanation is to be preferred to less but the limits are empirical, that is, determined by experience in the real social world. Many things cannot be observed and, for major social phenomena, there can be no control group. (Neither can there be in much of natural science; we are not alone here.) Empiricism implies induction, or inference from observations. Experiments in social matters are severely limited for obvious ethical reasons. Hence social scientists must take advantage of those opportunities that occur thanks to changes in laws or social policy. Beatrice Webb pointed out that, in fact, social experiments happen all the time thanks to the actions of legislators.

An essential component of empiricism is a notion of probability. Certainty in knowledge is not attainable and all results and inferences from data must remain hypothetical. Levels of probability can be determined with some precision in some kinds of investigation, but even this is often not possible. The more thorough and comprehensive the testing the greater confidence one may have in the results, but mistakes are possible from the conceptualization of the problem through to data gathering, analysis, and the drawing of conclusions. A tentative and humble stance is required.

[28] François Poullain, *Equality of the Two Sexes*, 7.
[29] Henri de Saint-Simon, *Mémoire sur la science de l'homme, Oeuvres*, 11: 26.
[30] Marianne Weber, *Max Weber*, 604.

Objectivity is a goal; it will never fully be achieved. Subjective views guide the choice of research questions and any source of inspiration is legitimate for the formulation of hypotheses. For their testing, however, objective procedures must be followed. Every attempt must be made to put aside the biases of one's own class, religion, gender, and political and social views. *Rationalism,* as a term, will be avoided here because so many different definitions have been applied to it over the centuries. Durkheim, for example, considered that his positivism, meaning his whole, objectivist, approach to methodology, was a consequence of his rationalism.[31] Yet the term has also been used to imply the validity of purely mental processes in the search for truth, quite the opposite contention.

Nominalism is a defining characteristic of empiricism. That is, names are chosen for reasons of convenience and do not constitute knowledge as such. A definition can be more or less useful but not true or false. In contrast with the philosophy of idealism, there is no notion that anything has an essence or a defining characteristic, the understanding of which constitutes knowledge.

Critics, feminist and other, have often portrayed empiricist methodology as derivative from the natural sciences. Empirical social scientists are seen as slavishly adapting the methods of another discipline to their subject. Yet the social sciences themselves have a history at least as old as that of the natural sciences. A good case can be made for dating the social sciences back to the fifth century B.C. The first known borrowings are *from* the social sciences *to* the natural. For centuries there was little specialization, but the same people wrote, thought, and did research in both the natural and the social sciences. (This is discussed in my *Early Origins of the Social Sciences,* but it is hardly my discovery.) Unity of method historically has simply meant a common commitment to the search for evidence in the real world as opposed to deduction from authorities or revelation from on high. There is no necessary implication of any particular kind of research method or quantification.

The Distinctive Contribution of Women
Dale Spender in *Women of Ideas* argues convincingly that women writers existed in much larger numbers than had been realized and were not isolated cases. The same holds more specifically here for women

---

[31] Emile Durkheim, *Règles de la méthode sociologique,* ix.

methodologists. Citation practices in the past were not rigorous; indeed in the case of the earliest women they were quite haphazard. Nonetheless, it is clear that these women knew of and used each other's work. They wrote reviews of each other's books in their lifetimes, and appreciative obituaries at each other's deaths. In some cases personal friendships and active collaboration grew. Mary Hays helped nurse Wollstonecraft in the last days of her life. Nightingale sent her reports to Martineau, who wrote popular versions of them for the press. They commiserated over setbacks in lobbying. Mary Jo Deegan's excellent *Women in Sociology* describes a powerful network which was active during the "golden era" of women in sociology, from 1890 to 1920 (15).

Women, of course, did not have the institutions men have had to support each other's work. Until the very last period of this history women were entirely excluded from universities. No schools ever arose to promote their work. There were no graduate students to complete unfinished work, write biographies, interpretations, or defences. No institutions formed to bring out collected editions or otherwise promote the *oeuvre*. Deegan shows how the first women to get into university positions in the United States were later removed, their work erased, their networks dispersed and destroyed after World War I (18). Few biographies of any kind were written of these women. Some of those that were constituted vicious putdowns or prurient leerings. An inordinate amount of attention was devoted to the woman's sex life and/or marriage. More scholarly work has recently been done, but the habit persists of referring to these women methodologists by their first names. Biographies which do so tend to be negative and trivializing.

Still, in spite of all these obstacles, a number of the early women methodologists circulated their books, articles, and manuscripts to other women for constructive criticism. There are numerous examples of generous discussion of a colleague's or predecessor's works. Roland wished that she could have written history like Macaulay. Tristan regretted the eclipse of Wollstonecraft. The women themselves had a sense of being involved in a collective enterprise, and the connections between and among them will be made clear. Many of the women were excellent stylists; these are not women who, in an expression of Alexandra Kollontai, had "to search for a word in her pocket."

In political theory the women range from the royalist conservative through democratic republican to the founders of modern socialism. Yet there are some common threads. A stress on positive social bonds appears often. Women theorists' approach to social compact theory differed from that of the men in that they routinely dismissed the extreme, conservative views of Hobbes and Rousseau. This was not the way things could have happened, the women argued, suggesting the influence of positive, mother-children links. The projected war-of-all-against-all found no credence among these thinkers. Even conservative theorists like Astell and classical liberals like Martineau were less "pure" than their male counterparts, admitting *some* role for social responsibility/government intervention. Women methodologists, in short, tended to be critical of the political theory of possessive individualism. As women today are more supportive of the welfare state and government intervention in the economy, so were women in past centuries.

Women theorists were decidedly less keen to support military institutions than their male counterparts. Rather than glorifying war they showed its futility, bravado, and brutality. There was great interest in social institutions to reach and maintain peace. None of this is to say that there was a common position among women methodologists on any of these issues, any more than there is now. Common themes there were, and these will be pointed out in the chapters to follow. These women theorists have been ignored in the general (male) literature on political theory both when their views converged with those of the dominant sex and when they departed from them. Neither originality nor solidarity sufficed to win lasting recognition for the women founders of the social sciences.

Chapter 2

WOMEN
AND THE EMERGENCE
OF EMPIRICISM

ethodological battles of the seventeenth century centred around the defence and modernization of idealism against the rise of scepticism and materialism, the understanding of social institutions and the "mechanical philosophy." All these factors came together in the emergence of empiricism.[1] The seventeenth century saw the development of scientific method and the emergence of modern mathematics. While the period is more known for the rapid development of the natural sciences, important steps were also taken in the social sciences. The Puritan Revolution prompted much social rethinking and theorizing. Statistics on births, deaths, and economic conditions began to become available. Quantified data were increasingly cited in the development of social and political theory.[2]

Women participated in this evolution of the social sciences in two distinct ways. First, they were the victims of Platonic and Aristotelian idealism and its adaptations, all of which ranked the ideal over the material, mind over body, male over female. These women had much to gain by the intellectual revolution that overthrew the old schools. Second, women found great use for the rising notion of social convention. Customs that had demeaned and limited them could be exposed,

---

[1] See my *Early Origins of the Social Sciences* for more background on the development of empiricism, the debate with idealism, and the broader intellectual/historical context.

[2] On the seventeenth century historical background, especially the role of scientific method and the social sciences see: Christopher Hill, *Intellectual Origins* and *World Turned Upside Down*; Richard H. Popkin, *History of Scepticism*; Charles Webster, *Great Instauration*; Margaret Wiley, *Subtle Knot* and *Creative Sceptics*; Keith Thomas, *Religion and the Decline of Magic*; R.F. Jones, *Ancients and Moderns*; Peter Mathias, *First Industrial Nation*; H.R. Trevor-Roper, *Religion the Reformation and Social Change*; Charles Wilson, *England's Apprenticeship*; Basil Willey, *Seventeenth Century Background*; Margaret C. Jacob, *Radical Enlightenment*; Donald Pennington and Keith Thomas, *Puritans and Revolutionaries*; Michael Hunter, *Science and Society in Restoration England*; R.S. Woolhouse, *Empiricists*.

by reason, as mere prejudice, not in the nature of things. The Puritan Revolution in Britain, simply by provoking social change, made further changes possible.

The defeat of mind/body dualism was crucial for the assertion of equality between the sexes and for the valuation of women's bodily role in child-bearing. A nonhierarchical dualism, of course, is logically possible, although "separate but equal" treatment tends to have fostered separateness more than equality in actual practice. Dualism could also, in theory, favour women. Or women could be accorded equality by ranking the ideal over the material and granting women equal souls. Although some feminists did precisely this, the centuries-long association of idealism with the denigration of women made theirs an esoteric argument. Proponents of the ideal/corporeal hierarchy did not typically question the male/female hierarchy. Nicolas Malebranche, a priest and as thorough an idealist philosopher as could be found in the seventeenth century, argued the inferiority of women's intellect on grounds that they/we have soft brains.

The re-emergence of an understanding of social convention (as opposed to divinely given immutable laws) was essential to achieving women's equality. If the subordination of women was conventional it could be changed; if it had been decreed by nature or divine plan, it could not. Feminists obviously could and did use these arguments. Conceptually, as with mind/body dualism, there is no necessary reason for natural theology or the interpretation of divine will to have relegated women to subordinate roles and status. Natural theology arguments could be devised to argue for equality, as could interpretations of divine will. Yet such arguments did not emerge. In fact empiricism, not idealism, became a tool for women in the struggle for equality. Defenders of idealism tended to insist on limited roles and low status for women.

There are three important early sources for the promotion of the concept of social convention so crucial for feminist theory. Thomas More used the radically different social conventions of Utopia to criticise those he opposed in real-life Britain. Michel de Montaigne in his *Essays* showed the variety of human conventions that had actually developed. He argued throughout for a more sceptical, probing, tentative approach to knowledge. The Puritans in the seventeenth century actively promoted different social institutions, rejecting the status quo to establish the Kingdom of God on earth.

Criss-crossing this debate about the nature of women and their place was the debate about how knowledge could be attained. The emerging empiricists held that knowledge had to be sought through the senses, by observation in the real world duly processed, reflected on, and criticized. Empiricists argued against intuition, introspection, or deduction from principles as much as they argued against the acceptance of traditional authorities as sources of knowledge. This gave empiricism a democratic flavour, for anyone could criticize received knowledge on the basis of their own observations. Women empiricists would make much of this feature of empiricism. As Astell's major biographer observed, "Baconian empiricism ... equalized the starting places of the sexes in the quest for knowledge."[3]

Lockean psychology played a crucial role here. The portrayal of the mind as a piece of white paper, on which sensations are made, compared, and then generalized into concepts, was empowering for both women and other disadvantaged groups. The theory gave enormous scope for education — that which was written onto the blank paper. It made possible the nurture over nature arguments which have fuelled reform movements ever since. Sarah Scott used Lockean psychology in her utopian novel, *Millennium Hall* (1762), as she described the plight of women in the real world of the eighteenth century. The only "probable means of mending mankind" was the education of the young, when the mind was as "a sheet of white paper" (1).

Meanwhile, the old guard kept to Aristotle, as interpreted by Aquinas and entrenched as official doctrine. Aristotle had originally included a substantial measure of empirical observation in his methodology, even if he ranked knowledge of forms and purpose higher than that received from the senses. He himself did a considerable amount of empirical work in biology. He certainly never advocated making a dogma of his teaching, let alone the establishment of penalties up to capital punishment for disagreeing with him. Platonic revivals added new elements to idealism but did not alter the fundamental suspicion of the senses in acquiring knowledge and preference for purely intellectual processes. Descartes's dualism was an attempt to integrate the two worlds, but it ultimately shared more with the idealist than the empiricist. Other modern idealists put more stress on reason, less on God and accepted authorities, as the source of knowledge. Yet the rejection or downgrading of sense information continued.

Women took part in all aspects of the methodological debate of the seventeenth century, from the defence and modernization of idealism

---

[3]   Ruth Perry, *The Celebrated Mary Astell*, 70.

through adaptations of Cartesianism to the dissemination of Montaigne's scepticism and the promotion of empiricism.[4] Anne, Viscountess Conway, was a mystic and extreme idealist connected with the Cambridge Platonists. The Electress Sophia of Hanover, later Princess of Wales, supported her countryman Leibniz against Newton. My main focus, though, will be empiricism, the methodology that gave women and other disadvantaged groups the wherewithal to fight the prejudices, laws, and customs that held them down. With its dualism Cartesianism played a more complicated role. At its simplest and most sceptical it was a powerful tool for fighting established authority and custom; rebuilt into a system it was not.

Britain was the main source of modern empiricism and women played a part, against all odds, in its development.[5] At this time women were nearly completely excluded from institutionalized education. Most of the women founders of the social sciences came from the very small number of girls who were given a good private education, usually by their fathers. **Thomas More (1478-1535)** was a radical, socialist, materialist, empiricist of the sixteenth century. He advocated equal educational and occupational opportunities for women and made an early, cogent plea for empiricism. Both were set out in the original utopian novel, then and now a relatively safe way to advance heretical ideas. More's utopian society was relatively egalitarian and most decidedly empiricist in its approach to knowledge. Women as well as men could become scholars, in both cases from any occupational background. The Utopians were fond of learning and were open to new discoveries. As befits empiricists they were modest in their claims for truth. They had no appreciation of such idealist concepts as essences or

---

[4] Good general sources on these women and the period are: Margaret Alic, *Hypatia's Heritage*; Bonnie S. Anderson and Judith P. Zinsser, *A History of their Own*; Susan Groag Bell, *Women from the Greeks to the French Revolution*; Edmond de Goncourt and Jules de Goncourt, *The Woman of the Eighteenth Century*; Samia I. Spencer, *French Women and the Age of Enlightenment*; Carolyn C. Lougee, *Le paradis des femmes: Women, Salons, and Social Stratification*; David Williams, "The Politics of Feminism in the French Enlightenment"; Paul Fritz and Richard Morton, *Woman in the 18th Century*; Léon Abensour, *La femme et le féminisme avant la Révolution*.
[5] Doris Mary Stenton, *The English Woman in History*; Ada Wallas, *Before the Bluestockings*; Katharine M. Rogers, *Feminism in Eighteenth-Century England*; Barbara Kanner, *The Women of England*; Moira Ferguson, *First Feminists*; Lawrence Stone, *The Family, Sex and Marriage in England 1500-1800*; Hilda L. Smith, *Reason's Disciples*; Myra Reynolds, *The Learned Lady in England 1650-1760*; Bridget Hill, *Eighteenth-Century Women*; Alice Browne, *The Eighteenth Century Feminist Mind*; Sheila Rowbotham, *Hidden from History*.

"man-in-general" but sought useful knowledge for application. More's mother was an educated woman and he carried on the tradition by teaching his daughters the classics. His eldest daughter, **Margaret Roper (1505-?)**, translated Eusebius' *History of the Church from Christ to Constantine* from Greek to Latin. She corresponded with Erasmus and, at age nineteen, translated one of his exegetical treatises. A resourceful and courageous woman, Roper saved her father's body from the last indignity after execution: she bribed an executioner for her father's head after it had been taken down from display on London Bridge, thus saving it from being tossed in the Thames in lieu of burial.

Michel de Montaigne (1533-1592) was key to the development of modern empiricism by reviving ancient scepticism, promoting a tentative, hypothetical approach to knowledge. Even without certain knowledge, he argued, there was much we could learn and apply. Meanwhile the search should go on. A man of his time, Montaigne was no advocate of women's rights. At best his *Essays* show some sensitivity to the injustices women suffered. Nevertheless, he contributed indirectly to the emergence of early feminism, for his methodology inspired the young Marie de Gournay, who was one of the first people to recognize the originality and usefulness of his "constructive scepticism" and the first known writer to have applied the approach to arguments for women's equality. Montaigne was still little known at this time. As his "adopted daughter," Gournay served first as secretary for the fifth edition of the *Essays*, 1592, then for decades after his death as editor and negotiator with publishers. Interspersed she did her own work: fiction, translations, poetry, and two short essays arguing the equality of the two sexes.

Marie le Jars de Gournay (1565-1645)

Born in Paris, where she lived most of her life, Marie le Jars belonged to a respectable family which later fell on hard times. She learned Latin and Greek at home largely through her own efforts. When she was age fifteen her father bought the feudal rights to Gournay; the family moved there and took the name. Gournay was eighteen or nineteen when she first read the original, short, edition of the Essays. *She immediately recognized their significance and wrote with enthusiasm to their author. The two met in Paris in 1594 (Montaigne, then Henry IV's negotiator, had been captured, imprisoned, and assumed dead). Her own father was by then deceased and Montaigne was fifty-five. He made her his "adopted daughter," visited the family,*

Marie de Gournay
Phot. Bibl. Nat. Paris

encouraged her to write, and discussed his Essays with her. After his death **Marie le Jars**
Mme de Montaigne asked Gournay to take over the editing of the next edition. **de Gournay**
Gournay not only brought out the 1595 edition, with her own preface, but
continued to edit and promote the work until her own death.

Gournay became head of her family on her mother's death. Later she
moved back to Paris, where she lived alone, frugally but independently. She
had her own modest salon, and Cardinal Richelieu was her patron. The idea
of the French Academy may have derived from meetings chez elle. She
was close to people who promoted it and satirized by those who opposed
it. Gournay's fictional writing is not our concern here except to note its use
of feminist themes and digressions to discuss social institutions.

Recommended biographies are: Marjorie Henry Ilsley, A Daughter of the
Renaissance and, in French, Mario Schiff, Marie de Gournay.

Marjorie Henry Ilsley, in her biography *Daughter of the Renaissance*,
described Gournay as not the only woman "to have suffered during
her life and after her death from the malice of pamphleteers and the
ill will of prejudiced and narrow minded men" (7). Nor should we be
surprised that Gournay was criticized for altering the *Essays* — even
by those who denied she played any role as editor (73) — nor that she
was accused of exploiting the name of Montaigne, with scarcely any
recognition of her fifty years of service editing and publishing his work.
Yet, Gournay was a conscientious and meticulous editor by the
standards of the time.

Her preface of 1595 staunchly defended Montaigne. Later Gournay
retracted the piece for its lack of restraint. In time she repented her
repentance and published another defence. She justified both
Montaigne's coining of new terms and his unorthodox, free-flowing
style. New ideas required new forms:

> One can represent common imaginations only with common words;
> whoever has conceptions or thoughts out of the ordinary must
> search for unused terms to express them.[6]

For those accustomed to the rigours of the scholastic syllogism,
Montaigne's wandering must have seemed undisciplined, but his editor
realized that a more cautious approach to knowledge required a new
form. The term "essay" literally means a try, admitting the lack of firm

[6] Marie de Gournay, preface, *Les éssais de Michel de Montaigne*, 1657, from 1635
edition. Translations from French works are my own.

conclusions, let alone proof that the truth has been attained and all alternatives refuted. The *Essays* are laced with cautions, a practice thoroughly contrary to scholarly convention. Gournay defended Montaigne against accusations of ignorance which arose from his modest reluctance to claim knowledge — he actually had his motto, *que sais-je?* carved into the beams of his study. She cited the chapters on epistemology (the "Apology of Raimond Sébond") and on medicine as evidence of Montaigne's learning.

Gournay translated Latin and Greek passages for the new edition. She added sources for Montaigne's numerous, and often inaccurate, quotations and paraphrases. This, she explained, was not easy to do, for as well as being incorrect, some citations were at odds with the original sources. Sometimes Montaigne had mixed several sources together. She defended his use of Bordeaux regional expressions. She also defended her "father" on charges of impiety (the *Essays* in fact were put on the Vatican's *Index* of forbidden books, but not until much later, in 1676). She acknowledged that some errors in the text remained, blaming the printers for not making indicated corrections.

In her two short essays on equality Gournay used Montaigne's method, raising an issue and gradually bringing in evidence from all sides with which to consider it. "Egalité des hommes et des femmes" was published in 1622; "Grief des dames" followed in 1626, making Gournay "the most ardent advocate of women's equality."[7] She brought to the debate a modern theory that early environment and habits, the "climate" in which one lives, account for the differences in human beings. The subordinate position of women was due, she maintained, neither to the will of God nor to Nature but to the ever changing caprices of man. She appealed to common sense and reason against custom and authority, including that of the church. Gournay claimed equality, neither more nor less. Human beings differed from animals by having a soul; physical differences were for purposes of propagation only. She cited eminent men where they shared her views on equality.

Gournay's chief argument, and one to be repeated over succeeding centuries, was that women's lesser achievements resulted from defects in their education. The human species was created male and female and neither sex was complete without the other. She advanced numerous arguments recognizable today as feminist theology. She noted the disparagement of books by women authors by men who did not deign to read

---

[7] Ilsley, *Daughter*, 201.

those books, learn from them, or find out if they themselves could achieve as much. She joked about the mustached doctors with their weak and base conceptions, frequent contradictions, numberless failures, and blind judgment. She criticized their assertion of "universal differences" between the two sexes. Although she conceded that in general women were inferior to men, she blasted the logic of using general assumptions to condemn all women or any particular woman's work.

Gournay introduced the second essay with a rueful:

> Happy are you, reader, if you are not of this sex, which is forbidden all advantages and deprived of liberty ... Happy are you, again, who can be wise without committing a crime, your being a man allowing you everything prohibited to women, any action of yours taken as being of noble purpose, sublime and exquisite judgment.[8]

Poullain's *Equality of the Two Sexes* (see below) would offer more comprehensive and polished arguments than anything in Gournay, but that was at the end of the seventeenth century and shows the benefit of the Cartesian method. If Gournay seems suggestive and brief she was nonetheless the real pioneer. "How often she led the attack," remarked biographer Ilsley, yet how little has she been recognized for her originality.[9] She was an early, consistent advocate for women and promoter of a key element of empiricism, constructive scepticism.

Gournay's immediate successor was **Anna van Schurman (1607-1678)**, a Dutch scholar who was also a sculptor, engraver, musician, and painter.[10] In 1638 she published a paper in Latin, translated into English in 1659 as "The Learned Maid; or, whether a maid may be a scholar?" A 1645 French translation also circulated widely. Short and succinct, the work opened audaciously by answering the question in the affirmative. Van Schurman admitted that women would not be allowed to use their learning in the professions, but argued that that should not debar them from knowledge. If women were excluded from colleges, the injustice of which she did not argue, they could still study privately (29). Women should not be excluded even from studies in law, the military, church, court, or university, although her main concern was access to the arts and sciences (5). Van Schurman did not follow Montaigne or Gournay in using the essay form but kept to the conventional syllogism. In content she stressed that women had rational souls, given them by God. They needed solid employment for their

---

[8]   Marie de Gournay, *Fragments d'un discours féminin*, 129.
[9]   Ilsley, *Daughter*, 200.
[10] Joyce L. Irwin, "Anna Maria van Schurman."

minds. Later in life she retreated from this stress on intellect in favour of religious commitment.

Voltaire joked that Descartes had been condemned in France for the only part of his philosophy that was true.[11] Why **René Descartes (1596-1650)** should have been such a threat will become clear shortly with Poullain's radical challenge to male supremacy, which used the method of Cartesian doubt. Descartes's scepticism and materialism shocked at first, not surprisingly in seventeenth-century France when scholasticism was still the official philosophy. His materialism was later downplayed, the idealism stressed, the scepticism ignored, and the certainty re-established. In the meantime, Cartesian doubt was used to argue for the equality of women.

The *Discourse on Method* was a short work, written in French so that women could read it as well as men.[12] Descartes's longer *Meditations, Principles of Philosophy*, and *Rules for the Direction of the Mind* were written in Latin. The *Discourse* was outrageously democratic in its claims. Anyone — even women — could contribute to knowledge and anyone could challenge the findings or claims of anyone else, including those of a bishop or professor. At a time when decisions regarding truth were made by established authorities like faculties of theology, and backed up by royal censors, Descartes was radical indeed. Galileo's condemnation by the Inquisition occurred just at the time Descartes was preparing the *Discourse* for publication. No wonder he took the precaution of living in Protestant Holland instead of France.

Published in 1637, the *Discourse* opens with a bold claim. Good sense was the most equally distributed thing in the world, so abundantly provided that even those who were difficult to satisfy in other respects hardly wanted more of it. Good sense or reason was naturally equal in all people. Descartes then went on to deride the existing store of knowledge in all fields. His thorough, unrelenting scepticism was dangerous to those for whom certainty in knowledge was required for religious belief. Descartes had been well educated, learning the sciences as well as Latin and philosophy. Yet he found fault in everything he had been taught:

> I learned to believe nothing too certainly of which I had only been convinced by example and custom. Thus little by little I was delivered from many errors which might have obscured our natural vision and rendered us less capable of listening to Reason.[13]

[11] Voltaire, *Letters concerning the English Nation*, 88.
[12] See Charles Adam, *Descartes. Ses amitiés féminines*.
[13] Descartes, "Discourse," *Philosophical Works*, 1: 87.

Cartesian doubt led back to certainty. "I think, therefore I am" became the basis for re-establishing confidence in one's own being and powers of reason. For the authorities, however, this was not good enough, for assurance was based on subjective persuasion and the exercise of one's own reason. When Poullain used the method of Cartesian doubt he, too, became bold in his assertions, now for the equality of women.

The **Princess Elisabeth of Bohemia (1618-1680)**, as well, grew more confident in her powers of reasoning when she used his method. Descartes's scientific work was in mathematics, astronomy, and optics. Princess Elisabeth encouraged him to deal with social questions, which he did in a short treatise on the passions, published just before he died. The two corresponded for many years.[14] Descartes, Elisabeth's senior in years as well as education, served as the princess's mentor, encouraging her to read and to use her mind, which she did. Their correspondence was published after her death as *Lettres sur la morale*. The early letters show Elisabeth to have been diffident, asking for advice, eager to learn. Later she became more sure in her own abilities, posing tough questions and pointing out contradictions in Descartes's logic. She found inconsistencies in his theological opinions. Today's feminist theologians and ethicists might find her listening to another voice, rejecting abstractions for their paradoxes, calling for more practical criteria for making moral judgments. She noted how princes did not observe the rule of "do unto others as you would have them do unto you" when the other was a subject.[15]

One of Princess Elisabeth's letters to Descartes politely challenges his reassertion of certainty after the exercise of sceptical doubt. Empiricist methodologists, notably Gassendi and Mersenne, advanced similar arguments, but Elisabeth's is noteworthy for its succinctness. She complimented Descartes's method of reasoning as the "most extraordinary" and "the most natural" because it did not teach anything new but pulled from the mind things people had not before realized that they knew. She did not know how "to get rid of" doubt to attain the tranquility of which he had spoken:

> For there are illnesses which remove completely the capacity of reasoning and, as a result, the capacity of enjoying a reasonable satisfaction, other illnesses which reduce the force and prevent one from following the maxims which good sense has forged, and which

---

[14] On the relationship see Jack Rochford Vrooman, *René Descartes*; René Descartes, *Correspondance avec Elisabeth* and *Lettres sur la morale*; Erica Harth, *Cartesian Women*, 67-68.

[15] Elisabeth to Descartes, in Descartes, *Oeuvres*, 4: 522.

> leave the most moderate person subject to be carried off by the
> passions and less able to separate out chance events. (4: 269)

Elisabeth asked Descartes to resolve these problems. He replied to
her queries but could not explain away the fundamental difficulty. Nor
does his treatise on the passions answer the problems she raised.

Another letter of Elisabeth's reached to the heart of Descartes's
dualism, pointing out its inherent contradictions. The princess presented
the problem as her own lack of understanding, how "the soul (unex-
tended and immaterial) can move the body" to which Descartes had
attributed weight. Nor could she understand how this force could carry
the body towards the centre of the earth. "We must first be persuaded
that a body can be pushed by something immaterial," yet elsewhere
Descartes had demonstrated that to be impossible. The princess could
not conceive how the immaterial could be the negation of the material,
which had no communication with it.

> I declare that it would be easier for me to concede the materiality
> and extension of the soul than give the capacity to move a body and
> to be moved to an immaterial body.[16]

As well it was difficult to understand how a soul/mind, as Descartes
had described it, having had the faculty and habit of reasoning, could
lose it by certain unhealthy airs. From being able to subsist without
the body and having nothing in common with it, how could the soul or
mind then be ruled by the body?

Elisabeth, in short, rejected the central principles of Cartesian dualism. She evidently saw no need for a strict separation between
mind/soul and body/matter. The notion that something corporeal could
think and direct its own movements was not repugnant to her. She
apparently did not continue in her philosophical reflections. Later she
became abbess of a Lutheran convent. In this capacity she helped Anna
von Schurman and her community, who lived in the vicinity.

François Poullain de la Barre (1647-1723)

François Poullain was a young writer and teacher when he wrote his
first radical plea for women's equality. He became a priest, then
converted to Protestantism and became a pastor, all the while using
the Cartesian method to argue for the equality of women.[17] The inferior status of women provided the ideal test for the method, bringing

---

[16]   Elisabeth to Descartes, in Descartes, *Lettres sur la morale*, 11.
[17]   On Poullain's life and work see Marie Louise Stock, *Poullain de la Barre: A
Seventeenth-Century Feminist*.

its searching doubt and rejection of authority to a subject of long-established authority and unquestioned tradition. In *The Equality of the Two Sexes* (1673), Poullain applied the Cartesian method to the common opinion that women were less fit and intelligent than men and ought to be subordinate to them. Not only did he conclude this supposition to be wrong but, using arguments of fact, argued that women were *better* designed for scholarship than men! Self-interest and custom were the basis for men's belief that women were made for them (15). Men took advantage of their superior physical strength, especially during women's times of pregnancy. Poullain's causal explanations included both physical factors, like the constitution of the body, and social factors, like the system of education, to show how women were disadvantaged (23-29).

Poullain accepted Descartes's radical democracy of reason, which Astell, we shall soon see, rejected.

> The domain of reason has no boundary; it has an equal jurisdiction over all people. We are all born to be judges of the things that affect us. (117)

Poullain used Cartesian doubt to sweep away the conventional arguments, founded on prejudice and tradition, for male supremacy. Differences between the sexes concerned only the body; the mind was sexless (85). Not only could women learn any scientific subject as well as men, they could exercise functions in government, law, the church, and even the military (121). As had Gournay, Poullain went far beyond most demands for women's equality for centuries. He highlighted the materialist component of Cartesianism, even using it to argue for the superiority of women. Women's brains "are arranged in such a way that they receive impressions of objects easily," even the weakest and the lightest impressions, which tend to escape persons constituted differently (that is, men). Women retain impressions better and are more skilled in presenting them (131). Poullain showed the differences between women and men in approaching a problem. He also showed considerable sensitivity to sexist language.

Poullain's work attracted little attention at the time. There is no evidence that Astell knew it although other advocates for equality did. An anonymous translator published an English version in 1677, with the title *The Woman as good as the Man*.

Anne Conway (1631-1679)

Conway, born Anne Finch, was a daughter of the speaker of the House of Commons. Her brother was a student of the Cambridge Platonist Henry More. She was educated by tutors in Latin, Greek, French, and apparently some Hebrew before marrying. In spite of suffering greatly from headaches she managed to carry on her scholarly work. For thirty years she corresponded with Henry More and received visits from him at the Conway country estate in Warwickshire. A Quaker convert, she was greatly respected both for her piety and learning. She wrote her one book, The Principles of the Most Ancient and Modern Philosophy, *in Latin, in the 1670s; scholars differ as to precise years. It was published posthumously in Latin in 1690 and in English in 1692.*

There are essays on Conway in Doris Stenton, English Woman *and the introduction to her* Principles. *See Jane Duran, "Anne Viscountess Conway."*

Anne Conway has become a source for some feminists and environmentalists because of her conceptualization of continuities in nature. She considered everything to be spirit and the division between living and nonliving arbitrary. Yet Conway's nature was not only fiercely hierarchical but expressed a male/active female/passive dichotomy as well. This makes her an anomalous model, as the excerpts to follow will show. Except for her Quakerism, her work is typically treated as derivative of her neo-Platonist friend Henry More. Yet there are places where she departs from his neo-Platonism and these are of particular interest to feminists.

On the one hand Conway rejected the Cartesian doctrine that only humans could think. She considered that there was some thought in all animals, indeed in all of nature. Matter and spirit were inextricably linked so that everybody and everything was spirit. Yet she portrayed animal nature negatively, even arguing that transformation into animal nature might be a punishment for degenerate human behaviour. "No man that lives carnally and after the manner of beasts can enter into the kingdom of heaven" (186). While all creatures were composed of both body and spirit, so had they also an active and passive principle, or a *"more active and more passive principle,* which may fitly be termed male and female by reason of that analogy a husband has with his wife" (188). The active/passive dichotomy was accompanied by a light/dark dichotomy, which again has a connotation of good and evil: "The spirit is an eye or light beholding its own proper image, and the body is a tenebrosity or darkness receiving that image" (189).

Conway's female principle, however, was not so passive as the original Aristotelian formulation. In reproduction the female seed both retained the image and spirit of the male and mixed female spirits with it:

> And therefore whatever spirit is then strongest, and has the strongest image or *idea* in the seed, whether it be the masculine or feminine, or any other spirit from either of those received from without, that spirit is predominant in the seed and forms the body, as near as may be after its own image, and so every creature receives his external form. (189)

This is something of a feminist declaration of independence in idealist philosophy. Spirit and body were both creatures with no essential differences. On the other hand spirits had dominion over bodies and moved them, a conventional Platonic teaching. Thus, her all-is-one conceptualization of nature incorporates a rigid hierarchy. Conway rejected the Cartesian and empiricist notion that the instruments of sense and thought are sexless, and thus that women are equally able to pursue knowledge.

Mary Astell (1668-1731)

Mary Astell was born in Newcastle to a respectable family with landed gentry connections. Her father was a prosperous coal merchant and member of the ruling guild. The family had been royalists in the Civil War and Astell early and always held to that cause. She was educated by a clergyman uncle, a published poet but an alcoholic who was fired from his post as assistant curate. He had attended Cambridge University when Platonism was prominent there and taught it to his niece. She also learned Latin, English literature, and some theology. From a young age she was deeply religious. She shared also the staunch conservative politics of the established church: the divine right of the sovereign to rule and no toleration for dissent. There were money problems on the death of Astell's father, when she was aged twelve. Her uncle/tutor died the following year, her mother six years later.

On her mother's death Astell was left with enough money to live for a year. Undaunted, at about age twenty she set off alone for London. She established herself in Chelsea with a network of aristocratic, wealthy women friends who shared her concern for women's education and gave her financial support. A gentlewoman in distressed circumstances, she did not work for money and her publishing apparently earned her little. Once she was helped by an archbishop. These experiences demonstrated the need for a

Mary Astell kind of community for women and presumably helped shape her proposal for a college for women. Astell never married. Apparently negotiations were once under way but broke down. At a time when respectable women did not live alone, she did. She was the last member of her family, predeceased by her younger brother.

Astell believed in the direct approach. Soon after her arrival in London she wrote the Cambridge Platonist John Norris, noting an error in his logic. An exchange of correspondence ensued, published in 1695 at Norris's initiative and under his name, as Letters concerning the Love of God. Astell was seeking a mentor in Norris. He obliged to a point, encouraged her work, but kept the subject of their correspondence largely to his own interests. Astell obviously shared much of the piety of the Cambridge Platonists, but both the Letters and her other methodological writing show her independence in key areas. Another work, The Christian Religion (1705), again shows the religious foundation for Astell's belief in women's equality, now with interesting ethical arguments. Tightly argued, with numbered paragraphs and more than 400 pages long, it was attributed to the dean of Canterbury.

Astell's methodology appears mainly in her books on women, beginning with the witty and provocative Serious Proposal for the Ladies, part 1 of which appeared in 1694, the longer part 2 in 1697. This was her most popular book, four editions of which were published by 1701. Some Reflections upon Marriage, based on an actual case demonstrating the legal disabilities of women, was published in 1700. Her publisher, who shared her conservative politics, probably commissioned her polemical pamphlets. In 1704 Astell published Moderation truly stated, a tract with no moderation whatsoever. Her last book, An Enquiry after Wit, opposed the moderation and accommodation for dissent of the Earl of Shaftesbury and John Locke. In the course of showing that the real enemy was deism, Astell made a number of points on methodology that help to flesh out her position. Apparently she planned to write a compendium on natural philosophy for women but did not.

The same year that her last tract came out, 1709, Astell turned to more practical endeavours. Frustrated in her project of a women's college, she now organized a charity school for girls in Chelsea. She found the backers, selected staff, and gave overall supervision. The school's foundation included a stipulation that it always be under the direction of women. In her fifties she had cataract problems, and an illness requiring respite from London air. Astell died at age sixty-five of breast cancer, despite a mastectomy without anaesthetic. "Astell Street" in Chelsea is named after her.

Recommended biographies: Ruth Perry, The Celebrated Mary Astell **Mary Astell**
(Celebrated) and Florence M. Smith, Mary Astell. *Shorter essays on her can
be found in Doris Stenton,* English Woman; *Ada Wallas,* Before the Blue-
stockings; *Margaret Hunt,* Women and the Enlightenment; *Bridget Hill,*
The First English Feminist; *Hilda L. Smith,* Reason's Disciples. *See also
Joan K. Kinnaird, "Mary Astell and the Conservative Contribution to English
Feminism."*

Mary Astell, "arguably the first systematic feminist theoretician in
the West,"[18] was at the same time a pioneer methodologist. Her work is
an eclectic combination of Cartesian doubt and Lockean caution and
aversion to system. While for Descartes doubt was a phase after which
certainty was re-established, for Locke reason for doubt remained and
certitude was never possible. In both substance and tone Astell resem-
bled Locke, whose *Essay concerning Human Understanding* had been
published in 1690, and which was to define empiricism for the next
century.

Adhering to the conventions of her class and sex, Astell published
her books anonymously. *A Serious Proposal to the Ladies* was officially
"By a Lover of her Sex," *The Christian Religion*, by a "daughter of the
Church of England," *Moderation truly stated* by Tom Single. She was,
however, known as the author, and her books were much talked about.
Her treatment of women as men's intellectual and moral equals was
attacked by anti-feminists of the day, but was otherwise appreciated as
provocative. Jonathan Swift satirized her. She had an early and excellent
imitator in, probably, Judith Drake, with *An Essay in defence of the
Female Sex*. Daniel Defoe praised her proposal for a women's college.
The scientist John Evelyn cited her approvingly in his *Numismata*. Yet
little of her correspondence, and no journals or early drafts, have
survived. When Ruth Perry was conducting the research for her biography, a mere four letters were known, those because their recipients
were men important enough to have their letters collected. Perry
unearthed another forty letters. We must be grateful to an amateur
historian/dressmaker, George Ballard, for a fifteen-page essay recording the essential facts of Astell's life, published in his *Memoirs of Several
Ladies of Great Britain* (1752). For this he interviewed friends of Astell,
notably the Anglo-Saxon scholar Elizabeth Elstob. (He found her nearly

---

[18] Catherine R. Stimpson, "Foreword," in Ruth Perry, *The Celebrated Mary Astell*,
xi.

destitute, teaching at a girls' school.) It was not until 1916 that Florence Smith's doctoral thesis gave us a full-length biography. This work, however, ignored Astell's redoubtable feminism. Astell has more recently attracted interest as an early feminist, but is still little recognized as a methodologist and political polemicist.

Astell's fierce opposition to Locke's liberal politics, toleration of dissent, and leanings to Unitarianism have tended to influence commentators to treat her as an opponent of Locke's empiricism also. True, she adopted Cartesian terminology, but so did Locke. Clearly she shared the more certain, less sceptical approach of Malebranche and the Cambridge Platonists for reasons of religion, but she also differed with them. She used Arnauld and Nicole's *Logic of Port Royal*, which stressed the idealism of Cartesianism, downplaying the scepticism and material elements. Yet Astell did the opposite, drawing on Descartes when he was cautious and sceptical, not accepting his system building. Nor did she use Descartes's animal/machine imagery, instead using "machine" in a pejorative sense. She had greater confidence than Locke in the possibility of certain knowledge, but altogether is closer to Locke on methodology than to Descartes or Malebranche. Unlike Locke she would allow some, (very limited) place for innate ideas. Her first major biographer saw the common ground: "whatever her attitude toward Locke, she is much influenced by him."[19] More recent commentators, on the other hand, have taken the Cartesian language at face value, ignoring the qualifications and differences.

Astell's letters to John Norris show her desperate desire for learning and frustration at the barriers:

> Hitherto I have courted truth with a kind of romantic passion in spite of all difficulties and discouragements, for knowledge is thought so unnecessary an accomplishment for a woman that few will give themselves the trouble to assist them in the attainment of it.[20]

She asked for a system of principles she could rely on, "to initiate a raw disciple in the study of philosophy" (101). Deferential as she was to her mentor there is the occasional spark of independence. Norris recommended Malebranche's vision-in-God conceptualization, a qualified version of which she accepted for a time. By her last letter she had totally rejected this position, that God is the only efficient cause

---

[19] Florence M. Smith, *Mary Astell*, 61.
[20] John Norris, *Letters concerning the Love of God*, 78. I have modernized spelling and punctuation in quotations from this and other early work.

of all our sensations. She argued the refutation well and succinctly. If the sensations we feel do not come from bodies, but are simply what God pleases to cause, we might as well feel cold from fire and heat from water:

> Since God may as well excite sensations in our souls without these positive conditions as with them to what end do they serve? And then what becomes of that acknowledged truth that God does nothing in vain, when such variety of objects as our senses are exercised about are wholly unnecessary. Why therefore may there not be a *sensible congruity* between those powers of the soul that are employed in sensation and those objects which occasion it? (279-80)

To Astell it seemed more agreeable to the majesty of God and divine order to say that God produced our sensations through Nature than to affirm that they are brought about directly through divine power (282). In *A Serious Proposal* Astell dismissed the vision-in-God methodology with irony: "Whatever the notion that we see all things in God may be as to the truth of it, it is certainly very commendable for its piety" (96).

A Serious Proposal to the Ladies became a work of methodology in the course of arguing the importance of education for women. To deal with education Astell had first to treat the underlying issue of how anyone acquires knowledge. The argument for women's requiring and deserving knowledge in turn derives from Astell's theology:

> For since God has given women as well as men intelligent souls, why should they be forbidden to improve them? (18)

It was cruel and unjust to exclude women from knowledge. Women's faculty of thinking should be employed on the noblest object, not trifles. She warned that "as exercise enlarges and exalts any faculty, so through want of using it becomes cramped and lessened" (19). However Cartesian her terminology, Astell insisted that "we know not anything by intuition, or immediate view, except a few first principles" (81). Otherwise knowledge was acquired by reason and deduction. Here she distinguished three modes of thinking: faith, science, and opinion, each with its own limits relative to the functioning of the human intellect:

> Knowledge in a proper and restricted sense and as appropriated to science, signifies that clear perception which is followed by a firm assent to conclusions rightly drawn from premises of which we have clear and distinct ideas. Which premises or principles must be so clear and evident, that supposing us reasonable creatures, and free from prejudices and passions, which for the time they predominate

as good as deprive us of our reason, we cannot withhold our assent from them without manifest violence to our reason.

But if the nature of the thing be such as that it admits of no undoubted premises to argue from, or at least we do not at present know of any, or that the conclusion does not so necessarily follow as to give a perfect satisfaction to the mind and to free it from all hesitation, that which we think of it is then called opinion. (81)

If the medium used to prove a proposition is authority, the conclusion we draw from it is a matter of faith and belief.

Moral certainty is a species of knowledge whose proofs are of a compounded nature, in part resembling those which belong to science, and partly those of faith. (81)

We do not conduct the whole process ourselves, but depend on others for proofs, deducing from circumstances and principles. We often deceive ourselves by inclining alternately to both extremes.

Sometimes we reject truths which are morally certain as conjectural and probable only, because they have not a physical and mathematical certainty, which they are incapable of. At another time we embrace the slightest conjectures and anything that looks with probability, as moral certainties and real verities, if fancy, passion or interest recommend them; so ready are we to be determined by these rather than by solid reasons. (81-82)

The "moral certainty" expression Astell used is of ancient origin, going back to the constructive scepticism of fourth century B.C. Greece. Closer to Astell's time the moderate wing of the Church of England, the Latitudinarians, used similar terms to refer to probable knowledge for which there is evidence short of certainty. John Wilkins used precisely that term in *Of the Principles and Duties of Natural Religion*, published in 1675. Astell vehemently rejected the tolerant approach of these "broad church" divines. Yet her methodological views show considerable moderation.

Astell did not include the senses in her enumeration of the ways of knowing in *Serious Proposal*, for properly speaking we are conscious of what we perceive rather than knowing it. "And also because that light which we suppose to be let into our ideas by our senses is indeed very dim and fallacious, and not to be relied on till it has passed the test of reason" (82).

Although it is not our subject here, Astell was also keen to argue the common ground between faith and science. She held that, while there was a great difference between immutable science and variable and uncertain opinion, the difference between faith and science was not so great as usually supposed. The question was not one of certainty but of the way of proof. Science involves following a process based on clear and evident principles, while faith depends on the witness of another. In matters of faith we cannot see so clearly and distinctly as to be unable to disbelieve. Faith has a mixture of will in it. But as it was a fault to believe in matters of science, where we should expect demonstration and evidence, so also was it an error to require scientific process for objects not proper to it. It would be ridiculous to reject music because we do not taste or see it. Each area has its own sphere:

> Whoever has not seen Paris has nothing but human authority to assure him there is such a place, and yet he would be laughed at as ridiculous who should call it in question, though he may as well in this as in another case pretend that his informers have designs to serve, intend to impose on him and mock his credulity. Nay how many of us daily make that a matter of faith which indeed belongs to science, by adhering blindly to the dictate of some famous philosopher in physical truths, the principles of which we have as much right to examine, and to make deductions from them as he had?
>
> To sum up all: We may know enough for all the purposes of life, enough to busy this active faculty of thinking, to employ and entertain the spare intervals of time and to keep us from rust and idleness, but we must not pretend to fathom all depths with our short line. (84)

We should be sober and recognize that we know very little if we make our *own* reason the standard of all truth. It is certain that nothing is true but what is conformable to reason, and as certain that there are many truths which human reason cannot comprehend.

> Therefore to be thoroughly sensible of the capacity of the mind, to discern precisely its bounds and limits and to direct our studies and inquiries accordingly, to know what is to be known, and to believe what is to be believed is the property of a wise person. To be content with too little knowledge, or to aspire to over-much is equally a fault, to make that use of our understandings which God has fitted and designed them for is the medium which we ought to take. (84)

Astell's understanding of "reason" was strictly qualified. Sceptical as she was of the reliability of the senses, so also was she of reason. Contrary to a common contention of idealists, she held that there are many truths our minds cannot comprehend. Nor did education result in any privileged access to reason. The difference between a doctor and a ploughman was not that one searched after knowledge while the other had nothing to do with it. Rather whoever had a rational soul ought to employ it about some truth or other in order to make true judgments, however extensive that person's knowledge might be. Yet the capacity to reason varied. Astell saw no reason why there might not be as great a variety in minds as there was in faces (85). Here she departed absolutely from the idealists with their singular Reason or Mind. Like Locke she used the plural for understandings and minds, and referred to "every individual understanding" and our "own particular minds."

Descartes, in the opening passages of the *Discourse on Method*, had argued everyone's equal capacity to reason. Astell's rejection of this key tenet is perfectly clear in *A Serious Proposal*. She repeated it with even more force in *An Enquiry after Wit*:

> Good sense is discerned only by the few who have it; for one may
> modestly say that it is not the birth-right of every reader, though
> more are born to than make use of it. (18)

In the same book she also indulged in a humorous putdown of two other elements of idealism, reliance on reason and on the goodness of God/nature not to deceive us. Thus she "demonstrated," by reason, that Columbus did not discover America:

> The plain homespun philosophy of looking into ourselves may also
> do us wondrous service in rectifying our errors about this pretended
> discovery ... *Reason* will tell us that it is not consistent with the good-
> ness of nature, which has no malice, to suffer such rich and deli-
> cious countries to be concealed from us, and our arts and sciences,
> our polite way of living, and all the improvements of this hemisphere
> have made, to be unknown to the other. A universal Being can have
> no interest opposite; and therefore can have no malice. And, if there
> be a general Mind, it can have no particular interest. This is
> demonstration! And so good night to *Columbus* and all his fine
> discoveries. (97-98)

In a more serious vein Astell exhorted modesty, caution, and consciousness of our own defects and imperfections in seeking the truth. In *A Serious Proposal* she described the exercise of understanding as passive and judgment as belonging to the will. The understanding, properly speaking, erred only in being too narrow. This gave guidance as to how we should proceed in seeking knowledge:

> Non perception we cannot help; a finite mind, suppose it as large as
> you please, can never extend itself to infinite truths. But no doubt

it is in our power to remedy a great deal more than we do, and probably a larger range is allowed us than the most active and enlightened understanding has hitherto reached. Ignorance then cannot be avoided but error may; we cannot judge of things of which we have no idea, but we can suspend our judgment about those of which we have, till clearness and evidence oblige us to pass it. (90)

Astell devoted some space to showing how easy it is to go wrong through impetuosity and volatility of thought, too warm an imagination, and too active a spirit. We skip nimbly from one idea to another without observing due order and connection, being content with a superficial view, a random glance, taking in appearances without penetrating the subject. Unrelated ideas rush in and the mind entertains all comers, however impertinent. But:

> Truth is not often found by such as won't take time to examine her counterfeits, to distinguish between evidence and probability, realities and appearances. (91-92)

It was conceit that made people think they could pierce to the bottom of things with the first glance.

> We love grandeur and everything that feeds our good opinion of ourselves, and therefore would judge offhand, supposing it a disparagement to our understandings to be long in examining, so that we greedily embrace whatever seems to carry evidence enough for a speedy determination, how slight and superficial soever it be. Whereas did we calmly and deliberately examine our evidence, and how far those motives we are acted by ought to influence, we should not be liable to this seduction. (94)

To cool this impetuosity and achieve a sedate and steady mind required making the "animal spirits" more calm and manageable. This is similar to Malebranche's advice on controlling unruly passions but there is a marked difference. While the idealist philosopher blamed all error on the senses, so that to attain knowledge one had to close the door and blinds and concentrate the mind, Astell considered that both body and mind could be at fault and both needed help:

> The body and the mind do so reciprocally influence each other that we can scarce keep the one in tune if the other be out of it. We can neither observe the errors of our intellect, nor the irregularity of our morals whilst we are darkened by fumes, agitated with unruly passions, or carried away with eager desires after sensible things ...

> Without attention and strict examination we are liable to false
> judgments on every occasion, to vanity and arrogance, to imper-
> tinent prating of things we do not understand, are kept from
> making a progress because we fancy ourselves to be at the top
> already. (92)

To think to good purpose we must realize how often we have not done
so up to now, suspect our quick judgments, and not give our imagina-
tions leave to ramble.

Astell's stress on governing the passions may seem old-fashioned
now, but much of her advice has not dated at all. If the impetuosity of a
warm imagination could be cooled, and the extravagances of a disor-
derly one regulated, "we should not be deceived by the report of our
senses, the prejudices of education, our own private interest, and readiness to receive the opinions whether true or false of those we love"
(94). We have to divest ourselves of our own interests. "Not to engage
ourselves so far in any party or opinion as to make it in a manner necessary that that should be right, lest from wishing it were, we come at
last to persuade ourselves it is so" (95).

> In sum, whatever false principle we embrace, whatever wrong
> conclusion we draw from true ones, is a disparagement to our think-
> ing power, a weakness of judgment proceeding from a confused and
> imperfect view of things, as that does from want of attention and a
> hasty and partial examination. (94)

We cannot even list all false reasonings and generalizations we fall
into, "for there are innumerable errors opposite to one single truth."
Apart from the general causes already mentioned, there are the various mixtures of the "passions, interests, education, conversation and
readings, and so forth of particular persons." The best way to improve
the understanding, to guard it against errors, was to regulate the will:

> not to judge of anything which we do not apprehend, to suspend
> our assent till we see just cause to give it, and to determine noth-
> ing till the strength and clearness of the evidence oblige us to it.
> (95)

Elsewhere in a pamphlet Astell advised the reader to exercise Cartesian doubt, not to take bare words on trust, but to see "with his *own*
eyes and to judge according to his *own* understanding," to be of no
party because some great man is, or the opinion is popular, serves well,
or has long been held.[21]

---

[21] Astell, *Moderation truly stated*, 2.

Norris had urged Astell to read Malebranche, the philosopher most opposed to materialism and the mechanical philosophy then gaining support. It is not clear whether or how much she acted on this advice, or what she might have learned indirectly, for she did not read French. If Astell had read *Recherche de la vérité* where it described the "delicate brain fibres" of women and children she might have been put off. Malebranche affirmed the superior sensitivity of women for frivolous things like fashion and taste, but:

> For the most part they are incapable of penetrating truths a little difficult to discover. They cannot use their imagination to develop complicated and difficult questions. They consider but the outer shell of things and their imagination lacks the force and breadth to get to the bottom and compare all parts without being distracted.[22]

Malebranche conceded, as the exception that proves the rule, that some women had firmer minds than some men. Generally, however, women's brain fibres remained as soft as children's while men's developed. Since women and children did not teach or do research their errors did not cause much harm, "for one hardly believes the things they put forward" (1: 268).

Truth was external, objective, singular, and beautiful according to *A Serious Proposal*. Our ideas are false when they have no conformity to the real nature of the thing whose name they bear (99). Since truth is one there should be no contradictions in opinions if we all act only for love of truth (114). "Thinking conformably to the nature of things is true knowledge" (121). We should be passionately in love with truth, sensitive to her excellency and beauty, "to embrace her how opposite soever she may sometimes be to our humours and designs, to bring these over to her, and never attempt to make her truckle to them" (95). We should be far from disliking a truth because it touches us close to home or plainly shows us our errors.

To help women use their minds properly Astell set out six rules, quite similar to the four rules Descartes gave in his *Discourse on Method*. Her third and fourth rules are rough paraphrases of his precepts. Her first resembles the first rule of Arnauld and Nicole's *Logic of Port Royal* (306). Astell addressed women explicitly and used nonsexist terms like "person" in her "natural logic." ("Mankind" and even "Man" appear, but much less often than in other authors.) She advised that just as diligence makes for riches so the use of our powers improves and

---

[22] Malebranche, *Recherche de la vérité*, in *Oeuvres complètes*, 1: 267.

increases them:

> The most observing and considerate is the wisest person, for she lays up in her mind as in a store-house, ready to produce on all occasions a clear and simple idea of every object that has at any time presented itself. And perhaps the difference between one woman's reason and another's may consist only in this, that the one has amassed a greater number of such ideas than the other, and disposed them more orderly in her understanding, so that they are at hand, ready to be applied to those complex ideas whose agreement or disagreement cannot be found out but by the the means of some of them. (105)

Here Astell has joined a Lockean development to the Cartesian base, going on to explain how a medium is necessary when relations cannot be discerned by intuition or a simple view.[23]

A Serious Proposal gives the following as rules:

> Rule I. *Acquaint ourselves thoroughly with the state of the question, have a distinct notion of our subject whatever it be, and of the terms we make use of, knowing precisely what it is we drive at ...*
>
> Rule II. *Cut off all needless ideas and whatever has not a connection to the matter under consideration ...*
>
> Rule III. *To conduct our thoughts by order, beginning with the most simple and easy objects, and ascending as by degrees to the knowledge of the more composed ...*
>
> Rule IV. *Not to leave any part of our subject unexamined ... dividing the subject of our meditations into as many parts as we can and as shall be requisite to understand it perfectly ...*
>
> Rule V. *Always keep our subject directly in our eye, and closely pursue it through all our progress ...*
>
> Rule VI. *To judge no further than we perceive, and not to take anything for truth which we do not evidently know to be so.* (105-07)

Astell noted that in some cases we are forced to be content with probability, but advised doing so only when it is plainly necessary. That is, we have to stay with probability when either we have no proofs of a constant and immutable connection with the ideas to which those proofs connect, or we cannot perceive the connection. Astell was conceptually far from the idealists on the Continent and the Cambridge Platonists close to home. The remedy in situations of uncertainty was the ancient one of suspension of belief: if we lack the means to pass

---

[23] Florence Smith, *Mary Astell*, 60.

judgment properly or we have never considered the matter before we should suspend judgment until we can be better informed. This is precisely what the ancient sceptics taught, what Montaigne revived, and what the Latitudinarians continued: we must make decisions on the basis of available information, while continuing the search. "Sceptic" in Greek means an inquirer or searcher, not someone who doubts.

Astell's case for women was part of a more general argument that all people had been given rational minds, which God intended to be used:

> If therefore he has given to mankind a rational mind, every individual understanding ought to be employed in something worthy of it. The meanest person should think as *justly*, though not as *capaciously*, as the greatest philosopher. (98)

There can be little purpose in thinking well if we do not live well. Women were to learn to think methodically the better to perform their obligations. Here Astell argued that knowledge was needed in all walks of life, not just the liberal professions. Women need knowledge to raise their children properly (129). The whole world is a single woman's family, an argument "maternal feminists" would use in the struggle for the vote in the early twentieth century.

Feminists who hold to the view that women form their moral ideas differently from men will find interesting antecedents in Astell. One of the best books we could study, she stated, especially in regard to morality, is "our own heart." One reason we are not more proficient in useful knowledge is because we do not duly consult it (143). With the idealist philosophers Astell was committed to reason over passion, but would allow the passions a much greater role than would they. The soul should have dominion over the body, which was to be an instrument for the mind and no more (137). It was not a fault to have passions, which were natural and unavoidable. The point was to govern them, "to maintain the empire of our reason and freedom of our will, "not to be enslaved to any appetite" (147). God was too kind and bountiful to deny us any pleasures befitting our nature. Astell's correspondence with Norris shows her balking at his excessive otherworldliness. If the sole object of love were God, what were creatures for, she countered. Nor, important as reason was, would she allow it the power to determine the principles of faith, which could only be known by revelation.[24] Astell, again, is in direct line with Montaigne, Bacon, and the scientists of the Royal Society.

---

[24] Astell, *Christian Religion*, 50.

Astell's religious views led her to prefer the spiritual world to the material world, but she would not dismiss the latter as rank or loathsome as so many idealists did. Nor could she keep the two spheres far apart. Descartes had found the union of body and soul so problematic that he invented a fictitious function for the pineal gland to make the link. While Astell instead simply asserted the connection and mutual influence of body and mind, she could not go so far as Locke to consider that matter just possibly might be able to think.

At the time Astell wrote women never had been and were not admitted into any university or college in Britain. Henry VIII closed the ancient abbeys and convents where women had learned and taught. Anna van Schurman had argued in "The Learned Maid" that women could be scholars in spite of their exclusion from colleges. Astell now sought the practical remedy: the establishment of a college for women. This she put in language unusually circumspect, even diffident. Seminaries were thought proper for men; they even enjoyed the bounty of noble lady foundresses. "Why should we not think that such ways of education would be as advantageous to the ladies?" (157) Why, indeed, should we despair of "finding some among them who will be as kind to their own sex as their ancestors have been to the other?" Novelist Daniel Defoe supported the proposal, using Astell's arguments in his *Essay upon Projects* (1697). Astell is thought to have lined up a backer, possibly the future Queen Anne, to provide £10,000 to establish such a college. Regrettably, the idea was opposed by Bishop Burnet, who thought it smacked of popery. (Astell herself never worried about popery; deism and Unitarianism were so much worse.) Her own stated intentions were evidently ignored: "Our institution is rather *academical* than monastic," she explained. Only the very ignorant or malicious would pretend that we would imitate foreign monasteries (157).

Astell's political views can be given only passing mention but several comments must be made. First, her Toryism, for all its insistence on the subject's duty to obey the sovereign, at the same time gave onerous obligations to the privileged. There is even a hint of the Utilitarian principle of the greatest good to the greatest number, which emerged in the eighteenth century. She at least required that the collective good be considered. In *The Christian Religion* Astell affirmed a preference for the good of her neighbour over her lesser good:

> A less evil suffered by me is not so bad in itself as a greater suffered
> by my neighbour. Therefore it is not reasonable, and consequently

not best, that my neighbour should endure an evil to procure me a
good not equal in degree to that evil; or that I should refuse pain or
loss to procure for another a good that outweighs it. (202-03)

God was no respecter of persons and absolutely did not "will a good to
any one of his creatures that tends to the greater evil of another, but ...
always wills the greatest good" (203). More specifically, "it is much
better that I should want some of the conveniencies of life than that
any of my neighbours should want the necessaries" (204). Astell here
seems to have moved past red Toryism if not quite to liberation theology. "Nor is it only charity but justice that requires our superfluities
should be laid upon our indigent brethren," she went on, defining superfluities as "all that exceeds the necessities and moderate conveniences
of life." Goods were "committed to our stewardship to no other end or
purpose but that they should be spent in supplying our neighbour's
wants" (205). Similarly, in *A Serious Proposal*, she affirmed:

When we consider that we are but several parts of one great whole,
and are by Nature so connected to each other that whenever one
part suffers the rest must suffer with it, either by compassion or
else by being punished for the want of it, we shall never be so absurd
as to fancy we can do ourselves a service by any thing injurious to
our neighbours. (138)

Consistent and clear as Astell was in resisting the "possessive individualism" then emerging, she was ignored in the scholarly debate.
Stimpson credits her with "the first feminist critique of possessive individualism,"[25] but C.B. Macpherson's classic analysis, *The Political Theory
of Possessive Individualism*, does not even mention her.

Astell's Toryism made for an obvious contradiction, for the divine
right of the sovereign to rule had its corollary in the right of a husband
to rule his wife. In *Some Reflections upon Marriage* Astell accepted this
principle, warning women of the risky consequences of their choice of
"a monarch for life." She advised the single state for many, acknowledging that if all so chose that would be the end of the human race (87).

A spectacular case of husbandly abuse prompted Astell to write *Some
Reflections upon Marriage*. The victim was her Chelsea neighbour and
acquaintance, the Duchess of Mazarine. The book, however, sets out
Astell's general views on marriage. In the course of making the case
for an educated wife, which she held to be in the husband's interest as

---

[25] Catherine Stimpson, "Foreword," in Perry, *The Celebrated Mary Astell*, xii. See
also Catherine Gallagher, "Embracing the Absolute," on how Astell's Toryism
contributed to her feminism.

well, Astell again turned to issues of methodology. Radical arguments for the equality of women were backed up with Biblical exegesis. This indeed gives a sense of *déjà vu* to much of the Christian feminism of recent decades, for example: "The Bible is for us, and not against us, and cannot without great violence done to it, be urged to our prejudice" (112).

Astell maintained that she was not stirring up sedition or undermining "masculine empire," but she did not advise a wife to think her husband's folly was wisdom or his brutality the love and worship promised in the marriage oath, for "this required a flight of wit and sense much above her poor ability and proper only to masculine understandings" (96). Women had an equal ability to make intellectual judgments:

> Nor can error, be it as ancient as it may, ever plead prescription against truth. And since the only way to remove all doubts, to answer objections, and to give the mind entire satisfaction, is not by *affirming*, but by *proving*, so that everyone may see with their *own* eyes, and judge according to their *own* understandings; she hopes it is *no* presumption to insist on this natural right of judging for herself, and the rather, because by quitting it, we give up all the means of rational conviction. Allow us then as many glasses as you please to help our sight, and as many good arguments as you can afford to convince our understandings; but do not exact of us, we beseech you, to affirm that we see such things as are only the discovery of men who have quicker senses, or that we understand and know what we have by hearsay only, for to be so excessively complaisant is neither to see nor to understand. (98-99)

Astell's claim for equality, in short, was inextricably intermixed with an affirmation of the empiricist approach to knowledge. Understandings, again in the plural, worked from sense data and observation could be improved with instruments. The Creator, moreover, made everything in "number, weight and measure" (52).

Astell was sarcastic when describing men's claim to freedom for themselves while denying the same rights to women. Was it "not then partial in men to contend for and practise that arbitrary dominion in their families, which they abhor and exclaim against in the state?" If arbitrary power is evil in itself it ought not to be practised anywhere, no more in families than in kingdoms:

> If all men are born free, how is it that all women are born slaves? ...
> And why is slavery so much condemned and strove against in one

case and so highly applauded and held so necessary and so sacred in another? (107-08)

Astell had an unsentimental view of social contract: "Covenants between husband and wife, like laws in an arbitrary government, are of little force, the will of the sovereign is all in all" (43). This was fact; she would not answer for the rightness of it. Similarly she pointed out that usurping the rights of others, though they might submit out of prudence, nonetheless left everybody free to regain their rights when they had the power and opportunity:

I do not say tyranny *ought*, but we find in *fact*, that it provokes the oppressed to throw off even a lawful yoke that fits too heavy. (89)

Injury would be returned for injury, crime for crime. Both parties were guilty, but the aggressor was doubly so, having the ruin of a neighbour to answer for as well as the injury he caused. As a call to arms this is timid enough, but clearly there were limits to submission. So also were there in domestic tyranny. Divorce was allowable in cases of "irreclaimable vice and cruelty" (10).

Astell, also in *Reflections upon Marriage*, drew an analogy between a husband's domination over his wife and that of humans over nature. Environmental consciousness was an extremely rare strain of thought in seventeenth century Europe, so her understanding of stewardship and questioning of anthropocentrism are all the more remarkable:

Perhaps we arrogate too much to ourselves when we say this material world was made for our sakes. That its glorious Maker has given us the use of it is certain; but when we suppose anything to be made purely for our sakes because we have dominion over it, we draw a false conclusion. (52)

Further: "None of God's creatures, absolutely considered, are in their own nature contemptible; the meanest fly, the poorest insect has its use and virtue" (52-53).

An article written by Astell to promote the practice of smallpox inoculation shows that she was acquainted with the only social statistics then available, the bills of mortality. Along with the irony and expostulation so much her style, her article cites a treatise by a Fellow of the Royal Society. She made the case for inoculation on the basis of comparative mortality rates. While one in six of those who had smallpox died of it, not one in fifty inoculated (scarcely one in many hundreds) died.[26] Even the small number suspected of dying after inoculation could be

---

[26] Astell, *The Plain Dealer*, 241.

explained by extenuating circumstances. She praised the writer of the treatise for undertaking to resolve, "by *clear matter of fact*, to establish or explode this practice." He had "with an unwearied application and the most stedfast impartiality, informed himself of its success throughout all parts of the kingdom" (240). Specifically, he had examined forty years of the bills of mortality and all the case material available on inoculation. Astell next credited the "reason and the courage of a lady for the introduction of this art" (243). This, of course, was Mary Wortley Montagu, who had learned of the practice in Turkey, used it on her own children, and induced the royal family to try it. Wortley Montagu and Astell thus become the first women to apply their knowledge of method to preventive health; many more followed them.

Astell's favourable views of science can also be seen in her intention to produce a compendium on natural philosophy. Her biographer George Ballard recorded in the manuscript of his *Memoirs of Several Ladies* that she had divided the subject matter into several branches, as she thought proper. She "earnestly solicited some learned ladies of her acquaintance" to choose the sections of work they were most capable of cultivating. She undertook to do the remaining parts herself. None of the women, however, was willing "to enter upon this employment." What progress Astell made Ballard did not know (MS 74: 510). This intriguing part of Ballard's manucript did not make it into the published version.

It appears that Astell did not write but rather inspired the next work promoting empiricism in the struggle for equality, *An Essay in Defence of the Female Sex*. The author, probably **Judith Drake**,[27] made the same claim for equality as had Astell, Gournay, and company: all souls are equal. There are no innate ideas but all notions are derived from our external senses:

> I shall not enter into any dispute whether men or women be gener-
> ally more ingenious or learned; that point must be given up to the
> advantages men have over us by their education, freedom of
> converse and variety of business and company. (28)

Great allowance had to be made for the disparity in those circumstances:

---

[27] Florence Smith, *Mary Astell*, Appendix 2 makes a strong case for Judith Drake, not Astell, as the author of *An Essay in Defence*. See also Moira Ferguson, *First Feminists*.

> I see therefore no natural impediment in the structure of our bodies;
> nor does experience or observation argue any; we use all our natural
> faculties as well as men and our rational too, deducting only for the
> advantages before mentioned. (33)

The author appealed further to the experience of simpler creatures,
where no differences in sense or understanding between males and
females can be found, no constraint of custom or law, no differences
in education or bias. Like other empiricists, but unlike Astell, Drake
insisted that the differences between humans and animals were
gradual.

Men's claims for superiority are not objective "as men are parties
against us and therefore their evidence may justly be rejected." If
women had written any histories, "time and the malice of men have
effectively conspired to suppress them" (40). Men did not allow
anything to be transmitted that would show the weakness and ille-
gality of their title to power, which they still exercised arbitrarily.

The essays of that "wonderful" Bacon were praised, while Locke
was the great master of the art of reasoning:

> The greatest difficulty we struggled with was the want of a good art
> of reasoning, which we had not, that I know of, until that defect was
> supplied by the greatest master of that art, Mr. Locke, whose Essay
> on Human Understanding makes large amends for the want of all
> others in that kind. (61)

We were to learn directly from Nature, "the great book of universal
learning" (56).

Drake's claim, as was Gournay's and that of many others, was for
liberty. Fetters, even of gold, were fetters still, and the softest lining
could not make them as easy as liberty (41). Again custom is a negative force; women were held back by the "tyranny of custom" (26). *An
Essay in Defence of the Female Sex* sparkles with wry observations.
There are wonderful putdowns of male academic games:

> Men measure themselves by their vanity, and are greater or less in
> their own opinions according to the proportion they have of it; if
> they be well stocked with it, it may be easy to confute, but impossible
> to convince them. (98)

> Men love as little to have their reputation as their chimneys over-
> topped by their neighbours; for they think by that means their names
> become dark as their houses do smoky by the other. (105)

Damaris Cudworth Masham (1658-1708)

The daughter of the Cambridge Platonist Ralph Cudworth, Damaris Masham was raised in an intellectual household where she was encouraged and trained to take part in the life of reason. She was a skilled linguist, fluent in Latin, French, and Hebrew. She used Lockean educational principles to raise her one son, who evidently benefitted sufficiently from the experience to be on good terms with Locke. Sir Francis and Lady Masham invited Locke to spend his last years with them at their country estate. He accepted on condition that he be a paying guest. Damaris Masham was at his bedside, reading him psalms, when he died. Locke himself was much impressed with her ability and references to her by other male scholars are unusually respectful. Masham was buried in the middle aisle of Bath Abbey, but there is no memorial to mark her.

See Ada Wallas, Bluestockings *and Katharine M. Rogers,* Feminism.

It is a pity that Mary Astell and Damaris Masham could not have become friends. They had much in common methodologically, less so theologically; politically they were poles apart. Masham shared the toleration and liberalism of her friend John Locke, while Astell deplored it as treason and ruin. Yet both women supported education for women when few others did. And, if Astell was the stronger feminist, Masham was the more able critic of Malebranche's sexism.

Both of Masham's two books on methodology were published anonymously, but were known to be her work: *Occasional Thoughts in reference to a vertuous or Christian Life* (c. 1694) and *A Discourse concerning the Love of God* (1696). Each advances Lockean empiricism and repudiates idealism, especially that of Malebranche and his English disciple Norris. Each contains extensive discussion of theological questions. *Occasional Thoughts* is a defence of the life of reason, for women as well as men, but is cautious in its expectations for knowledge. Understandings and minds appear in the plural, implying a diversity of possibilities. As they were for other advocates of women's equality of this period, to Masham habit and custom were corrupting, reason the source of pleasure and satisfaction (5). The *Discourse* blames custom and education for many of the mischiefs we suffer (58). The right kind of education was required. In *Occasional Thoughts* Masham argued that we should not presume too much but be aware of the "inaccountableness" of divine wisdom to our understandings (111). We humans are only a small part of the "intellectual creation," and our abode on earth but a "very inconsiderable proportion of time to millions of ages," and nothing to eternity. We are little able to judge of the "divine economy" (112).

Masham was not the firebrand feminist her contemporary Astell was, but *Occasional Thoughts* makes an eloquent plea for the education of women. The need for that education flows directly from her Lockean psychology. Women should be responsible for the first eight to ten years of education of their children, both boys and girls. Hence women themselves have to be educated even for the sake of male education, quite apart from their own needs (190). To the quality of tenderness must be joined "a well informed understanding" (191). Thus women needed knowledge of languages, Latin as well as English, arithmetic, geography, and history. "The impressions received in that tender age" were of exceeding consequence to men "throughout the whole remainder of their lives, as having a strong and oftentimes unalterable influence upon their future inclinations and passions." Hence the need to admit mothers to education "for the right forming of the minds of their children of both sexes" (8). Yet those most solicitous about education "have usually employed their care herein but by halves" with little thought "in reference to the one whole sex" (7). By omitting women from education the pains taken in educating boys would often prove to be ineffectual.

Girls, Masham observed, were brought up in "traditionary opinions" instead of reason (162). Even if Nature were kind in bestowing talents on the female sex, through want of cultivating them this bounty was usually lost. Thanks to the "ignorance of men" science was believed improper for women; so little was taught them that knowledge of it could not be expected from them. Masham was scathing about the double sexual standard. "Virtue" for women meant chastity only, while for men many qualities were understood (154). Women were, as a consequence, hindered from aspiring to any form of excellence (21).

Masham's social analysis reveals a remarkable lack both of Euro- and anthropocentrism. For near four hundred years, "if the historian says right," morality was more exemplary among pagan native people than their "exterminators" who called themselves Christians, and were guilty both of deplorable "injustice, cruelty and oppression" and of introducing previously unknown vices to America (57). There was no sharp distinction between people and animals, who differed in reason "in kind or degree." Yet any advantage humans had because of their superior capacity for reason did not given them licence, for humans were designed to be subject themselves to reason. Masham carefully referred to the "appearance" that animals were intended to be subject to humans (66).

In 1690 Norris directed his *Reflections upon the Conduct of Human Life* to Masham on the mistaken assumption that she had lost her eyesight. His point was that she need not regret this loss, for the senses were not reliable sources of knowledge in any event. Masham learned of Norris's intention and wrote him to try to stop him. He went ahead nonetheless. Her *Discourse concerning the Love of God* was intended to show the "unservicableness" and "injuriousness" of a hypothesis lately recommended to the world by Norris (1-2). She did not think there was any danger that his "abstruse" hypothesis would become general opinion, but she admitted that it had the attraction of novelty. Masham would expose the "weakness and extravagance" of Malebranche's related doctrines of occasionalism and the vision-in-God, discussed above with Astell. Her own ontology, which she justified with theological arguments, was decidedly materialist. She rejected outright the Malebranche "hypothesis" that God was the sole cause of all sensation, that creatures had no ability to influence us but were only "occasional causes of those sentiments which God produces in us" (9). In arguing against Malebranche Masham appealed to the inherent democracy of empiricism:

> Every man indeed cannot so handsomely compose his system as
> Father Malebranche, but every man has as much authority to
> impose it upon others, or to be credited without proofs. (103)

Masham's repudiation of Malebranche was much more decisive and consistent than Astell's of the year previous. Unlike Astell she was proficient in French and she presumably knew Malebranche better from primary sources. Significantly for women, she lambasted Malebranche for his contention that children became sinners through physical union with their mothers. Although both "the apostle and reason" assure us that there was no transgression where there was no law, for Malebranche this was a necessary consequence of his idealism (107). Masham seems to have well understood the misogyny of Malebranche's position and reacted strongly to it. She lacked Astell's wit in argument but was considerably more precise and thorough at trouncing Malebranche.

Catharine Trotter Cockburn (1679-1749)

Trotter's father, a naval captain, died of plague en route to Turkey, his pension was irregularly paid, and the family had to live off relatives. At age sixteen Catharine Trotter had the first of her many plays produced in London, a tragedy in five acts. She later moved to Kent and, through Bishop and Mrs

Gilbert, became acquainted with the Cambridge Platonists living there, **Catharine**
notably John Norris. When this group began to attack Locke's Essay *Trotter* **Trotter**
published a defence, in 1702, against the advice of her friends. Locke traced **Cockburn**
her through the bookseller and sent her his appreciation. The spunky author
also sent a copy to Leibniz. Trotter married a clergyman and turned to other
work. She wrote another defence of Locke in 1726.

See Edmund Gosse, "Catharine Trotter, the Precursor of the Bluestockings"
and Doris Stenton, English Woman. *A two-volume* Works of Mrs. Catharine
Trotter Cockburn *includes a life of the author and the defence of Locke.*

Locke's *Essay concerning Human Understanding* was to be enormously influential in the eighteenth century, but when it first appeared
in 1690 it was attacked. The second person to come to its defence was
Catharine Trotter, a playwright and poet, later a writer of weighty tomes
on religion. Aware that a woman's name on her book would prejudice
readers, Trotter not only left off her name but wrote in the masculine.
Although it is not our concern here, a major motive for her was to
defend Locke against charges of impiety. Trotter's work is limited by
the fact of her scant education. Still, there is no doubt that she understood Locke's approach to methodology, chose it over the idealist alternatives preferred in her circle, and found it empowering. The dedication states that Locke's *Essay* gave her the courage to encounter an
opponent to it.

> The Essay of Human Understanding is a public concern, which
> everyone has a right and interest to defend. It came too late into
> the world to be received without opposition, as it might have been
> in the first ages of philosophy, before men's heads were prepos-
> sessed with imaginary science. At least, no doubt, if so perfect a
> work could have been produced so early, it would have prevented
> a great deal of that unintelligible jargon, and vain pretence to knowl-
> edge of things out of the reach of human understanding, which
> makes a great part of the school-learning, and disuse the mind to
> plain and solid truth.

Instead, Locke was reserved for a curious and learned age, to break in
upon the sanctuary of vanity and ignorance, "by setting men on considering first the *bounds of human understanding,* to help them in a close
pursuit of true and useful knowledge."[28] Was it possible for a lover of

---

[28] Catharine Trotter Cockburn, *A Defence of the Essay of Human Understanding,*
dedication.

the truth to be unmoved or to silently allow injurious insinuations against so excellent a design?

In the preface Trotter argued that Locke's *Essay* had helped to fix morality upon a solid foundation. Since the "science of true morality" was of the "most universal and highest" concern to humanity, those writers who established it on the clearest, most obvious, and most solid grounds did the best service to religion. By contrast, well-meaning men attempted to support religion on metaphysical notions, false and abstruse reasonings. Locke had dared to go against the "established monarchy over men's judgments" and so was considered a "troublesome and dangerous innovator" by those who had "imbibed the opinions of reverenced authors" and were unwilling "to unlearn all their former knowledge, to examine what they have been taught for first principles not to be questioned" (1). It took a "mighty force of reason and generous courage to break through all the prejudices of men and free them from a willing slavery" (2). The *Essay* removed the obstacles to truth, showed the method of attaining it more clearly and effectually, and was written "in an exacter method" than any before it (3). Whatever we can know at all must be discoverable through Locke's principles, ideas derived from sensation and reflection.

Trotter seems to have been less concerned about the scope for error than Locke had been, but she did affirm limits to knowledge based on the possibilities for observation. We are as ignorant of the "nature" of a thing as we are of the soul. We cannot know *what* it is, but can have clear ideas of the operations of thought. The immateriality of the soul/mind was "highly probable" but such should not be used in arguing for the soul's immortality (42). Thinking matter, as Locke had held, was not impossible (47). Trotter's defence of Locke includes an embryonic discussion of the greatest-happiness principle of Utilitarianism, to which subject we next go. God made happiness "the necessary motive of all our action" and gave us faculties to judge what is fit (11).

Utilitarianism

Two British male contributors should be cited for their influence on social theory and sex equality. **Francis Hutcheson (1694-1746)** was a major instigator of utility theory. He did not quite coin the term "the greatest good for the greatest number," but his formulation was close. As early as 1725 he referred to an internal moral sense — reason — by which we judge true and false, moral good and evil. Society ought to be directed so that our actions produce "the greatest and most extensive good in our power."[29] In *A System of Moral Philosophy*, published posthumously from his lecture material, Hutcheson described the purpose of laws in terms of the utility principle, using "good" and "happiness" interchangeably here as elsewhere. "The end of all laws should be the general good and happiness of a people" (2: 310). Hutcheson went further than other democrats by insisting that although they did not have the same rights as humans, animals did have some rights. Unnecessary cruelty was cruel and unjust, to be condemned as showing inhuman temper (1: 311).

The "monstrous power" civil laws gave to husbands over their wives was not only unjust, but imprudent, unnatural, tyrannical, and unmanly (2: 165). The conceded superiority of men to women in body and mind did not give men a right to govern women. There were exceptions to male superiority, in any event, and women were superior in other respects. Marriage should be a partnership of equals, including joint management of property. Hutcheson himself had experienced, and abhorred, the negotiations over property which were then a feature of bourgeois marriages. He argued also for the need for economic equality. "A democracy cannot remain stable unless the property be so diffused among the people that no such cabal of a few could probably unite in any design" with sufficient wealth to support a force superior to that of the rest (2: 247).

John Millar (1735-1801) was a student of Adam Smith, who had been a student of Hutcheson. Millar, in turn, taught James Mill, father of J. S. Mill. He worked for the great reform causes of the day: parliamentary and electoral reform, the abolition of slavery, prison reform, and workers' education. His *Origin of Ranks* (1779) is an early example of class analysis. It includes a lengthy chapter on the rank and condition of women in different historical periods from primitive to recent times. Here Millar was later proved wrong on some points, but he did much to correct the historical record. He noted instances of women holding political and economic power in other and earlier societies. In short, he challenged the theory of universal patriarchy. His wife's share in this book cannot be precisely determined, but it is known the women of this large family took part in intellectual debate, and that she was consulted about his work.

Both Millar and Hutcheson were writers fully committed to Enlightenment, liberal ideas, and both were exceptional in their day for their

---

[29] Hutcheson, "Correspondence," in *Collected Works*, 7: 4.

favourable attitudes to women. Hutcheson, moreover, was a founder of the utility theory still so roundly condemned for its notions of quantification and objectification. Yet he was not only a proto-feminist and democrat, but sensitive to ecology as well!

Mary Wortley Montagu (1689-1762)

The Rt. Hon. Lady Mary Pierrepont was born in London and had noble ancestors on both sides of the family; her father, a marquess, was later made a duke. Her intellectual tastes and rebellious nature surfaced early. She hid from her governess to work in her father's library where, with the help of a dictionary and a grammar, she taught herself Latin. Later she learned French, Italian, and Turkish. In 1712 she eloped with Edward Wortley Montagu to avoid an arranged marriage with someone she loathed. Wortley Montagu was an acceptable and wealthy suitor but had refused to entail his estates for the couple's prospective heir. The elopement prompted the first destruction of her journal, the first of many destructions of her papers. Four years later she set off with her husband for Turkey, where he was appointed British ambassador. The normal appointment was five years but he was replaced after little more than a year. Her letters home, the first of which were published in 1763, the year after her death, made her literary reputation.

Wortley Montagu's great practical contribution to humanity was the introduction of the smallpox vaccination to Britain at a time when the disease killed enormous numbers of people. She had learned of its efficacy in Turkey, where she had her six-year old son "engrafted." She also had her daughter vaccinated on return to England. Wortley Montagu had herself suffered from the disease earlier. In 1722 she published an article on vaccination, signed by "a Turkey merchant," out of compassion for those "abused and deluded by the knavery and ignorance of physicians."[30] She was under no illusion as to the opposition she would meet by destroying such a considerable part of the income of the medical profession. Yet she persisted in advocating its use with friends and family, convincing the Princess of Wales to have the royal children done. Voltaire in his English Letters (letter 11) credited Wortley Montagu with saving many lives and urged that France follow suit.

Back in England Wortley Montagu anonymously published a political journal, The Nonsense of Common-Sense. *She is sometimes credited with the powerful and witty* Woman not Inferior to Man, *published under*

---

[30] Robert Halsband, "New Light on Lady Mary Wortley Montagu's Contribution to Inoculation," 401.

Mary Wortley Montagu in Turkish Costume

the name of "Sophia, a person of quality," in 1739. Another polemical work, Woman's superior excellence over Man, 1743, is less sure in attribution. There are sufficient similarities in style and point of view between the two and her known letters to make her authorship likely. The fact that there are no letters referring to either publication proves nothing, for undoubtedly any such letters would have been destroyed. A stronger point against her authorship is that, in 1738-39, she was ardently pursuing a younger Italian scientist and left England in the summer of 1739 with the hope of living with him. Yet in this period she managed to write and publish the polemical Nonsense of Common-Sense, of which there is no mention in her surviving letters.

Wortley Montagu left for the Continent with her husband's consent, apparently with the condition not to return. The elusive and bisexual Count Algarotti joined her only in 1741 and sporadically after that, preferring to travel and later returning to his home in Italy. Her only contact with her daughter for twenty-two years of exile was through letters, which again are of great interest. This unconventional arrangement caused problems for the family. The daughter married a political earl, Lord Bute, later prime minister; the son turned out to be a rascal but succeeded his father in Parliament. Her daughter, to whom Wortley Montagu left her estate, burned volumes of her diary and strictly censored the letters she did permit to be published. Some letters are known to have been burned. Wortley Montagu returned to England only after her husband's death and herself died soon after of breast cancer.

Publication of the Turkish letters began soon after her death, without family consent. Essays, poems, and the European letters were published later. As well as her own writing Wortley Montagu translated and adapted a French farce on arranged marriage, with a feminist twist — the heroine wanted to find out if her prospective husband had good character.

Robert Halsband's The Life of Mary Wortley Montagu is still the only recommended full-length biography; see also his introduction to The Complete Letters (CL); George Paston, Lady Mary Wortley Montague and her Times; chapters in Katharine M. Rogers, Before their Time; and Margaret Alic, Hypatia's Heritage.

If the author of An Essay in defence of the Female Sex was Astell's first disciple to get into print, Mary Wortley Montagu was her chosen successor. As a young girl Lady Mary Pierrepont was much influenced by reading Astell's Serious Proposal. The two women later became friends. On the surface this seems an unlikely friendship, the worldly Wortley Montagu with her title, money, and court connections and the ascetic and pious Astell, an impoverished gentlewoman. The two shared a love of intellectual life, a belief in education for women, and conservative politics.

When Astell in 1724 wrote a preface to Wortley Montagu's letters she was handing on the torch.[31] The *Letters*, she wrote, exceeded all in "delicacy of sentiment and observation, that easy gracefulness and lively simplicity."

> I read with transport, and with joy I greet
> A genius so sublime and so complete,
> And gladly lay my laurels at her feet.[32]

Alas, this "most ingenious author" had condemned her manuscript to obscurity during her life.

> However, if these *Letters* appear hereafter, when I am in my grave,
> let *this* attend them in testimony to posterity, that among her contem-
> poraries *one woman*, at least, was just to her merit.

Astell appreciated her friend's inclusion of women's society as well as her literary merits:

> I confess I am malicious enough to desire that the world should see
> to how much better purpose the ladies travel than their lords, and
> that whilst it is surfeited with male travels, all in the same tone and
> stuffed with the same trifles, a lady has the skill to strike out a new
> path and to embellish a worn-out subject with variety of fresh and
> elegant entertainment ... The reader will find a more true and accu-
> rate account of the customs and manners of the several nations with
> whom the lady conversed than he can in any other author. (3: 467)

The *Turkish Letters* or *Embassy Letters* cover the two-year period the Wortley Montagus were away, the months of travel, and the stay in Turkey itself. Wortley Montagu plainly intended the letters to be published, but not in her lifetime. Nor could Astell persuade her other-wise. Wortley Montagu left the material carefully edited and rearranged. The letters are "clearly an accurate record of her experiences and obser-vations" but were "pseudo-letters," with personal comments excised.[33] The author kept an album as a permanent record of the letters' contents, distributing the material among her various correspondents. They

---

[31] Perry, *Celebrated*, 277.
[32] Astell, Appendix 3, in Mary Wortley Montagu, *Complete Letters*, 1: 466.
[33] Halsband introduction, *CL*, 1: xiv.

sparkle with life, reporting an exotic culture with sensitivity, wit, and a sure eye for detail. Commented her biographer, Halsband:

> These letters contributed greatly to the exchange of ideas between Islamic Turkey and Christian Europe. By virtue of their clear-sighted observation, their expansive tolerance, and their candid sympathy for an alien culture, they are Lady Mary's valid credential for a place in the European "Enlightenment." (1: xiv)

Otherwise put, Wortley Montagu was researching and writing the sociology of her day. She kept the albums with her the whole of her expatriate life, giving them to an English clergyman in Rotterdam en route back to England, obviously not trusting them to her family.

Wortley Montagu may have exaggerated the novelty of a land trip across Europe to Turkey, but she was correct in assessing the rarity of her access to women's society in Turkey. She had seen sights "as you never saw in your life and what no book of travels could inform you of" (1: 310). It was death for a man to be found in women's quarters. Other accounts of voyages to the Levant were "generally so far removed from truth and so full of absurdities I am very well diverted with them. They never fail giving you an account of the women, which it is certain they never saw" (1: 367). She discovered that Turkish women had enormous privileges and more liberty than English women, contrary to expectation. The custom of veiling in public facilitated clandestine affairs. "This perpetual masquerade gives them entire liberty of following their inclinations without danger of discovery" (1: 328). On the whole, women were the only free people in the empire. While the law permitted four wives she knew of no "man of quality" making use of the liberty, nor would a woman of rank permit it. Turkish women resumed their social life soon after giving birth, which Wortley Montagu preferred to the English confinement of a month or more (1: 380). Later she commented that nowhere were women treated with more contempt than in England (3: 40).

For three weeks in Adrianople, en route to Constantinople, Wortley Montagu and her husband stayed with a Muslim scholar. Daily conversation with him "gave me opportunity of knowing their religion and morals in a more particular manner than perhaps any Christian ever did" (1: 317). She described Islamic teachings and practices and explained the differences between the sects, all with great sympathy. To her correspondent she said:

> You see that I am very exact in keeping the promise you engaged me to make, but I know not whether your curiosity will be satisfied

with the accounts I shall give you, though I can assure you that the desire I have to oblige you to the utmost of my power has made me very diligent in my enquiries and observations. It is certain we have but very imperfect relations of the manners and religion of these people, this part of the world being seldom visited but by merchants who mind little but their own affairs, or travellers who make too short a stay to be able to report anything exactly of their own knowledge. The Turks are too proud to converse familiarly with merchants etc., who can only pick up some confused informations which are generally false, and they can give no better an account of the ways here than a French refugée lodging in a garret in Greek street could write of the Court of England. (1: 315-16)

Later letters reveal a sense of the similarity of social institutions despite superficial differences:

Mankind is everywhere the same: like cherries or apples, they may differ in size, shape, or colour, from different soils, climates, or culture, but are still essentially the same species.

She would go even further: "All animals are stimulated by the same passions, and act very near alike, as far as we are capable of observing them" (3: 15). Nowhere in Wortley Montagu's surviving work is there a thorough treatment of methodological issues but there is sufficient to show, as above, a general empirical orientation. Another letter explicitly praises Locke for making "the best dissection of the human mind of any author I have ever read" (3: 239).

As a young woman Wortley Montagu felt the limitations of her sex, but did not then question that it was inferior. Still, women needed education for their moral development. She had written Bishop Gilbert Burnet to ask his advice on her translation of Epictetus:

My sex is usually forbid studies of this nature, and folly reckoned so much our proper sphere we are sooner pardoned any excesses of that than the least pretensions to reading or good sense. We are permitted no books but such as tend to the weakening and effeminating the mind, our natural defects are every way indulged, and it is looked upon as in a degree criminal to improve our reason or fancy we have any. We are taught to place all our art in adorning our outward forms, and permitted, without reproach, to carry that custom even to extravagancy, while our minds are entirely neglected, and by disuse of reflections, filled with nothing but the trifling objects our eyes are daily entertained with. This custom, so long established and industriously upheld, makes it even ridiculous to go out of the

> common road, and forces one to find many excuses, as if it was a
> thing altogether criminal not to play the fool. (1: 44)

There was hardly a character in the world more despicable or more
liable to ridicule than the learned woman, who was considered to be
impertinent, vain, and conceited. Wortley Montagu did not here argue
the equality of the two sexes, accepting that God and Nature made
women a lower part of nature. (She was only twenty-one at the time
and unmarried; she did not repeat this argument.) Still, "the careless
education" given women made them liable to corruption by men. She
ended by quoting Erasmus in support of women's reading Latin. It was
no more indecorous for women to be able to converse with eloquent,
learned, and wise authors than it was for German women to learn
French to be able to speak with francophones (1: 46).

In numerous places Wortley Montagu decried the "false reasoning"
which led to women being debarred from the advantages of learning.
Men fancied that "the improvement of our understandings would only
furnish us with more art to deceive them, which is directly contrary to
the truth." It was ignorance that led to idleness and ill conduct (3: 26).

In her mature years Wortley Montagu asserted the equal capacities
of women even in her *Letters*. Her anonymous work goes even further,
as we shall see later.

> The same characters are formed by the same lessons, which inclines
> me to think (if I dare say it) that Nature has not placed us in an infe-
> rior rank to men, no more than the females of other animals, where
> we see no distinction of capacity.

She then went on to joke that "if there was a commonwealth of rational horses (as Doctor Swift has supposed) it would be an established
maxim amongst them that a mare could not be taught to pace" (3: 27).

Wortley Montagu accepted the doctrine that a wife owed obedience
to her husband and claimed never to have disobeyed hers. This made
her wary of marriage and she hoped that her granddaughters would
be "lay nuns." On her grandson's birth she predicted an easy way for
him as a male (he was later Primate of Ireland):

> I am never in pains for any of that sex. If they have any merit there
> are so many roads for them to meet good fortune, they can no way
> fail of it but by not deserving it. We have but one of establishing
> ours, and that surrounded by precipices, and perhaps, after all, better
> missed than found. (3: 83)

Letters to her daughter regarding her granddaughter's education
give her views both on the how and why of women's education and the

disabilities educated women still faced. Since the young Lady Mary both desired and was capable of learning she should be indulged in it. Yet she should be no more a linguist than was necessary to read books in the original, to avoid the corruption and injury of translation. True knowledge consisted in knowing things, not words. Wortley Montagu then cautioned that her granddaughter must conceal whatever learning she attained — as she would hide a physical disability (3: 20-24). Parading learning only served to arouse envy and hatred. If her granddaughter had her own passion for learning, history, geography, and philosophy would furnish her with materials for a long and cheerful life. Wortley Montagu regretted the deficiencies, superstition, and false notions of her own education.

Wortley Montagu's partisan political writing came out in a journal she edited, *The Nonsense of Common-Sense* (1737-38). It was ostensibly unallied, but in fact supported the Walpole government as a reply to a liberal journal, *Common Sense*. The masthead advertised "To be continued as long as the author thinks fit, and the public likes it." The publication lasted nine issues. Wortley Montagu promoted the domestic wool industry (against silk imports), supported lower interest rates, and generally approved of "sin taxes." Despite the fact that her husband had voted against Walpole's Gin Act she supported it. Never a democrat, she showed contempt for the lower classes while dishing out patronizing advice.

Wortley Montagu described herself as a moralist. From earliest childhood she had seen the wheeling and dealing of patronage politics and did not like it. As a young wife she had unsuccessfully prodded her MP husband to look to his career. She was scathing in an unpublished satire written about the time of *The Nonsense of Common-Sense*.[34] As a corrupt arm or leg had to be lopped off to save the body, so also Parliament, this essential part of the body politic, had to be put to an end (46). Even Walpole, whom she supported, got no better than "as honest as his present post gives him leave to be." The king would govern better if he did not have to give out patronage appointments to blockheads, she argued (47).

One number of *The Nonsense of Common-Sense* was devoted to the situation of women. Here, as later, Wortley Montagu stressed that women needed to be reasonable creatures or corrupt morals would

---

[34] Wortley Montagu, "An Expedient to put a stop to the spreading Vice of Corruption," in the re-print of *Nonsense of Common-Sense*.

result. She became one of the early users of the expression "human-kind" in making the argument:

> Men that have not sense enough to show any superiority in their
> arguments hope to be yielded to by a faith that, as they are men, all
> the reason that has been allotted to human kind has fallen to their
> share. I am seriously of another opinion. (27)

Sophia, an anonymous author, who may have been Wortley Montagu, made the case for women's equality in *Woman not Inferior*. That reason/mind/soul had no sex was a view shared with Astell. Like Astell also, Sophia used wit, invective, and sometimes sarcasm to score points. Between arguments of reason, refuting the prejudices against women, the author brought in her own positive examples. Experience, she pointed out, showed what women could do when given the chance. It was convention, not nature, that kept them from matching men in performance. If Wortley Montagu was indeed Sophia, she went further than Astell, attacking the right of men to rule over women. If not, she is still a powerful voice as an analyst of the condition of women and advocate for education.

> If this haughty sex would have us believe they have a natural right
> of superiority over us, why do not they prove their charter from
> nature by making use of reason to subdue themselves ... Were we
> to see the men everywhere, and at all times, masters of themselves
> and their animal appetites in a perfect subordination to their ration-
> al faculties, we should have some colour to think that nature
> designed them for master to us. (2-3)

Instead male supremacy was based on nothing better than custom and superficial appearances, not reason or evidence:

> How many things do these mighty wise creatures hold for
> undoubted truths without being able to assign a reason for any one
> of their opinions! The cause of which is that they suffer themselves
> to be hurried away by appearances ... Where they want evidence in
> the principles fallacy helps them to fill up the vacancy with seem-
> ings in their inference. In a word, as they suppose without reason
> so they discourse without grounds; and therefore would have as
> strongly maintained the negative of what they assert if custom and
> the impression of the senses had determined them to it after the
> same manner. (3)

If men were to govern women, Sophia demanded, they must back up their claim with proofs that women could not govern themselves (19).

Brute strength was not a sufficient ground; if it were, the lion would
have a better title over the whole creation than men. But:

> A little experience is sufficient to demonstrate how much fitter we
> are to be guardians over [men] than they are to be such over us. (21)

A young woman on a farm was qualified to be mistress of it when men
her age were still under the supervision of masters (a similar point is
made in several places in Wortley Montagu's *Letters*). Women were
debarred from the sciences, government, and public office by no proof
of science. The diversity in performance between men and women
stemmed from differences in education, exercise, and external impressions, opportunities for which were socially determined. Given the
same advantages of study allowed men, women would keep pace with
them in all the sciences and all branches of useful knowledge. Moreover, "There is no science, office or dignity which women have not an
equal right to share in with the men" (55). Given the opportunity,
women could teach at universities, and practise and teach medicine.

Even barred from the medical profession, women had, with no
reference to Galen or Hippocrates, invented an infinity of reliefs.

> The observations made by women in their practice have been so
> exact and built upon such solid reason as to show more than once
> the useless pedantry of the major part of the school systems. I hardly
> believe our sex would spend so many years to so little purpose as
> those men do who call themselves *philosophers*, were we to apply
> to the study of nature. We could point out a much shorter road to
> the desired end. We should scarcely do like some men who waste
> whole years (not to mention many of them who dwell for life) on
> mere *Entia Rationis*, fictitious trifles, nowhere to be found but in
> their own noodles. (42)

Since the chief fruit of learning was a just discernment of true from
false, Sophia held that women would "apply ourselves to the observation
of ourselves and the different objects which environ us, in order to find
out in what they relate to us or differ from us, and by what applications
they may be beneficial or obnoxious to us" (43-44). Wortley Montagu
had described just this sort of thing in her letters, describing the practice of smallpox inoculation in Turkey, which was always conducted
by women.[35]

Sophia/Wortley Montagu held that the military arts had no mystery
beyond any other. Women could read a map as well as men and divide

---

[35] Wortley Montagu, *CL*, 3: 338.

forces into battalions. Like men, women came in different degrees of strength (49). The author, whose values were decidedly anti-militarist, was not arguing for a military role for women but simply puncturing machismo. She wanted to establish that women did not lack courage — remember Boadicea — and that her sex was not despicable (56). Humanity and integrity made us abhor "unjust slaughter" and prefer "honourable peace to unjust war" (51).

Wortley Montagu's letters similarly derided war. Recognizing the vast increase in useful and speculative knowledge, she maintained that many palpable follies persisted. Of these war was "the most glaring, being full as senseless as the boxing of school boys" (3: 17). While her elusive friend Algarotti was composing panegyrics for whoever might win, Wortley Montagu thought that the naturalist collecting butterflies was better employed. The lofty Pindar who celebrated war and "the divine Homer who recorded the bloody battles most in fashion, appear to me either to have been extremely mistaken or extremely mercenary" (3: 220).

It was only custom that made it an oddity for a woman to declaim the sciences from a university chair. Women had public authority vested in them as reigning queens. Why could they not then hold such subordinate offices as minister of state, privy councillor, general, or admiral? There was "no science or public office in a state which women are not as qualified for by nature as the ablest of men," asserted the author of *Woman not Inferior*, not even the church (45). Women could understand, compare, and interpret Scripture, the church fathers, and canons. It was a "positive law" of God that had kept women from becoming priests, not any natural incapacity or unworthiness. It would be presumptuous to inquire why, but Sophia did presume. Possibly, knowing men's general tendency to impiety and irreligion and women's natural propensity to virtue, God had confined religious functions to those who most needed them! Two centuries later Virginia Woolf would use a similar argument, now crediting a report of the Church of England, not God, with the observation that women were more virtuous than men, and so less needy of ecclesiastical office than they.[36] Sophia/Wortley Montagu also suggested that it would never enter women's heads to describe God as a "venerable old man" (42).

Polemical tracts naturally elicit responses, in this case sixty-six pages entitled *Man Superior to Woman* by "a gentleman." Wortley Montagu,

---

[36] Virginia Woolf, *Three Guineas*, 161.

or someone writing very much like her, retorted with 111 pages of *Woman's superior excellence over Man*, 1743. The sub-title gives a preçis of her case:

> A reply to the author of a late treatise entitled Man superior to Woman, in which the excessive weakness of that gentleman's answer to Woman not Inferior to Man is exposed, with a plain demonstration of woman's natural right even to superiority over the men in head and heart, proving their minds as much more beautiful than the men's as their bodies are, and that, had they the same advantages of education, they would excel them as much in sense as they do in virtue.

Woman's Superior Excellence noted the prodigious advantages education gave to men, which led to men's keeping women from making their full contribution:

> What incensed me the most was to consider the immense fund of knowledge and useful discoveries, which their groveling jealousy has by such means robbed the world of. (2)

Wherever women had any degree of equality of advantage with men "they have always run at least parallel with them" (68). Examples were given of the achievements of women scholars in other countries. Marie de Gournay's treatise on equality was particularly noted. Again, the democracy of empiricism was key. The only requirements for knowledge were sensation, reflection, and attention, in all of which women were not lacking (78).

Emilie du Châtelet (1706-1749)

The daughter of a baron and baroness, Châtelet was born Gabrielle-Emilie Le Tonnelier de Breteuil. She was a studious child, tutored at home by her father in English, mathematics, and sciences. She also learned Latin and Italian. At age nineteen she married the marquis du Chastellet-Lomont, by which name she is sometimes listed in library catalogues. (Voltaire modernized the spelling to Châtelet.) She had three children by her husband, two of whom lived. He was an army general, content to let her run the family's business affairs and "complaisant" about her many affairs. Her noble background and money enabled her to overcome some of the limitations of inadequate education; she hired noted scientists to teach her mathematics and physics. Still there were problems when, for example, a tutor claimed that she had stolen his work!

Voltaire had been a visitor in her parents' home, but their collaboration began only in 1734, when Emilie du Châtelet was twenty-eight and Voltaire

Emilie du Châtelet

forty. *He first made the trip to the Châtelet chateau at Cirey when tipped off*
about a warrant for his arrest; his English Letters *had already been burned*
by the public executioner. Châtelet offered him refuge and joined him shortly.
Voltaire had to escape again in 1736, this time to Holland, after publish-
ing Le Mondain, *a work whose materialist views Châtelet shared, and which*
she had influenced. Thus she had good reason for not publishing her own
work on the same subject, a translation/commentary on Mandeville's Fable
of the Bees *(available in Wade,* Studies on Voltaire, *131-87).*

An ancillary service of Châtelet's to scholarship was her good deed to
the great philosophe *Diderot when he was in prison. She intervened with the*
warden, a relative, and succeeded in getting better conditions for him so
that he could write.

Châtelet and Voltaire worked together at Cirey until the end of her life,
writing, performing his plays (in which she played the heroine), conducting
experiments, translating, and receiving scientific visitors. A laboratory as well
as a library was installed. Voltaire was preparing a paper on fire for the
Académie des sciences when, a month before the deadline, Châtelet
decided also to enter the competition. She did her experiments at night to
conceal them from Voltaire; her theoretical approach differed also from his.
Neither won but both papers were published as honourable mentions. Apart
from this paper, the only other work Châtelet published in her lifetime was
Institutions de physique *(1740), a treatise originally intended to be on*
Newton, but to which she then added a discussion of Leibnizian metaphysics.

Châtelet had completed her translation of Newton's Principia Mathe-
matica, *and was working on the commentary during her last pregnancy.*
The premonition that she would not survive the birth drove her to work day
and night to finish it. She did, had a normal delivery, then died a few days
later. The infant daughter, fathered by her last lover, also died soon after.
Châtelet's translation was published posthumously in 1759. Some of her
papers were published many years later: Grammaire raisonnée, *with a*
structuralist bent, and Discours sur le Bonheur. *Her vast manuscript on*
Biblical criticism remains unpublished while much of her writing on meta-
physics, which influenced Voltaire's own Traité de métaphysique, *was lost.*

Few women scholars have done well with their biographers, but Châtelet
fared particularly badly until recently. Ira Wade's Voltaire and Mme du
Châtelet and Studies on Voltaire *turned the tide, bringing out her own*
work and showing the collaboration with Voltaire. A major recent biography of
Voltaire includes one volume that deals with the collaboration: René Vaillot,
Avec Mme du Châtelet. *Her work in science has begun to receive more*
attention; see Londa Schiebinger, "Emilie du Châtelet and Physics," in The
Mind Has no Sex?, *59-65; Linda Gardiner, "Women in Science," in* Samia I.

Emilie   Spencer, French Women and the Age of Enlightenment, 181-93; Linda
du Châtelet   Gardiner Janik, "Searching for the Metaphysics of Science: the Structure and
Composition of Madame du Châtelet's Institutions de Physique," and Erica
Harth, Cartesian Women. 189-213.

> Recommended biographies: Ira O. Wade, Voltaire and Madame du Châtelet;
> Esther Ehrman, Mme du Châtelet; Nancy Mitford, Voltaire in Love; Theodore
> Besterman, "Emilie du Châtelet: Portrait of an Unknown Woman," in Voltaire
> Essays; in French, André Maurel, La Marquise du Châtelet.

Châtelet's intellectual "pretensions" were much mocked in her life-time, then, after her death she became known as Voltaire's friend and lover. Information about her contribution to methodology is hidden away in books such as Nancy Mitford's *Voltaire in Love*, which in fact deals seriously with Châtelet's scholarship. Publications of her work are sandwiched into publications on Voltaire, with acknowledgments in the subtitle, for example Ira Wade's *Studies on Voltaire with some Unpublished Papers of Mme du Châtelet*. There is still confusion as to her share in some work published in Voltaire's name. In the preface to *Elémens de la philosophie de Newton* Voltaire stated that the ideas had come from her, that he had only been the scribe. Certainly he would have known little of Newton were it not for her help. Nothing remains from the Voltaire-Châtelet correspondence, so the nature of her influence on him remains unclear. Enough material is available to know that Châtelet made an independent contribution to methodology and significantly influenced Voltaire's. There is little in her life to make her a source for feminists, but there are some apt remarks about the need for women to study and the prejudices women suffer. Châtelet died tragically young, at age forty-three, of puerperal fever after childbirth.

Châtelet dedicated her *Institutions de physique* to her son, later duc du Châtelet and an early victim of the Terror. The work expounds the philosophy of Leibniz as promulgated by his successor Wolff. Voltaire teased Châtelet as "ma wolvienne," was annoyed that she had departed from the Newtonian camp, and constantly urged her to return. The departure was never whole-hearted, however — Châtelet doubted Leibnizian metaphysics. She denounced scholasticism and Descartes in her work, focusing instead on experience and observation. A strong sense of the collective nature of knowledge pervades the whole book.

Châtelet maintained that hypotheses are needed in the acquisition of knowledge.

> One of the mistakes of some philosophers of this time is to want to
> ban hypotheses from physics, while they are as necessary as
> scaffolding in a house under construction. It is true that when the
> building is finished the scaffolding is no longer useful, but one could
> not have put the house up without its help. (9)

She described how hypotheses could become poison in philosophy
when passed for truths. They could be more dangerous than "the
unintelligible jargon of the school," absolutely devoid of sense.

> But an ingenious and hardy hypothesis, with some semblance of
> truth, entices human pride to believe it. The mind applauds the
> discovery of subtle principles and then uses all its sagacity to defend
> them. The majority of the great men who have created systems are
> examples; these are the great vessels carried by the currents. They
> make the most beautiful manoeuvres in the world, but the current
> carries them away. (10)

Châtelet has been credited with formulating a middle way between
Lockean empiricism and rationalism, relying heavily on inference from
observation but permitting some role for reason beyond that of the critical processing of sense information.[37] This is perhaps taking her "sufficient reason" concept too far. In discussing reason in *Institutions de
physique* she stressed the role of experience:

> Remember, my son, in all your studies that experience is the bâton
> which nature has given us blind people to lead us in our research; we
> cannot be sure with its aid to take the right road, but we cannot but
> stumble if we stop using it. It is experience that lets us know phys-
> ical qualities and it is our reason that makes us benefit from it and
> draw new knowledge and new light from it. (10)

She saw scientific research as a collective endeavour, according only
a modest role to herself:

> Physics is an immense building that surpasses the forces of a single
> person. Some contribute a stone, while others build whole wings, but
> all must work on the solid foundation given this edifice in the last
> century by geometry and observation. There are others who describe
> the design of the building and I am amongst this number. (12)

Leibniz was little known in France despite his great discoveries.
Châtelet conceded that obscurities undoubtedly remained in his metaphysics, but "it seems to me that he has furnished us, in the principle of
sufficient reason, with a compass capable of leading us in the moving

---

[37] Wade, *Studies on Voltaire*, 126.

sands of this science." Yet qualifications remained, for only "some points of metaphysics " could be demonstrated rigorously (13).

Châtelet criticized the subjectivity of Descartes's method of clear and distinct principles:

> This method serves but to extend disputes eternally, for those who have opposing sentiments have each one of them a clear, internal sentiment of what they advance. Thus no one is obliged to give way because the evidence is equal on both sides. It is therefore necessary to substitute demonstrations for the illusions of our imagination, and not admit anything as true except that which follows in an uncontestable manner from first principles that no one can doubt, and reject as false all that is contrary to these principles. (17)

Euclid, she noted, had not been content to call on lively, internal sentiments but on rigorous demonstration.

> It is, then, indisputably necessary to keep oneself from error to verify one's ideas, to demonstrate their reality and to admit nothing as indubitable that one cannot assure by experience or demonstration, that it contains nothing false nor chimerical. (20)

Voltaire's eulogy of Châtelet explains how she came to discuss Leibniz and then reject him. Voltaire credited her with giving a clarity it never possessed to the metaphysics, but then, having mastered it, she discovered its lack of foundation. Leibnizian monads and pre-established harmony, with Cartesianism, were systems that did not merit her attention:

> Therefore, having had the courage to enhance the work of Leibniz, she had the courage to abandon it.[38]

Châtelet's translation of Newton, still *the* French translation, includes also her own commentary.

Her *Discours sur le bonheur* was a personal account of a then popular subject, happiness, published half a century after her death. It differs from the standard by including, along with some Epicurean fare, the need for sensibility, health, virtue, passion, and altruism, an ability to entertain illusion. There are positive references to the methodologists Cicero, Montaigne, Locke, Newton, and Clarke. The essay is also the source of a significant statement on the particular need women have for knowledge:

> Love of study is certainly much less necessary to men for their happiness than it is for women. Men have infinitely more resources for

---

[38] Voltaire, "Eulogy of Madame la Marquise du Châtelet," in Ehrman, *Mme du Châtelet*, 85.

happiness than women, resources that are entirely lacking to
women. Men have many other ways to attain glory ... through war,
government and negotiation. (21)

Women are excluded, by their sex, from every kind of recognition.
When one happens to be born with a good enough mind, she has only
study to console her for all the exclusions and dependence to which
her sex condemns her.

Châtelet's "translation" of Mandeville's *Fable of the Bees* is misnamed,
both because she translated little of it, and because she added her own
extensive comments. Only a poet could properly translate poetry, she
believed. Her "translator's preface" is another source of her views on
women's scholarship and gives a neat maxim on the role of translators.
They were the "merchants in the republic of letters and they merit at
least this praise if they sense and know their force and undertake to
add nothing from themselves."[39] Châtelet noted the paradox that the
only profession demanding study to which women were admitted was
comedy, which was considered infamous:

We should reflect a little why for so many centuries not one good
tragedy, good poem, esteemed history, beautiful painting or good
book of physics has ever come out of the hands of a woman. Give
me a reason, if possible, why these creatures, whose understanding appears altogether so similar to that of men, seem, however, to
be stopped by an invisible force. (135-36)

She would leave it to the naturalists to search out the physics, but
until they found a reason, women would be right to complain about
their education.

For myself, I declare that if I were king, I would conduct this experiment in physics. I would correct this abuse that cuts out half the
human race. I would have women participate in all the rights of
humanity, especially those of the mind ... This new education would
do a great good for the human race altogether. Women would be
better valued and men would acquire a new subject of emulation.
I am persuaded that many women, thanks to the defects of their
education, either do not know they have talents or, from prejudice or
cowardice of mind, hide them. What I have learned from my own
experience confirms me in this opinion. (136)

Through chance Châtelet acquired friends who showed her that she
was a thinking creature. Then the world and dissipation succeeded in

---

[39] Châtelet, "Translation of Mandeville," in Wade, *Studies on Voltaire*, 133.

taking her entire time and mind. At the age when there was still time to
develop her reason she did not take her talents seriously, but only when
it was too late to develop them.

> This reflection did not discourage me. I was happy to have
> renounced the frivolous things of my life that occupy most women
> for all of their lives, wanting to use what remained of my mind and
> sensing that nature had refused me the creative genius necessary
> for finding new truths; I did justice to what I had and confined myself
> to disseminating clearly the discoveries of others that were not
> accessible thanks to language differences. (136-37)

Châtelet is here too modest about her abilities. What she added of
her own observations to Mandeville is of interest. Her line of approach
was similar to that taken later by the British moral philosophers and
the French Encyclopedists. Yet hers is a particularly early example,
well before Adam Smith's *Theory of Moral Sentiments* (1759), of the
attempt to explain the origin of morals and laws through the moral
sentiments. Châtelet was writing in 1735-37, before Montesquieu's
Spirit of Laws (1748), La Méttrie's *Man Machine* (1747), Helvétius' *De
l'Esprit* (1758), and Hume's *Enquiry concerning the Principles of Morals*
(1751). She was, as Voltaire had earlier done with his *English Letters*,
introducing English work to France. Her choice was Mandeville, not
Hobbes, a social compact not based on force or fear but which stressed
the role of positive social bonds, initially through the family. She
described Mandeville as an English Montaigne, but with even more
method, the author of the "best book on morality ever written" (137).

The commentary also shows a more modest presentation of what
was obviously a speculative exercise, a reconstruction of the origins of
civilization.

> Our mind is composed of different passions as our body is of bones,
> flesh, muscles etcetera. These passions govern us in turn and are
> the source of our virtues and vices. That is what I try to prove in the
> first chapter of this book. There one will see from where moral good
> and evil come, and I hope to convince the reader that man owes
> none of these ideas to religion ...
> Every animal desires its own happiness without regard to that of
> others. Thus those who have the fewest desires would seem to be
> the most able to live socially. Man being the animal with the most
> passions and desires would seem to be, for that reason, the one least
> apt for society. (142)

Yet, through the help of those same passions, the human being is the

only one capable of becoming sociable. Châtelet then quoted Mandeville on love as the beginning of all society, and continued her own
commentary:

> It would have been impossible to persuade people to sacrifice their
> particular interest for the good of society if one could not have given
> them something equal in return. (144)

Legislators found that pride furnished this return. No one was so despicable as to accept contempt willingly nor savage enough to be insensible to praise. Legislators then tried to persuade people that their
understanding, a faculty that raised them above other beings, must
control their senses and repress their desires.

To introduce this emulation legislators divided people into two
classes: the vulgar, who acted only to satisfy their own desires, and
those who could subordinate them for the good of society and humanity. Even the most corrupt people could be constrained to make *some*
sacrifices for the common good. All wanted to be in the higher class
even if, at the bottom of their hearts, they were of the vulgar.

> That is, or at least that may be the manner by which people were
> civilized, which proves well that the first rules of morality were
> invented by politicians to govern the multitude more securely. But
> these political foundations once laid, it was impossible that people
> not be civilized, and that all sensed that the way to satisfy their
> desires was to moderate them. People then agreed to name every
> action prejudicial to society a *vice* and to call all those actions that
> might reasonably result in justice *virtue*. (144)

Châtelet made an early and original contribution to the ongoing
debate of the origins of society, law, and morality. The different treatment of women distinguishes her theory markedly from work by male
theorists of the time and indeed for decades to come. Although it is at
least as plausible as accepted male accounts it never made it into the
debate! Nor was Châtelet an obscure or resourceless person, but one
with wealth, title, and connections. The work cannot be discussed here
for its influence, for it was not published at the time and could only have
had an indirect influence, through Voltaire. Yet it seems important in
this work of recovery to pay attention to what was a most interesting
contribution, even if it was lost. Those who ask if women theorists make
a difference should look at this distinctive work of Châtelet. As we leave
her we finally leave the reach of the seventeenth century. In fact she
did much more than interpret seventeenth-century theorists to her own
time and country, but her work was grounded in that endeavour.

Revisiting the Feminist Critique

Returning to the feminist critique of empiricist methodology discussed in chapter 1, disconfirmation appears with the very emergence of modern empiricism. As early as Marie de Gournay, Montaigne's editor, women used the emerging methods to further their rights and to claim access to the life of reason. Anna van Schurman was another early asserter of women's equality. Mary Astell did not share Locke's liberal politics or theology, but she did opt for his empiricism. Her intellectual mentor had been a Cambridge Platonist but she rejected his idealism for empiricism. Contrary to all expectation from the feminist critique, one of the first defenders of Locke's empiricism was a woman, Catharine Trotter. Damaris Masham, Locke's friend, also defended his empiricism, argued for education for women, and criticized the most extreme idealist philosopher of the day, Malebranche.

Lockean psychology made possible the argument of nurture over nature, that women's apparent inferiority was not grounded in biology but lack of education and opportunity. Lockeans accordingly argued for better education for both sexes. Masham was quick to see the democracy inherent in empiricism. Philosophers had no right to impose their system on others or to be credited with truth without proofs. This included the great idealists, especially the extreme sexist Malebranche.

While a number of contemporary women reject quantification in the name of women, there was no such repugnance as the new sciences emerged in the seventeenth century. Scarcely any quantitative data were available in this early period, but the early women methodologists used those that were: the bills of mortality. Astell cited comparative statistics to support the case for smallpox inoculation made by her friend Mary Wortley Montagu. Eminent writer of letters that she was, Wortley Montagu was another Lockean in methodological preference, an astute collector of social data, and an advocate of women's access to education. Châtelet was so committed to the Newtonian mechanical universe that she devoted years of her life, even her last months, to translating *Mathematical Principles of Natural Philosophy*. With Voltaire she encouraged the French to take up the new empiricist philosophy from Britain.

As we turn, in the next chapter, to methodologists in the last half of the eighteenth century, and the fullest expression of the Enlightenment, we meet writers even more sure of their convictions. They could be no more committed to education for women than some of the earlier writers, but we will see them being much more assertive in claiming it. We will see as well methodologists forcefully arguing the case for quantification, for mathematically based social sciences in which to ground the needed social reforms. As we have already seen, women found quantified data useful in their advocacy of equality and other worthy causes. As statistical theory and techniques advanced they would become even more committed to, and adept at, their use.

Chapter 3

FROM THE ENLIGHTENMENT TO THE FRENCH REVOLUTION

*T*he period known as the "Enlightenment" was a time of questioning and challenge to established authority for women as well as men. Theorists argued for such radical ideas as the citizenship of all the people of a country, instead of only the nobility, land owners, or some relatively small, privileged group. Women joined in these struggles for equality and liberty for all, some arguing specifically for their own sex. The need for education and the belief that all people were capable of it was prominent in the struggle. The desperate effects of certain laws and social institutions were described. That the great mass of the people were often hungry, dirty, and cold was no longer accepted as a necessary law of nature or divine command. Society could and should be organized to increase productivity and provide for the needs of all. Church and state, which continued to hold that such change was not possible, were denounced for their self-interest. Enlightenment writers used factual arguments against custom and authority as sources of knowledge.

Given that these were such central concerns of the Enlightenment it is remarkable that its proponents should have later come into such ill repute. True, in arguing for greater material production theorists did not realize that a time of mass consumption, over-packaging, waste, and pollution might later occur. In trying to put bread on people's tables they did not conceive of plastics in the oceans and gluts in the market. They were trying to combat poverty at a time when famines occurred regularly, epidemics wiped out thousands, and the vast majority of the population was — and was expected to be — illiterate.

A new approach to knowledge was a central part of Enlightenment philosophy.[1] That is, the people advocating these radical social views

---

[1] On the historical background to this period see: John Lough, *Introduction to Eighteenth Century France*; J.O. Lindsay, *Old Regime*; Frank E. Manuel, *Prophets of Paris*; J.H. Brumfitt, *French Enlightenment*; Nannerl O. Keohane, *Philosophy and the State in France*; F.C. Green, *The Ancien Regime*.

rejected the established idealist methodology required by the ancient universities, faculties of theology, and state censors. Theirs was not a new methodology in the sense that continuities with seventeenth-century empiricist methodology were strong. Voltaire had introduced Lockean empiricism to France and the rest of the Encyclopedists took it up. They, with the physiocrats, in turn became methodological models for later British empiricists, notably Adam Smith and David Hume. British-French exchanges have always been important, as we have just seen with Montaigne-Bacon-Descartes-Locke-Astell-Newton-Châtelet. Those exchanges would be no less vital as the eighteenth century progressed, with even more women participating: Macaulay, Wollstonecraft, and Hays in Britain, Roland and de Staël in France.

Yet, contemporary feminist opponents of empiricism view the Enlightenment as a particularly offensive period. Contemporary feminists "identify Enlightenment rationalism as a distinctly *male* mode of thought." The dichotomies of the Enlightenment are said to be "all part of the male/female hierarchy central to patriarchal thought ... absolute, monolithic and abstract."[2] One wonders how these critics could have avoided noticing the materialism, democracy, and, for most, scepticism. To be sure, some Enlightenment theorists got carried away with their own systems and were so criticized by colleagues. But contemporary feminist critics can find no good whatsoever in their work, only "dogmas of Enlightenment rationalism" (69), "Enlightenment errors" (78), and the "sterile dogmatism of Enlightenment epistemology" (82). Some contemporary commentators believe that the original Enlightenment happened only to men, that the feminist Enlightenment took place only in the 1960s and 70s. Even Sandra Harding, who defended feminist empiricism in *Feminism and Methodology*, had nothing positive to say about the Enlightenment. The term appears as something women are struggling against, or whose dubious benefits they have been denied (189). Phyllis Mack, in her "Women and the Enlightenment," grudgingly admitted that women had had an "Enlightenment of sorts," but that the impact of Enlightenment values was at least partly negative (9).

Writers who stressed the difficulties of acquiring knowledge and who opposed idealism for being abstract are now castigated for not understanding that knowledge is not achieved by abstraction and that it is always "situated" and "perspectival." For Susan Hekman, again,

---

[2] Susan Hekman, "The Feminization of Epistemology," 67.

the Enlightenment meant the nefarious effects of the dualisms of subject/object, rational/irrational, culture/nature, and fact/value. Note the non-sequiturs in her article in *Women and Politics*:

> The definition of women as exclusively objects and the definition of knowledge as objective and hence masculine has been a principal target of feminist criticism in the social sciences.[3]

No wonder that contemporary feminists have identified Enlightenment rationalism "as a distinctly *male* mode of thought" (67) but why is this identification necessary? We have already seen feminists/empiricists who have defined the mind as sexless and objectivity as a means of overcoming tradition and prejudice. Why is this whole history ignored?

> Liberalism is fundamentally an Enlightenment philosophy that sees knowledge as the acquisition of an object by a subject. (73)

Enlightenment philosophers did indeed treat knowledge, at least probable knowledge, as something that could be acquired, with much diligent work. Here they were opposing a regime which employed censors whose permission to publish was required, where books offending church or state were burned by the public executioner on courthouse steps. In the circumstances, isn't liberalism a refreshing change? That knowledge could be acquired by ordinary human beings was a radical idea, opposing as it did the accepted doctrine that only established authorities were legitimate sources of knowledge.

Feminists have criticized such other Enlightenment ideals as "the autonomous and self-regulating self, as reflective of masculinity in the modern West."[4] Another contribution in the same work condemned the Enlightenment in similar terms:

> Feminist notions of the self, knowledge, and truth are too contradictory of the Enlightenment to be contained within its categories. The way(s) to feminist future(s) cannot lie in reviving or appropriating Enlightenment concepts of the person or knowledge.[5]

Reading these contemporary feminist critics it is hard to know which they consider worse: liberalism or empiricism. Both are identified with the oppression of women.

> The only role for women in the liberal ideology is that of an object dominated by a male subject; liberal feminism is thus an epistemological impossibility.[6]

---

[3] Susan Hekman, "The Feminization of Epistemology," 75.
[4] Linda J. Nicholson, *Feminism/Postmodernism*, 5.
[5] Jane Flax, "Postmodernism and Gender Relations," 42.
[6] Hekman, "Feminization," 73-74.

But Enlightenment values empowered women! Instead of truth being determined by the Faculty of Theology at the Sorbonne or similar authoritative bodies to which women were not admitted, truth became a goal which all could seek, if none absolutely find. The criterion of objectivity meant that women could enter the fray. Empiricism was a great leveller and for that reason was feared by the holders of established authority. The definition of knowledge as objective, far from making it masculine, made it accessible to women.

Hekman, again in "The Feminization of Epistemology," favours a plurality of discourses, a "fusing of perspectives" over monolithic truth (66). She identifies herself with "anti-foundationalists," those who oppose the very attempt to ground knowledge rationally. But without some criteria of reason, assertions pass for argument and can only be refuted by other assertions. Judith Grant warns that "a theory which rejects reason and also wants to be democratic is highly problematic."
Such theories risk devolving into authoritarian non-theories more akin to religions. It is reason which makes discourse possible. Intuition and faith, by contrast, "cannot be challenged."[7]

An essay on women and the Enlightenment in a widely used anthology does much mischief with its derogatory portrayal: "Like the Revolution it helped to shape, the Enlightenment not only failed to improve women's lot but worsened it in some ways."[8] Writers who were relatively sympathetic to women are condemned for their failure to do more, while the institutions of monarchy, nobility, university, and church, which so thoroughly excluded women, are let off. The author could find good work from only one Enlightenment figure, Condorcet, whose failings she also underscored. Diderot was appropriately criticized for his derogatory essay on women, yet his sympathetic treatment of women elsewhere was not noted. Germaine de Staël got not a mention.

The age of the Enlightenment remained a difficult time for women because the new principles it advanced were not enacted. The French Revolution broke out in 1789 and soon deteriorated into the Terror, from which Napoleon seized power and launched war. Reading the feminist critics one might think the Encyclopedists and other reformers were in power, their decrees denying women their rights. Yet these

[7] Judith Grant, "'I Feel Therefore I am': A Critique of Female Experience and the Basis for a Feminist Epistemology," 113.
[8] Abby R. Kleinbaum, "Women in the Age of Light,"in Renate Bridenthal and Claudia Koonz, *Becoming Visible*, 217.

radicals, reformers, and revolutionaries were the dissidents and under-dogs. Their books were burned and they went to prison or into hiding when the authorities cracked down.

The Enlightenment helped to change public opinion toward a greater awareness of women's social and legal handicaps.[9] Montesquieu's *The Spirit of Laws* did at least this much, without advocating any radical change in relations. Holbach wrote sympathetically on women. Diderot, who also wrote some nonsense on women, showed great understand-ing of the legal injustices women suffered and the church's complicity in maintaining those injustices.[10] The *Encyclopedia* itself took no posi-tion, but included articles arguing both the equality and inferiority of women.

As before, the interaction between French and British writers was crucial. British liberalism had fed the French Enlightenment. Its defence then became the test of loyalty for later British liberals/reformers. The revolutionary hope for a new and better society even prompted the use of new terms, notably a "social science" on which to ground the "social art." We begin with a person central to all of these developments, Catharine Macaulay, a British liberal, defender of the French Revolu-tion, advocate for women's education, and the first of the methodolo-gists in this history to have visited the United States.

Catharine Macaulay (1731-1791)

The second daughter in the family, Catharine Sawbridge was given a good education at home. She early read Roman history and acquired a life-long taste for the humbler virtues of a republic. In 1760 she married a Scottish physician, George Macaulay, and settled with him in London; they had one daughter. When her husband died Macaulay had published the first volume of her History of England. *Succeeding volumes followed until the last appeared in 1783.* Loose Remarks on Hobbes's Philosophical Rudiments of Government and Society, *an attack on his individualistic politics of fear, was published in 1767. Another pamphlet, "Observations on a Pamphlet ... on the Causes of the Present Discontents" (1770), gives more on her own political views. "A Modest Plea for the Property of Copy Right" (1774) sought legislative relief for authors.* A Treatise on the Immutability of Moral

---

[9] Arthur M. Wilson, "'Treated Like Imbecile Children' (Diderot): The Enlighten-ment and the Status of Women," in Fritz and Morton, *Woman in the 18th Century*, 91.

[10] His novel, published in English as *The Nun*, is superb; *La Religieuse*, in *Œuvres*, 5: 1-171.

Catharine Macaulay, mezzotint by J. Spilsbury after C. Read, 1764
By Courtesy of The National Portrait Gallery, London

Truth *came out in 1783.*

In 1774 Macaulay moved to Bath and, after remarrying — a younger **Catharine Macaulay**
man, and even worse, one of lower social station — moved to Berkshire.
This lost her the support of many of her admirers. She visited France twice
in the 1770s, there meeting such notables as Benjamin Franklin and Turgot.
In 1785 she and her second husband, William Graham, made an exten-
sive trip to the United States. (Almost all her work appears with the name
Catharine Macaulay and that is how she is referred to here.) They met
George Washington there and she subsequently corresponded with him. A
supporter of the American Revolution, Macaulay was a positive figure for
the early American women's movement. In 1790, the year before her death,
she published Letters on Education *and her reply to Burke's attack on*
the French Revolution, Observations on the Reflections of Edmund
Burke on the Revolution in France. *Her last work, as her first, shows a*
profound commitment to liberty.

Recommended biographies: Bridget Hill, Republican Virago: The Life and
Times of Catharine Macaulay, Historian; *introduction to* Letters on
Education; *Doris Stenton,* English Woman; *Katharine M. Rogers,* Feminism. *Lucy Martin Donnelly, "The Celebrated Mrs. Macaulay," is a hostile*
putdown of her work.

Macaulay's work was both accessible and unusually well written.
Her eight volumes of history, shorter works on political theory and
theology, and several polemical tracts had appeared before she
published her major contribution to methodology, *Letters on Education,* in 1790. This makes her a prime example of the integration of
particular, historical work with a concern for empiricist methodology.
She integrated as well an academic interest in the structure of knowledge with a concern for application. Her loss to the history of methodology is regrettable for both reasons. Her pioneering work on environmental ethics has been just as much ignored in the history of that
subject.

Macaulay was widely known in her day. Her histories were popular
in Britain and were also available in French translation. Nor can one
explain her eclipse by the notoriety of her unconventional second
marriage, for the most correct and chaste of women methodologists
fell equally into obscurity. One suspects that her liberal political views,
including support for both the American and French Revolutions,
proposals for nonsexist education, and refusal to glorify war, might

better explain the loss of her place in the history of ideas.

Macaulay's Lockean empiricism is clear in her earliest writings on history and theology as well as in the more extensive *Letters on Education*. Her *Treatise on the Immutability of Moral Truth* praised Locke and Hartley as benefactors of mankind, for "knowledge of the mechanism of the human mind" was essential for the practice of religion and moral duty (xiii). Her preface to the *Letters on Education* began with a declaration: "Of all the arts of life, that of giving useful instruction to the human mind and of rendering it master of its affections is the most important" (i). Later in the book she affirmed: "As the senses ... are the only inlets to human knowledge, consequently human knowledge can only be gained by experience and observation" (237). She shared the Enlightenment confidence in the powers of reason, as opposed to custom and authority, and distrust of the powers of abstract logic. Reason might "indeed be confounded by sophistry, borne down by authority, or led into erroneous conclusions from false statements of facts and false positions," but she believed in the capacity of people to discern "the moral differences of things, whenever they are fairly and plainly proposed" (193). Authority and custom were often sources of error (195). Logic was used to defend errors. Experience showed that "in our widest deviations from the dictates of reason, the mind is often more in fault than the body" (295).

> Few persons reason so closely and so accurately on abstract subjects
> as, through a long chain of deductions, to bring forth a conclusion
> which in no respect militates with their premises. (203)

Experience was "the only efficacious instructor" — by giving us knowledge of relations and causation, it makes our reason a valuable gift beyond the instinctive powers of animals (23). Macaulay's "intuitive knowledge of certain truths" referred only to the mind's ability to make judgments. There were no innate ideas:

> In the economy of the human mind are comprehended the faculties
> of sensitive perception, with an intuitive knowledge of certain truths,
> called on this account self evident. Such as a perception of the difference in numbers, a certain intellectual consciousness, or power, by
> which the mind perceives the nature of its own operations and
> reflects on its intellectual ideas, a judgment in perceiving their agree
> ment and disagreement, through all the extent of relation and
> comparison, a power of generalizing and combining its ideas, in
> such a manner as to apprehend truths of the most abstract kind.
> (382-83)

Next there was a power of memory to call up the results of all the preceding operations. The mind delighted itself to combine truths, using its imagination creatively.

Macaulay was not impressed by academic games. Everyone could "acquire the jargon of terms, but the depths of science is only to be attained by genius." She scorned those who conversed in generals without entering into particulars to investigate the subject:

> Men like these, without the desire of attaining truth, wrangle but
> for victory ... if they have sense enough to see their mistakes, they
> never have candor enough to acknowledge them.[11]

However radical Macaulay's histories later came to seem, she was herself keenly aware at the time that she was writing to correct the record. Introducing this volume she noted that:

> Party prejudice and the more detestable principle of private inter-
> est have painted the memoirs of past times in so false a light that it
> is with difficulty we can trace features. (1: ix)

Her histories, unlike Hume's, were "meticulously documented" with original sources, from reading at the British Museum, yet her writing style was just as lively as his, even entertaining.[12] She shared the ancient purpose of writing history, that fear of a bad reputation in posterity might be the only hold on powerful rulers. Fame was the only reward in present times for the sacrifice of private interests for the public good. The only punishment the guilty had to fear was "eternal infamy." The weight of punishment, moreover, ought to be determined by the importance of the consequences of the crime. Equally, we ought to do justice to the memory of illustrious ancestors who struggled for liberty against tyranny.

The historian's task was to digest the voluminous collections of data available "to give a true and accurate sense of these to the public":

> I have ever looked upon a supposed knowledge of facts seen in the
> false mirror of misrepresentation as one of the great banes of this
> country ... Labour to attain truth, integrity to set it in its full light
> are indispensable duties in an historian. I can affirm that I am not
> wanting in those duties.[13]

Since the "common reason of mankind" sought liberty and virtue the fact of slavery had to be explained. Macaulay here argued that in every

---

[11] Catharine Macaulay, *History of England from the Accession of James I*, 1: xiii.
[12] Janet Todd, "Catherine Macaulay," *Dictionary of British Women Writers*.
[13] Catharine Macaulay, *History of England from the Accession of James I*, 1: x.

society there were a number to whom tyranny was in some measure profitable. The "doctrine of slavery" was defended by "fraud and sophistry," which she determined to expose. In her one-volume history Macaulay expressed cynicism about government: "Of all human errors, the errors of government are the seldomest corrected."[14] A monarchical form of government was especially liable to error, basing a society's welfare on the conduct of one individual, in this case the illiberal Queen Anne. The royal prerogative of making peers was one of the "most noxious" of monarchical powers (288). When conventional histories devote so much attention to war Macaulay's unambiguous contempt for it stands out:

> I know of no real advantages ... which can accrue to any people
> from success in arms but that of political security ... Victory only
> serves to facilitate the ends of domestic tyranny and is purchased
> with the addition of accumulated taxes, with public debts, and public
> slavery. (182)

She saw military achievements as signs of servitude and marks of folly.

Macaulay's pamphlet was both a trouncing of an opposing pamphlet and a statement of her own beliefs in the possibilities of government action. She conceded that her opponent had much to complain of:

> Whilst the obvious intent of this pernicious work is to expose the
> dangerous designs of a profligate junto of courtiers, supported by
> the mere authority of the crown, against the liberties of the consti-
> tution; it likewise endeavours to mislead the people on the subject of
> the more complicated and specious, though no less dangerous
> manoeuvres of aristocratic faction and party, founded on and
> supported by the corrupt principle of self-interest; and also to guard
> against the possible consequences of an effectual reformation in the
> vitiated parts of our constitution and government. A circumstance
> much to be dreaded from the active exertion of a vigorous and
> enlightened zeal in the great body of the people.[15]

Her opponent had entirely disregarded "a more extended and equal power of election, a very important spring in the machine of political liberty" (28). The machine imagery she used was positive.

She acknowledged that it was common to regard present evils as worse than past ones.

---

14 Catharine Macaulay, *The History of England from the Revolution to the Present Time*, 199.
15 Macaulay, "Observations on a Pamphlet," 7.

The offences of a present possessor of power throw a favourable shade over the equally atrocious crimes of his designing predecessors. The grievances attending his government, which are but the bitter consequences, or rather the fruits of seeds sown by his ancestors, are regarded as springing immediately from the particular policy of his administration; and thus, the causes of political evils being never traced up to their sources, it is not surprising that the generality of mankind are so unfortunately divided in their opinions concerning their cure. (8)

However sardonic her remarks, Macaulay held to the belief that government could be better. One had to recognize the power of private interests and construct government institutions to mitigate the dangers. "All systematical writers on the side of freedom plan their forms and rules of government on the just grounds of the known corruption and wickedness of the human character" (9). There was no "moral impossibility" to forming a system answering to just ends. "The wisdom of man is fully adequate to the subject" (13). Yet people in general were too fond of:

accustomed establishments, however pernicious in their nature, to adopt material alterations; and this propensity has ever afforded full opportunity to the interested to reject every part of reformation which tends effectively to establish public good on the ruins of private interest. (11-12)

Macaulay concluded firmly:

In tracing the origin of all governments we find them either the produce of lawless power or accident, acted on by corrupt interest. (12)

Moreover, the same circumstances held for the reformation of government as for its formation, for which her own country afforded a melancholy example. "In all the great struggles for liberty true reformation was never by the ruling party either effected or even intended" (12). The English Revolution left full opportunity for private interest to exclude the public good. Nor were the people helpless:

Take away the cause and the effect will cease; take away from the representative, by a quick and thorough circulating round of rotation, every such lucrative and corrupt prospect of private interest, and the warm contention for seats in Parliament, both on the side of governments and individuals, will sink into a coolness which will reduce such elections to the quiet calmness of a nomination for parish officers. (24-25)

The pamphlet ended with a caution not to expect too much:

> I would warn my countrymen from entering into any dangerous or even vigorous measures against the conduct of their present governors without exacting a political creed from leaders ... some particular promises of real public good. (31)

Before the American Revolution Macaulay urged more generous treatment of the colonists, warning against the "delusive hope" that government, by picking the pockets of the Americans, would spare taxpayers at home. If these are your thoughts, she cautioned in "An Address to the People,"

> little have you studied your own natures, and the experience of all ages, which must have convinced you that the want of power is the only limitation to the exertion of human selfishness; but should you be contented to bid defiance to the warnings of common policy, should you be contented to be slaves on the hope that the Americans will bear the greater part of the burden of your enormous taxes, be assured that such an alternative will never be in your power. No, if a civil war commences between Great Britain and her colonies, either the mother country, by one great exertion, may ruin both herself and America, or the Americans, by a lingering contest, will gain an independency; and in this case, all those advantages which you for some time have enjoyed by your colonies, and advantages which have hitherto preserved you from a national bankruptcy, must forever have an end; and whilst a new, a flourishing, and an extensive empire of freemen is established on the other side of the Atlantic, you, with the loss of all those blessings you have received by the unrivalled state of your commerce, will be left to the bare possession of your foggy islands; and this under the sway of a domestic despot, or you will become the provinces of some powerful European state. (25-27)

With the benefit of hindsight this seems to have been sound advice indeed for 1775, the year before the Boston Tea Party. Yet the advice of women political commentators not only went unheeded as advice, but it was ignored in the documentation of the period later. George Washington, however, did appreciate Macaulay. The Washingtons entertained Macaulay and her husband for ten days at Mount Vernon and, as president, Washington corresponded with her while working out the new constitution.

The *Letters on Education* contain a powerful and eloquent defence of empiricism, a manifesto for educational reform, and a plea for environmental ethics. In the preface Macaulay made, far too modestly, "some small claim to original thinking" (vi). Thanks to women's studies the analysis on women has been revived, but the methodology continues to be ignored, while the environmental ethics have scarcely been noted. The three are inter-related, for Macaulay shared both the empiricist view of animals on a continuum with human life and the belief that the foundation of moral behaviour was sympathy. Her rejection of the idealist mind/body dualism is key to her advocacy of women's rights. As well it gives a glimpse of a different approach to morality. Here also in the *Letters on Education* God is referred to in inclusive language, as "the universal parent" of creation (2).

With other empiricists and the ancient materialists Macaulay consistently noted the commonalities with animal life, although reserving rational powers to humans. The *Letters* actually open with a discussion of human/animal differences. Macaulay's ethics permitted the killing of animals, but it did not follow that their slaughter should delight the human mind. A cat worried its prey without considering whether or not it was doing evil, "but man has sympathy in his nature, and his knowledge of the relation of things causes him to put himself in the place of the sufferer, and thus to acquire ideas of equity" (196-97). Macaulay here used the moral sentiments ideas of Adam Smith and David Hume, but went much further than both in applying the ethics to animals. "Universal benevolence" was the goal, and those most active in spreading happiness and least cruel would enjoy a better state in the hereafter. All human virtue proceeds from equity.

> For had the mind of man been totally divested of this affection it would not in all probability have ever attained any ideas of equity. Yes, it was the movements of sympathy which first inclined man to a forbearance of his own gratifications, in respect to the feelings of his fellow creatures; and his reason soon approved the dictates of his inclination ... This being granted, all human virtue will be found to proceed from equity; consequently, if the principle of equity itself owes its source in the human mind to the feelings of sympathy, all human virtue must derive its source from this useful affection. (275)

Utilitarian Macaulay was, but she rejected the "absurd opinion" that rectitude was founded on the utility principle confined to the benefit of our own species. Here she criticized Hume. Utility had to be taken in a general sense; virtue consisted in "that conduct which is of general utility," not merely human advantage (193). The human being was not "lord of creation" unbound by any tie to nature (192). The virtue of benevolence should be cultivated in children by giving them animals to care for. Such care would provide agreeable and innocent amusement and, through knowledge of animal nature, children would be cured of prejudices founded on human ignorance, vanity, and conceit (125).

With Astell Macaulay held to a conception of knowledge as gender free. She reasoned that since the sense organs were the same in both sexes perceptions were the same for both (179). Differences between women and men then could only arise from different combinations of ideas. Yet the notion of a sexual difference in human character had, with very few exceptions, universally prevailed from the earliest times. "The pride of one sex and the ignorance and vanity of the other have helped to support an opinion which a close observation of Nature, and a more accurate way of reasoning, would disprove" (204). The differences were too flattering for men to impute them to accidents of opportunity. Macaulay cited Rousseau as a strenuous asserter of sex differences, noting that this concept coincided with the supposition that Nature intended the subjection of one sex to the other and gave the subject party an inferior intellect.

Of course there were real differences between the sexes, so unfavourable to women that Macaulay noted, "I was never an apologist for the conduct of women" (214). Yet, for all the vices and imperfections of women they had never done the damage men had in history. With Gournay, Poullain, Astell, Sophia, and a growing number of women's advocates she blamed poor education and opportunity for women's lesser performance.

> All those vices and imperfections which have been generally
> regarded as inseparable from the female character do not in any
> manner proceed from sexual causes, but are entirely the effects of
> situation and education. (202)

Women were corrupted by their situation and education. Their nervous system was "depraved" by a false notion of beauty and delicacy even before they came out of the nursery (207). This depravity influenced the mind, and consequently morals, more than was commonly believed. But women's moral education was, if possible, "more absurd than their physical":

> Every thing that ennobles our being and that renders us both innox-
> ious and useful is either not taught, or is taught in such a manner
> as to leave no proper impression on the mind. This is so obvious a

truth that the defects of female education have ever been a fruitful topic of declamation for the moralist; but not one of this class of writers have laid down any judicious rules for amendment. Whilst we still retain the absurd notion of a sexual excellence it will militate against the perfecting a plan of education for either sex. (208)

Letters on Education was no manifesto for political rights for women, but there were some succinct remarks about the legal disabilities from which women suffered:

For with a total and absolute exclusion of every political right to the sex in general, married women, whose situation demand a particular indulgence, have hardly a civil right to save them from the grossest injuries; and though the gallantry of some of the European societies have necessarily produced indulgences, yet in others the faults of women are treated with a severity and rancour which militates against every principle of religion and common sense (210).

Mind/body dualism has been so long used against women that Macaulay's very different approach is noteworthy. She was sceptical of the "mutual hostility between soul and body" which prevailed among our ancestors. She noted the daring fact that "some modern philosophers" (presumably Locke) maintained that humans were made of one substance only (294-95).

It is true that the mind receives all its intelligence through the organs of sense, and were it deprived of their assistance, it would be incapable of sentiment and consequently of giving birth to any idea. But in the contempt with which the severe moralist regards the sensual part of man, he does not take into consideration that the most sublime ideas we are capable of forming owe their origin to the impressions of sense; and that as all the virtuous as well as the vicious affections flow from these sources of intelligence, it may be found on a clear view of the subject, that a refinement in the sensual gratifications is necessary to the refinement of sentiment. (295)

There were implications from these fundamental points for both the organization of government, to be considered shortly, and methods of teaching and curriculum.

Having accepted Lockean psychology Macaulay had to be concerned with the order in which material was taught. If ideas are formed by a combination and comparison of ideas, obviously the earliest impressions would be the most influential, for they shape all subsequent thinking. Macaulay accordingly specified an order for teaching, beginning with Greek, Latin, the classics, and other languages, then going on to

political and social theory, metaphysics, and ancient myths. Ecclesiastical history and doctrinal controversy would not be taught until the
student was a well prepared age twenty-one. Mathematics and the
European tour also came late in the order. Logically,

> the new philosophy, which supposes the human character to be the
> mere creature of external impressions, would naturally prescribe
> the commencement of regulating education from the moment of an
> infant's birth. (36)

Macaulay indeed gave advice on the early care of young infants.

Education would be remarkably similar for the two sexes in her
system. "Let your children be brought up together; let their sports and
studies be the same" (50). As a result, men and women would be able
to enjoy friendships without passion. Girls would be sent on the European tour, normally the privilege of males. Macaulay herself had travelled and personally knew the advantages of direct contact with other
thinkers and cultures. Most of her advice, and her most radical reforms,
concern the education of girls.

> Confine not the education of your daughters to what is regarded as
> the ornamental parts of it, nor deny the graces to your sons. Suffer
> no prejudices to prevail on you to weaken Nature in order to render
> her more beautiful. (50)

Yet the practice of teaching girls needlework and such skills should
also continue. Boys should be given instruction in some, presumably
not the same, handicrafts. Practical knowledge should not be confined
to girls. Even the forming of a button was a better occupation than
hunting down harmless animals — a risk to a boy's neck and his
benevolence (65).

The explanation Macaulay developed of moral worth as the reason
that women need the same education as men, even without any expectation of radical change in their respective occupations, echoes that of
Gournay and Astell:

> I have given similar rules for male and female education on the
> following grounds of reasoning.
> First, that there is but one rule of right for the conduct of all ration-
> al beings; consequently that true virtue in one sex must be equally
> so in the other ... and, *vice versa*, what is vice in one sex cannot have
> a different property when found in the other.
> Secondly, that true wisdom ... is as useful to women as to men,
> because it is necessary to the highest degree of happiness, which
> can never exist with ignorance. (201)

The happiness of the two sexes was reciprocally dependent, so that until both sexes were reformed there was no expecting excellence in either.

Macaulay shared the Enlightenment faith in the possibility of progress. If people's external circumstances improved so would their manners. The mind and body were so closely connected that manners "will be barbarous where customs are gross" and virtue found where there was reasonable enjoyment (268). An improvement in the "useful arts" could improve human sentiments.

This acceptance of the sympathy principle had direct consequences for the organization of government. Sceptical as she was of the achievements of governments to date, Macaulay believed in the capacity of government to intervene to achieve social goals. Because people were influenced by their impressions/sensations they could be motivated by appropriate laws and precepts. Human passions, including the sociable ones, were latent in every mind, not activated until put in motion by some impression. The growth and prevalence of passions depended on repetition. With the proper use of laws, precepts, and customs, governments could improve human conduct.

Macaulay then asked if we could, by the spirit of our laws, prevent the operation of all impressions that led to cruelty in society.

> Did we encourage the operation of every impression which had a benevolent tendency, it appears probable that we should exalt the sympathizing feeling to a degree which might act more forcibly than the coercion of rigorous laws — to the restraining all acts of violence, and consequently all acts which militate against the public peace. (276-77)

Yet she warned that people could become inured to cruelty, as they were to the cruel slaughter of animals. Barbarous treatment of the offender did not necessarily lead to an increase in sympathy. In the case of cruelty to animals she recommended that a premium be paid for finding the least painful means of slaughter, then severe penalties established for those using other means; cruel sports should be discouraged by example and precept.

Macaulay cited Beccaria's excellent treatise *On Crimes and Punishments* concerning the effect of laws and practices on human behaviour (273). Unlike the great Italian law reformer, she was not opposed completely to the death penalty, but would restrict its use considerably. She opposed branding as a punishment. Executions should be private since brutality coarsened people's moral sentiments. Considering the arguments for and against capital punishment:

> Those who take the benevolent side of the question maintain that the
> depriving a citizen of his life is a breach of one of the fundamental
> obligations of government, and that there may be found a variety of
> punishments more fully adequate to the preservation of the public
> peace than acts of violence which shock the sensibility of the feeling
> mind and harden to a state of barbarism the unfeeling one.

She agreed that there were arguments for the opposing side, as well,
but good policy required taking as little life as possible. She added that
the melancholy ceremonies concerned with execution should be made
"as aweful as possible" (279).

So as not to shock the more compassionate, or steel the hearts of
the more insensible, all executions should be performed in private
(281). Apart from what governments could do to influence behaviour
through criminal sanctions, it had broad duties to act:

> The education of the people, in the most extensive sense of this
> word, may be said to comprehend the most important duties of
> government. For as the education of individuals is forever going on,
> and consists of all the impressions received through the organs of
> sense, from the hour of birth to the hour of death; public education,
> if well adapted to the improvement of man, must comprehend good
> laws, good examples, good customs, a proper use of the arts, and
> wise instructions conveyed to the mind. (274)

Macaulay's position on social compact theory was complex. She
rejected with scathing contempt the hardline approach of Hobbes and
those who "made a deity" of government or society, sacrificing the
dearest interest of individuals to it:

> Thus they reversed a very plain and reasonable proposition. Soci-
> ety with them was not formed for the happiness of its citizens, but
> the life and happiness of every citizen was to be devoted to the glory
> and welfare of the society. (271)

Yet citizens had duties to their governments. Curiously there was no
uniformity of opinion on such an important subject. Indeed there was:

> no speculation on which a greater variety of opinions have been
> formed, on which the prejudices of the species have been more at
> war with their interests, or on which the feebleness or the inactiv-
> ity of the reasoning powers have been more exposed, or which more
> proves man to be the slave of custom and of precept ...
> We have indeed made no accurate definitions either on the duties
> of government, or on the duties of a good citizen. (270-72)

Her feminist interests gave Macaulay reason to suspect the highly patriarchal prevailing male view of the early origins of society. "Domestic education," notably the teaching of good and evil, must have begun with the beginning of human life (237). As time went on, impressions accumulated and the powers of comparison and inference increased; moral judgments also increased. Yet even in the "solitary, natural state" there would be *some* education by parents, more in the rudest early societies, increasing as societies developed.

In a 1767 essay on Hobbes, Macaulay referred to the "maternal feeling" common to all animals.[16] Nature and reason contradicted Hobbes's position that the mother had a "natural right" to expose her children after birth (9). The human species was bound by reason, morality, and natural obligation. Parents and children were mutually bound. Macaulay's paraphrase of Hobbes is superb. He had set out to confute the received opinion "that man is a creature fit for society," drawing from those premises "that man cannot desire society from love, but through hope of gain" (1). The origin of all lasting societies was thus fear. Macaulay argued that Hobbes confounded absolute with limited powers (5). Regrettably he was not so much acquainted with the "science of policy" as he was adept in the art of confounding things. Macaulay's portrayal of early society is quite different from Hobbes's war of all against all. She pointed to positive bonds and positive teaching of moral rules right from the beginning of human life, a point also made in her *Letters on Education*. But her critique of "possessive individualism" has been no more discussed in the mainstream male literature than Astell's.

Also in this paper on Hobbes Macaulay expressly rejected the view that political equality and good government were incompatible. Rather each required the other (16). She then went on to discuss the place of a democratic constitution in a commonwealth (23).

Observations on the Reflections of Edmund Burke was both a reply to Burke's attack on the French Revolution and liberal institutions for Britain, and another opportunity to oppose Hobbes's conservative social compact theory. Macaulay showed how "the fanatic atheist Hobbes" had, from "an original right in the people to choose their governors," gone on to contend that their posterity forever lost their native privileges and became "bound through the whole series of generations to the

[16] Macaulay, "Loose Remarks on ... Hobbes's Philosophical Rudiments of Government and Society," 9.

service of a master's will" (14). She scorned the "slavish adulation" the English people showed to royal administration. "None of the enslaved nations of the world address the throne in a more *fulsome* and *hyperbolical* style of submissive flattery" than the English (15). The sort of compliments Burke recommended would offend a wise and good prince and lead to unfortunate consequences. A false opinion of the rights and powers of citizens might:

> *enslave* the ductile mind into a state of passive obedience, and thus secure the peace of government. Yet in the same degree does it inflate the *pride* and *arrogance* of princes until all considerations of *rectitude* give way to *will*, the barriers of personal security are flung down, and thence arises that *tremendous necessity* which must be followed by a state of *violence* and *anarchy*. (17)

Macaulay tore into Burke's defence of custom:

> When the people, disdaining and rejecting all those fond opinions by which they have been *enslaved to misery*, assert their native right to forming a government for themselves, surely in such a case the builders are bound by no law of *duty* or *reason* to make use of these old materials in the structure of their new constitution, which they suppose to have been of an injurious tendency. The leaders of the French Revolution, and their followers, see *none of those striking beauties* in the old laws and rules of the Gothic institutions of Europe, which Mr. Burke does. They do not profess to have any of the spirit of antiquarians among them, and they have not perceived, in the experience of old or ancient times, a *perfect harmony* arising from *opposition* of interests; nor can they *understand* how such a combination can be formed as shall produce it.

The French, she noted, chose a simple rule for the model of their new structure, "yet regulated with all the *art* and *design* which the experience of ages affords to the wisdom of man" (34).

> They are accused of having entirely dismissed that useful guide *experience* from their councils, but they think they have made *the best use* of it; whether this opinion of theirs is founded in truth, time, and the future history of man, must evince. (34-35)

Later in the pamphlet Macaulay again argued against Burke's reliance on convention:

> If we say that *lawful* governments are formed on the authority of conventions, it will be asked, *who gave these conventions their authority?* If we grant that they derived their authority from the *assent of the people*, how came the people ... to exert such an authority at any

one period of society and not at *another?* If we say it was *necessity* that recovered to the social man the full rights of his nature ... *who is to be the judge* of this necessity? why *certainly* the people. (94)

When Burke argued that people needed governors to control their passions, Macaulay countered that these governors themselves had passions, for they were of the same nature as other people. Governed by the same principles and errors and "having no *common* interest with themselves which might lead them to preserve a salutary check over their vices, [governors] must be inclined to *abuse* in the *grossest manner* of their trust" (47).

The Utilitarian ethics which grew out of Scottish moral philosophy included the whole sensitive creation, meaning animals as well as human beings. Francis Hutcheson was crystal clear on this point in his writing, specifying the duty to avoid cruelty to animals. David Hume did not follow Hutcheson here, although he agreed that humans should avoid needless cruelty. Jeremy Bentham did take the Hutcheson view, although he accorded little attention to the subject in most of the great volume of his work. Macaulay's extensive treatment of cruelty to animals makes her the authentic spokesperson for the moral philosophy/Utilitarian position. In *Letters on Education* she devoted pages of vigorous debate and graphic detail to the ethical question and related religious teachings. She was as explicitly critical of Hume as she was of Plato and any philosophical position argued solely from the human point of view. Yet Macaulay's work in this area has been ignored as much as her writing on political theory and methodology. An excellent anthology on Christian teaching on animals omits her entirely (forty-nine of the fifty works excerpted are of male authors).[17]

Mary Wollstonecraft (1759-1797)

Mary Wollstonecraft was born in London, the granddaughter of a success-ful weaver whose son lost most of the property passed on to him. The family, including six other children, moved numerous times. Wollstonecraft père drank excessively and abused his wife. At age fifteen Mary left home with-out consent. She later helped her sister, who had married young, to leave her abusive husband. She was self-supporting from the age of nineteen, working as a companion, teacher, head of her own school, and governess in a noble family in Ireland. She learned her radical politics from a group

---

[17] Andrew Linzey and Tom Regan, *Animals and Christianity.*

Mary Wollstonecraft, by Sir John Opie
By Courtesy of The Tate Gallery, London

of Dissenters, led by Richard Price, in the same town as her school, Newing- **Mary**
ton Green. She then turned to writing for her living, translating from French, **Wollstonecraft**
Italian, and German for the radical publisher, Joseph Johnson, reviewing
books and publishing her own.

Her first book, Thoughts on the Education of Daughters (1786),
gave Lockean advice on infant care and teaching. She next translated Of
the Importance of Religious Opinions (1788), by Jacques Necker, father
of Germaine de Staël. Fame came with A Vindication of the Rights of
Men, a fast and furious defence of the French Revolution, supporting the
position taken by her friend Richard Price. This "first vindication" was
published anonymously in 1790, but promptly republished with her name.
In 1792 she published her second vindication, now on the rights of
"woman." Only then did she go to France, where she met the American
writer, Gilbert Imlay, and had a baby by him. There she did the research
for her more comprehensive book, Historical and Moral View of the
Origin and Progress of the French Revolution, published in 1794. Wollstonecraft witnessed the king being taken to trial and literally saw blood
in the streets. After leaving France in 1795 she travelled in Scandinavia,
partly on business for Imlay, who by then had tired of her. Her Letters
written ... in Sweden, Norway and Denmark, published 1796, were
well received as social and political observation. Other stories and essays
were published posthumously. One collection, Original Stories, with illustrations by William Blake, includes Lockean theory on education and environmental ethics.

In 1796, at a tea party at the home of Mary Hays, Wollstonecraft again
met the anarchist theorist, William Godwin. They married when she became
pregnant, but she died from infection after giving birth. Their daughter, Mary
Godwin Shelley, became a writer and is most known for her story of the
graduate student Frankenstein and his monster. Wollstonecraft's first daughter
committed suicide young.

Wollstonecraft evidently learned her radical politics from religious dissenters
but remained an adherent of the church. She was buried after a religious
service in St. Pancras Churchyard. Still she was not left in peace, but hers
and Godwin's remains were moved when the railway station was built.

Recommended biographies: Eleanor Flexner, Mary Wollstonecraft; Ralph
M. Wardle, Mary Wollstonecraft; Claire Tomalin, The Life and Death of
Mary Wollstonecraft; Emily W. Sunstein, A Different Face; Moira Ferguson
and Janet Todd, Mary Wollstonecraft; Edna Nixon, Mary Wollstonecraft;
Emma Rauschenbusch-Clough, A Study of Mary Wollstonecraft; chapters

Mary in Alice Rossi, Feminist Papers *and C. Kegan Paul,* William Godwin: His
Wollstonecraft Friends and Contemporaries; *in French, Paule Penigault-Duhet,* Mary
Wollstonecraft. *On her journalism see Ralph M. Wardle, "Mary*
Wollstonecraft, Analytical Reviewer."

When we realize how much these early advocates for women had
written on rights to education and participation in intellectual life Wollstonecraft seems less original than she might on first impression. Many
of the points commonly associated with her name had at least been
suggested two centuries earlier by Gournay and in considerable detail
a century earlier by Astell. Macaulay also, an acknowledged source for
Wollstonecraft, added considerably to the analysis in the preceding
generation. Wollstonecraft was not "the only audible voice raised to
assert that women, as well as men, had an inalienable right to freedom,
that they too were human beings."[18] But she did go further than her
predecessors in opening up the issue of political rights for women and
in specifying the demand for economic independence and access to
traditional male occupations. She was attacked in her lifetime and
ignored after her death. Perhaps the tragic events of her life — two
attempted suicides, an illegitimate child, and a marriage prompted by
pregnancy — threatened suffragists of the Victorian era. *A Vindication*
of the Rights of Woman (1792) was republished in the nineteenth
century, but seems not to have been a source for the suffrage movement in England. Wollstonecraft was read by American suffragists but
broader recognition is relatively recent. Her life and work inspired both
the great English novelist Virginia Woolf[19] and the pioneer American
anthropologist Ruth Benedict.[20] Wollstonecraft is now standard fare in
women's studies. Yet her advocacy of empiricism is still little known.
Her contribution to political theory on equality, social class, ideology,
and the origins of society is still ignored in mainstream political science.
There are now several good biographies of her, a collected letters, and
even — those most rare tributes to women scholars — two critical
editions of her *Vindication of the Rights of Woman* (1982 and 1988), a
scholarly collected works (1989), and a compilation of her three major
Political Writings (1993).
Wollstonecraft's review of *Letters on Education* shows that she was

---

[18] Eleanor Flexner, *Mary Wollstonecraft*, 12.
[19] Virginia Woolf, "Mary Wollstonecraft," *Second Common Reader*, 168-76.
[20] Benedict's essay on Wollstonecraft was published posthumously in Margaret
Mead, *An Anthropologist at Work: Writings of Ruth Benedict*.

not yet, in 1790, much of a feminist. She opened by complimenting Macaulay as a "masculine" writer and closed with disparaging remarks about "female" literary works.[21] The review cites the book at length and contains little original material apart from theological disputes with Macaulay. Wollstonecraft, however, was learning; her second vindication would be a radical manifesto for women's equality.

A Vindication of the Rights of Woman (*VW*) was dedicated to Talleyrand, defender of the French Revolution and author of a report on a new system of public education for France. His proposal would separate girls from boys at age eight, hence Wollstonecraft's attempt to convince him to reconsider. She argued that women should be able to advance, instead of retarding, "the progress of those glorious principles that give a substance to morality" (18). Men claimed the freedom to be allowed to judge for themselves respecting their own happiness. Why not women? "Who made man the exclusive judge, if woman partake with him the gift of reason?" (22) The basic argument, in short, was the same as Astell's, although Wollstonecraft never mentioned her and may not have read her. Also like Astell, Wollstonecraft understood reason as the basis of the difference between humans and animals and a gift of God.

Since women did not at that time show an equal capacity to reason Wollstonecraft had to argue, as had earlier advocates for equality, the disabilities of women's education, not defects in nature, as the cause of their inferiority. Hence the ancient Greek distinction of *nomos* (norm/law) and *physis* (nature) again becomes key. Women did not perform so well as men in many respects, nor did the people of France who rose up against tyranny always act in accordance with reason and justice. The explanation for both was defects in education and opportunity, the result of bad social institutions. Both women and the French population, given better education and a better social environment, would perform better. Intellectual and moral development were so closely linked that improvement in either would help the other. Education, Wollstonecraft wrote in *An Historical and Moral View of the Origin and Progress of the French Revolution* (*H&M*), could change "the natural laws of humanity" for better or worse (132).

Time alone would tell, once women could get a "masculine" education, whether sex differences were fundamental or accidental.

> I only contend that the men who have been placed in similar situations have acquired a similar character ... men of genius and talents

[21] Mary Wollstonecraft, review of Catharine Macaulay, *The Analytical Review*, 241, 254.

have started out of a class in which women have never yet been
placed. (VW, 170)

Girls should be given the same exercises as boys, "that we may know
how far the natural superiority of man extends" (187). While Astell
sought a place for privileged women in the life of reason Wollstonecraft
wanted women also to be able "to study the art of healing, and be physicians as well as nurses," study history and government, and run farms
and businesses (312).

Indeed, the ability of women to earn their own subsistence was the
true definition of independence (187). Without that their morality would
be limited; virtue could not be expected from women until they were
in some degree independent of men (299). When absolutely dependent on their husbands, women were forced into being cunning, selfish,
and mean.

How much more respectable is the woman who earns her own
bread, by fulfilling any duty, than the most accomplished beauty.
(315)

A chapter on national education set out the reasons for a state-run
school system in which girls and boys would be taught together (355).
Wollstonecraft admitted that she had earlier favoured private education but experience had led her to change her mind. This chapter also
sets out her views on the treatment of animals. "Humanity to animals,"
which was not a national virtue, should be inculcated as part of national
education (364). Further, the transition from "habitual cruelty" to
animals to "domestic cruelty over wives, children, and servants" was
easy. The implications for humans of cruelty to animals was not the
only reason for her concern, however, for Wollstonecraft had some
sense of what is now called "deep ecology":

Justice, or even benevolence, will not be a powerful spring of action
unless it extend to the whole creation. (365)

Those who could see pain and not be moved would soon learn to inflict
it. Again, for Wollstonecraft as for Macaulay and other Utilitarians, the
ethical case was firmly grounded on the psychology of sensation. Her
Original Stories, written for children in 1788 and first published in 1796,
include advice on the benevolent treatment of animals. God, as creator
of the world, was the creator of all its inhabitants, including the meanest
creatures. All were meant to be happy, and God provided nourishment
for them all.[22]

It is true that Wollstonecraft made the customary separation between rational human beings and the "brute creation." Yet it is equally clear that the ability of humans to reason did not engender any right to treat other creatures cruelly. For Wollstonecraft, who took her ethics from her faith, reason gave people "pre-eminence over the brute creation." Yet it was virtue that exalted one being over another. Rational creatures were to "crown the whole," rising in excellence above love of self to more sublime emotions, which were prompted by the discovery of the wisdom and goodness of God.

Wollstonecraft advanced her famous claim to the right to vote in a seemingly casual digression in the *Vindication of the Rights of Woman*:

> I may excite laughter by dropping a hint, which I mean to pursue some future time, for I really think that women ought to have representatives, instead of being arbitrarily governed without having any direct share allowed them in the deliberations of government. (311)

There was no hint that women might themselves be elected as representatives.

The claim for equality in rights was always linked to responsibility. Without rights there could be no duties (307). Morality would never "gain ground" when "one half of mankind be chained to its bottom by fate, for they will be continually undermining it through ignorance or pride" (299). In the *Vindication of the Rights of Men* (*VM*) she had already argued that true happiness arose from friendship, which could only be enjoyed by equals (*VM*, 10). In the second vindication she further asserted that, if woman was not "prepared by education to become the companion of man she will stop the progress of knowledge and virtue, for truth must be common to all" (*VW*, 20). Wollstonecraft argued vehemently against Rousseau's contention that women controlled men through their feminine charms. Women, she held, were degraded by the trivial attentions paid them by men, while otherwise being kept in ignorance.

> This is the very point I aim at. I do not wish them to have power over men, but over themselves. (*VW*, 140)

Against the double standard she argued that men should be more chaste (*VW*, 38).

It is clear in each of her three major books that Wollstonecraft's quest for equality was for all people, not just her sex. Distinctions of rank were corrupting, for respectability was accorded not from the performance of duty but station in life (*VW*, 306). Every profession in which power was based on the subordination of ranks was injurious to

---

[22] Wollstonecraft, *Original Stories*, in *Works*, 4: 367-72.

morality. As well as the armed forces, Wollstonecraft cited the church. The clergy had more opportunity than the military to develop their intellects, but "subordination almost equally cramps their faculties." Blind submission was imposed at college and could be seen thereafter in "the servile dependent gait of a poor curate and the courtly mien of a bishop. And the respect and contempt they inspire render the discharge of their separate functions equally useless" (*VW*, 51).

Wollstonecraft's anti-military views flowed from her more general contempt for systems of rank. A standing army was "incompatible with freedom, because subordination and rigour are the very sinews of military discipline, and despotism is necessary to give vigour to enterprizes that one directs" (*VW*, 49-50). Like women without education, military men were "sent into the world before their minds have been stored with knowledge or fortified by principles." Not a comparison likely to make her popular, the consequences were similar: soldiers, like women, acquire superficial knowledge and "practise the minor virtues with punctilious politeness" (*VW*, 62).

In her analysis of class inequality Wollstonecraft described the "property" the poor have in their labour. She used the labour theory of value in her first vindication but drew more radical implications from it than did contemporary theorists (*VM*, 51). She described the extreme suffering of the poor in France, "their property the fruit of their industry, being entirely at the disposal of their lords, who were so many petty tyrants" (*VM*, 16). She showed how laws were "the champion of property," not of life and liberty. While small fines were meted out for the life of a person, the death sentence protected the property of the rich (*VM*, 19-20). Similarly, in the second vindication she held that "most of the evils" that made this world a dreary scene flowed "from the respect paid to property" (*VW*, 298).

Like Burke and the conservatives, Wollstonecraft had a notion of society as an organic whole, but she mocked his "servile reverence for antiquity" and "prudent attention to self-interest." Under his principles the slave trade would never have been abolished (*VM*, 23). "Charity is not a condescending distribution of alms but an intercourse of good offices and mutual benefits, founded on respect for justice and humanity" (*VM*, 12).

Wollstonecraft's political analysis includes both a fierce denunciation of the actual, corrupt, practise of politics and a belief that government could play a role for good. In fact, people were exploited by their governments as well as by their employers. "The clogged wheel of corruption" was "continually oiled by the sweat of the laborious poor, squeezed out of them by unceasing taxation." People's own money was "extorted by the venal voice of a packed representation" (*VM*, 43). She deplored the "taxes on the very necessaries of life," which enabled "an endless tribe of idle princes and princesses to pass with stupid pomp before a gaping crowd" (*VW*, 311). Her history of the French Revolution shows her deep conviction of the goodness of ordinary people, especially given the help of education. She admitted that "acts of ferocious folly" had been committed, yet:

> I feel confident of being able to prove that the people are essentially good and that knowledge is rapidly advancing to that degree of perfectibility when the proud distinctions of sophisticating fools will be eclipsed by the mild rays of philosophy. (*H&M*, 72)

In the meantime, representation was "only a convenient handle for despotism" (*VW*, 311). No wonder she was less than enthusiastic about the vote and in no hurry at all for women to enter Parliament!

> Experience, I believe, will show that sordid interest, or licentious thoughtlessness, is the spring of action at most elections. (*VM*, 85)

The fact that nature made people unequal, in physical and mental powers, did not justify inequality in society but gave government one of its purposes: to destroy this inequality and protect the weak (*H&M*, 7). Laws could be changed. Property laws should be, to make for a more equal division of property among all children of a family (*VM*, 50). While her future husband was an anarchist, Wollstonecraft, just as egalitarian in ideals, lined up with the Utilitarians to give government duties:

> A truly benevolent legislator always endeavours to make it the interest of each individual to be virtuous; and thus private virtue becoming the cement of public happiness, an orderly whole is consolidated by the tendency of all the parts towards a common centre. (*VW*, 306)

Wollstonecraft's commitment to empiricism is coupled with a disdain for scholasticism, tradition, authority, and abstract methods. Against Burke she argued for points "to be demonstrated and not determined by arbitrary authority and dark traditions" (*VM*, 37). She scorned the work of "seminaries of learning in Germany, where formerly scholastic, dry theology, laborious compilations of the wanderings of the human understanding, and minute collations of the works of the ancients had consumed the fervour of youth and wasted the patience of age" (*H&M*, 237). Macaulay had used the image of inlets for the sense organs.

Wollstonecraft now used it in *Original Stories* for the connection to ethics:

> Knowledge should be gradually imparted and flow more from example than teaching; example directly addresses the senses, the first inlets to the heart; and the improvement of those instruments of the understanding is the object education should have constantly in view and over which we have most power. (*CW*, 4: 359)

By comparison we have little power over the "quick perception of truth" of the mind. "Over this subtile electric fluid how little power we possess and over it how little power can reason obtain" (*VW*, 247). A habitual association of ideas meant a habitual slavery. Hence the "baneful effect on women" from the "dry employments of their understandings" (*VW*, 247-48).

As a Lockean Wollstonecraft paid close attention to early education. The poor education given women had debilitating effects on their character. "Is it surprising," she asked, "when we consider what a determinate effect an early association of ideas has on the character that [women] neglect their understandings and turn all their attention to their persons?" (*VW*, 246) Yet until women were led to exercise their understandings they should not be satirized for attachments to "rakes" or being "rakes at heart," when it appeared to be the inevitable consequence of their education (*VW*, 253). Like Locke and other empiricists she used "understandings" in the plural.

Wollstonecraft was not averse to natural science models, including mechanical ones. She disapproved of seeing nature "through the medium of books without making any actual experiments" (*H&M*, 235). She credited Newton with following Descartes's example by displaying "the mechanism of the universe" with wonderful perspicacity (*H&M*, 236). Causal knowledge was the object, for everything was affected by natural causes. Yet she recognized the usual empiricist limits to knowledge:

> I know that the human understanding is deluded with vain shadows and that when we eagerly pursue any study we only reach the boundary set to human enquiries ... The *cause* we were pursuing melts into utter darkness. (*VM*, 77)

Her history of the French Revolution ended with a medical analogy of disease and cure. The philosophical eye must look into nature and weigh the consequences of human action to discern the cause of so many dreadful effects. (*H&M*, 522)

Germaine de Staël, whose writing career began as Wollstonecraft's ended, was much more given to the terminology of "political science," but Wollstonecraft, too, used the expression. The terrible happenings of the French Revolution were due to the tenacity and smallness of mind of political actors, who were destitute of both "legitimate patriotism and political science" (*H&M*, 300). The improvement of manners was a harbinger of reason, "and from the ratio of its advancement throughout society we are enabled to establish the progress of political science" (*H&M*, 497). She credited the Encyclopedists not only with useful knowledge but for turning the attention of the nation to the principles of political and civil government. She referred also to the "science of government" when discussing the possibilities of slow and gradual change (*H&M*, 357).

Mary Hays's obituary of Wollstonecraft in the *Monthly Magazine* praised both her concerns for women and her broader analysis of civil institutions. Wollstonecraft had been "quick to feel and indignant to resist the iron hand of despotism, whether civil or intellectual."[23] Apt as Hays was in describing her friend's merits she was overly optimistic in judging their results, that her "impassioned reasoning and glowing eloquence" would soon shake "prejudice to its foundation so that it tottered to its fall" (233). Yet Hays was correct, if impolite, in predicting that "the rights of woman, and the name of Wollstonecraft, will go down to posterity with reverence when the pointless sarcasms of witlings are forgotten."[24]

Mary Hays (1760-1843)

Mary Hays was born to a middle-class, dissenting family living in Southwark. She became a Unitarian and associated with the radical Unitarian minister Joseph Priestley and former minister William Godwin. She once became engaged, and was planning a secret wedding, when her fiancé died of fever. Much later she fell in love again but, alas, this was unrequited. (Both Hays and Wollstonecraft shocked society by pursuing men.) She never married.

In 1791 Hays published a pamphlet defending the Unitarian form of worship, using the pseudonym "Eusebia," after the author of the first church history. The pamphlet a success, Hays was encouraged to write more. She published articles in progressive journals and met with other radicals who used the same publisher, Joseph Johnson. She read Mary Wollstonecraft's

---

[23] Mary Hays, "Mrs. Godwin," *Monthly Magazine*, 232.
[24] Mary Hays, "On the Influence of Authority and Custom on the Female Mind and Manners," *Letters and Essays*, 21.

Mary Hays Vindication of the Rights of Woman *soon after its publication and wrote* Wollstonecraft, *sending her her own essays for comment. This collection appeared in 1793 as* Letters and Essays, Moral and Miscellaneous *(L&E), and is a major source for Hays's views on methodology, politics, and women. Godwin encouraged her to write more on women's issues.*

Her first feminist novel, Memoirs of Emma Courtney, *was published in 1796, her second,* The Victim of Prejudice, *in 1799. By this time English reaction to the French Revolution was strong enough to force radicals into exile or anonymity. Priestley and his wife left the country after an attack by a mob; Thomas Paine was convicted of treason for his* Rights of Man; *the radicals' own publisher went to prison for sedition. (Hays was a frequent visitor.) Her powerful argument for feminism,* An Appeal to the Men of Great Britain in Behalf of Women, *was published anonymously in 1798. This was in part a sequel to* A Vindication of the Rights of Woman. *Wollstonecraft had intended to write one herself, but died before she was able to do so. Also in this period Hays wrote articles for the progressive* Monthly Magazine; *sometimes she signed them, sometimes she signed herself "a woman." Her topics included equality, the relative influences of nature and nurture, and mental illness.*

Her six volumes of Female Biography *were published in England in 1803; an American edition followed in 1807. Her* Memoirs of Queens *(1821), also shows the considerable political roles women have actually played.*

For biographical background see Gina Luria, Introduction to Appeal *(1974 reprint), 5-15; or Gina Luria, Introduction,* Letters and Essays *(1974 reprint) 5-15; Terence Allan Hoagwood, Introduction,* Victim of Prejudice *(1990 facsimile), 3-12; Burton R. Pollin, "Mary Hays on Women's Rights in the* Monthly Magazine."

Mary Hays, like her friend Mary Wollstonecraft, was a consistent, unmitigated radical, a supporter of the French Revolution and the overthrow of custom and prejudice in favour of principle and reason. Her advocacy of rights for women employed the same denunciation of custom and prejudice. Her political writing was ignored by conservatives and radicals alike but, with the benefit of hindsight, appears to have been remarkably prescient. Her arguments include pioneering statements of Christian feminism. With no genteel aversion to publication, Hays published boldly in her own name, reverting to anonymity only when forced to by circumstances. She is, effectively,

Wollstonecraft's successor. Having learned from her, Hays reviewed Wollstonecraft's work, wrote a eulogy of her, and continued the defence of women's equality after her mentor's death. She was one of Wollstonecraft's last visitors, called in by Godwin to help nurse her on her death bed. Hays then became the butt of the sexist jokes and sexual innuendo that had earlier been directed at Wollstonecraft.

Hays's paper, "Thoughts on Civil Liberty," is a short, passionate statement packed with observations which have stood the test of time. It has the particular merit of relating the situation of women to the more general issue of liberty. Contrary to conventional wisdom, then and later, Hays held that women were *more* committed to liberty than men, because they had been sensitized to the abuses of power by government's acting against their interests. "As women have no claim to expect either pension or place they are less in the vortex of influence" (*L&E*, 11-12). Here as elsewhere Hays argued that prejudice and custom were the culprits. She wondered "by what infatuation and magic so many hug their chains and bow down before the idol in power ... but when the progress of corruption is traced and the force of habit acknowledged, our wonder ceases" (12). Yet reason and principle would ultimately win out:

> It needs little of the spirit of prophecy to predict that the present
> just and liberal notions on the subject of civil government, which
> like a flood of light irradiate Europe, will in future periods produce
> certain, though slow effects; the feeble efforts of prejudice and inter-
> est must in the end give way to truth, however gradual may be their
> declining struggles. (13)

The effects of privilege for the few and oppression of the many would inevitably lead to corruption and overthrow.

> A race of men born only to consume the "fruits of the earth," and
> set on high for others to maintain by the sweat of their brow, must
> necessarily be corrupt, for idleness engenders every evil. (15)

More specifically:

> It appears to me that all monarchical and aristocratic governments
> carry within themselves the seeds of their dissolution, for when they
> become corrupt and oppressive to a certain degree the effects must
> necessarily be murmurs, remonstrances and revolt. (17)

Yet Hays was no romantic extolling the benefits of revolution. Although she supported the French Revolution, she was conscious of, and frank about, the dangers. She shuddered at the state of political knowledge for:

> However I approve the principles, the desolations in a neighbour-
> ing country make me tremble at the very idea of the dangers (from
> the opposition of jarring interests) attending the practice. Posterity
> will, I have no doubt, reap the benefit of the present struggles
> in France, but they are ruinous and dreadful to those engaged in
> them. (17)

She even showed some sympathy with the French royal family as
persons, though not with their cause; they were, at least partially, the
victims of bad influences. She was aware also, much as she sought
change over custom, that the cure could be worse than the disease:

> The body politic in Europe in general seems at present like the body
> natural when struggling to expel offensive and morbid humours;
> the convulsive efforts threaten more immediate danger than even
> the lurking mischief, and there is reason to dread lest the patient
> expire under the operation of the powerful remedy. (19)

The paper includes an astute observation on the slowness of para-
digm change. A century and a half before Thomas Kuhn, Hays pointed
out that:

> "the most necessary part of learning (said one of the Grecian philoso-
> phers) is to unlearn our errors," and a conviction of the truth of the
> doctrine ... compels us to add it is also the most difficult. Novel
> truths, or rather truths represented in a new point of view, operate
> most forcibly on the rising generation where the memory is not
> preoccupied. (12-13)

Similarly, in a *Monthly Magazine* article, "The Talents of Women," she
noted how "all philosophy, and every truth, was at one period *modern,*
and reproached with its novelty" (784).

Hays was a firm believer in the power of government to intervene
in society, however uncomplimentary she was to the current holders
of power. Her contempt for the current British government included
some feminine sensibility on extravagance and waste, notably "exor-
bitant taxation," to defray the expenses of church and state (*L&E,* 12).
Yet:

> Surely legislation in which the peace and virtue of millions are
> concerned, cannot be the only subject that admits of no improve-
> ment. (*L&E,* 14)

She hoped that change could be made in Britain without revolution: "I
love peace and am one of those who 'faint when they do look on blood.'"
She prayed for a "wise and peaceful reformation of the gross corrup-
tions and abuses which deform the present system of government in

this country" (*L&E*, 14). She herself shrank from the idea of revolution in Britain, lacking courage for the martyr's crown. Those who suffered in endeavouring to benefit others, whatever the cause, unquestionably were martyrs. She wished that "the wisdom of the legislature may keep pace with the national light" (*L&E*, 16).

"On the Influence of Authority and Custom on the Female Mind and Manners," an essay also on the theme of liberty, opened fervently:

> Of all bondage, mental bondage is surely the most fatal; the absurd despotism which has hitherto, with more than gothic barbarity, enslaved the female mind, the enervating and degrading system of manners by which the understandings of women have been chained down to frivolity and trifles. (*L&E*, 19-20)

Women wasted so much time conforming to fashion that they had little leisure for intellectual improvement. The dignified and rational pursuits of life were too great a sacrifice to the god of wealth.

Hays shared with many earlier feminist theorists the belief that the sexes were alike in the most essential part of their being, their rational faculties. She defended Wollstonecraft's *Vindication of the Rights of Woman* on this point, predicting eventual victory, although she had no idea how long it would take:

> I am aware that some men of good sense and candor have supposed that the idea of there being no sexual character is carried in this most admirable work a little too far. Let them reflect for a moment on the extremes which the opposite opinion has produced and say from whence arises the most formidable danger? (*L&E*, 21)

Hays, however, did not go so far as Wollstonecraft in demanding equality for women. She accepted the exclusion of women from active politics (admittedly then a rough-and-tumble affair) and from certain professions. She explained that educated women would not necessarily neglect their domestic duties, observing that those contributions were undervalued by men, who did not have to do the work and whose arguments served their own interests (*L&E*, 29). She sought equality and companionship between the sexes. A great superiority of either side caused jealousy or painful constraint. She warned that "the love of arbitrary power, with morbid influence, corrupts the human mind." Vulgar people of every rank were terrified at women's asserting rights to activity (*L&E*, 22).

In a more philosophical letter Hays tried to answer the common charge that the doctrine of materialism promoted immorality. On the contrary, she argued, this system posed fewer difficulties than its free-will alternative. One could not give children a fine imagination or strong mental powers because those depended on physical makeup. But it was possible, by exhortation, example, well-proportioned rewards and chastisement, to encourage them to virtue and restrain them from vice.[25] Moral sentiments deeply impressed on the brain were as difficult to change as leopards' spots.

> If the powers of the human mind are produced by mechanism, however delicate and curious the machine, they must be subject to fixed and invariable laws. Let us trace our actions to their source; perception depends upon the circumstances in which we are placed, for we cannot perceive what exists not within the sphere of our observation, our judgment is an effect of our perception and will constantly be determined by the strongest motive; that determination produces a volition, that volition action. (*L&E*, 176-77)

In the same circumstances, we would do the same over again, but, since we do in fact learn from experience, circumstances will never be identical.

Hays accepted the convention that a masculine mind was a good thing, effeminacy a bad thing. Perhaps for this reason she avoided reference to God in the masculine, preferring inclusive nouns like "Deity," "Infinite Wisdom," "Parent of the universe," or "universal Parent." She also used the still rare expression "humankind" in the closing of her obituary of Wollstonecraft, "the benevolent friend of human kind."[26]

Hays's novel, *The Victim of Prejudice*, was daring in its treatment of women's issues, including illegitimacy, protracted sexual harassment, forcible confinement, sexual assault, the destitution of the "fallen" woman, imprisonment for debt, prostitution, murder, and execution. She used more melodrama than is now fashionable and the moral lessons lack no ambiguity. Her heroine received an unusual education which encouraged physical strength, the cultivation of reason, courage, independence, self-respect, and contempt for "the tyranny that would impose fetters of sex upon the mind" (169). At a time when heroines in novels were supposed to be morally uplifting models, Hays defended her unusual choice of anti-heroines. Moral issues could be dealt with, she maintained, and lessons drawn by showing the sordid side of life.

Responding to a doctor's "Essay on Insanity," Hays in 1800 entered into the debate on the causes and cure for mental illness. Her views of

---

[25] Mary Hays, "On Materialism and Necessity," *L&E*, 166-67.
[26] Mary Hays, "Mrs. Godwin," *Monthly Magazine*, 233.

the mind's being based on sensation led to a non-judgmental approach and the possibility of treatment. She deplored the "darkness, solitude, confinement and severity" which constituted the lot of mental patients. These conditions were "little calculated ... to divert the gloom of intense meditation or sooth the throbbings of despair." Instead she advocated humane, benevolent treatment.[27]

For Hays, as for other theorists who used sensation as a base, there were mutual influences between physical and social factors. This is well argued in her 1796 article on women's abilities.

> *Moral* circumstances may lay a foundation for *physical* differences
> years, nay ages, previous to our birth.

Moral causes mean "all circumstances which are fitted to work on the mind as motives or reasons and which render a peculiar set of manners habitual to us."[28] Forms of government and the various professions and callings had an influence. Using arguments similar to those of Hume, Smith, and Macaulay she suggested how moral sentiments developed:

> The human mind is of an *imitative* nature; nor is it possible for any
> set of men to converse often together without acquiring a similitude
> of manners and communicating to each other their vices as well as
> their virtues. The propensity to society is strong in all rational crea-
> tures; and the same disposition which gives us this propensity makes
> us enter deeply into each other's sentiments and causes like passions
> and inclinations to run, as it were by contagion, through the whole
> circle or knot of companions. (785)

Hays next argued that these sentiments gain force in succeeding gener-ations. People are more susceptible of impressions in infancy and retain what they learn early.

Hays disputed the contention that women's smaller size entailed any mental incapacity: "a smaller machine" could perform with equal precision (785). She used empiricist arguments to rationalize women's lesser performance. Granting that no female Homer, Newton, or Shake-speare had yet arisen, she pointed out that these were extraordinary phenomena, even for men with all their superior opportunities for acquiring knowledge.

> And none but a pedant or a sophist will attempt to establish general
> principles from individual exceptions. But in every country and
> period ... women have been considered and treated as inferior to

[27] Mary Hays, response to "Essay on Insanity," *Monthly Magazine*, 523.
[28] Mary Hays, "The Talents of Women," *Monthly Magazine*, 785.

men. Examine the history of the world, if, in all ages, the few have been found to subjugate the many; the weak, the strong; the designing, the virtuous? if treachery, perfidy, and cunning have prevailed over talents, valour, and honesty: tyranny and proscription can surely afford no certain criterion of mental, moral, or even physical superiority. (786)

Hays was quite unimpressed with men's "boasted superiority":

Wilder theories, absurder conclusions, more pernicious mistakes in morals, and errors in legislation, have too frequently blotted the page of history, and disgraced the annals of mankind, feebler woman could scarcely have effected. (787)

Her *Appeal to the Men of Great Britain* made the case for women in much the same way Macaulay and Wollstonecraft had. There was the same appeal to reason over custom and prejudice, with the same explanations for women's then lesser performance. A materialist basis for sense and thought underlay her claim to equality in reason. Women's "pains, their pleasures, their senses and their passions, their virtues and their vices are all of the same stamp, when nature gets fair play" (153-54). She again put forward utilitarian arguments which expressly use the language of pleasures and pains. Women's claim to the vote was still phrased in the subjunctive, even buried in a complicated argument for reason, liberty, and rationality against domestic tyranny:

You may talk to woman to eternity of the supreme felicity of pleasing you, though at her own expense, at the expense of her liberty, her property, her natural equality, at the expense of almost every gift with which God may have endowed her, and which you pretend to prune, to garble, or to extirpate at will; I say, you may preach thus to eternity, but you may never convince — while that never dying principle of which we have been speaking — while the voice of Nature pleads within us, and clearly intimates — that a greater degree, a greater proportion of happiness might be the lot of women, if they were allowed as men are, some vote, some right of judgment in a matter which concerns them so nearly, as that of the laws and opinions by which they are to be governed. (149-50)

Hays described the sad consequences of leaving women unrepresented as "arbitrary exclusion" and "mortifying distinction," men "governing the women without control, without representation, and without limitation," leaving them "exposed to every species of injury without a possibility of redress" (153).

Hays shared the conventional view of matter as inert unless and until it was animated by "the breath of life." Here she was so bold as to use not only sex-neutral expressions for the source, "Creator" and "Providence," but went even further, referring to "the common mother of mankind" (154).

Not the least of Hays's accomplishments is her six-volume *Female Biography or, Memoirs of Illustrious and Celebrated Women*. The work was alphabetically organized, so that Astell in the seventeenth century succeeds Aspasia of the fifth century B.C. *Female Biography* is a superb recounting, with lively writing and well-chosen anecdotes, of women who had made notable contributions in politics, science, literature, and the arts. In the preface Hays sets out her scholarly intentions for the work, notably her commitment to objectivity:

> Unconnected with any party and disclaiming every species of bigotry, I have endeavoured, in general, to serve the cause of truth and of virtue. Every character has been judged upon its own principles; the reflections, sparingly interwoven, have been such as naturally arose out of the subject; nor have I ever gone out of my way in favour of sects or systems. (vi)

The biographies, packed with interesting observations, read well. When William Thompson and Anna Wheeler launched their socialist manifesto for women's equality in 1825, they cited both Wollstonecraft and Hays as sources.

Marie-Jeanne Roland de la Platière (1754-1793)

Marie-Jeanne Phlipon was born in Paris, the daughter of a master engraver. Initially taught at home, then at a convent, she learned Latin and English as well as French. Later, on her own, she read natural science and the materialist Encyclopedists. She was religious as a child but lost her faith in adolescence and remained a sceptic. Her memoirs record the experience of being sexually molested as a child by a pupil of her father's. In 1780 she married a respected, progressive man twenty years her senior. They had one daughter. Mme Roland, in line with Rousseau's teaching on the role of women, assisted her husband in his administrative duties and technical publications. His appointments took them to Amiens and later Lyon, where she ran a salon for democrats. They travelled to England and Switzerland, countries preferred by progressives.

Both Rolands were active in the French Revolution, eventually with the more moderate Girondins; M. Roland for a time met with the Jacobins. Both demonstrated for the abdication of the king, whom M. Roland had twice served as minister. In 1792 M. Roland protested the king's refusal to sign

Marie-Jeanne Roland, miniature

certain decrees passed by the Assembly and was promptly fired. Mme Roland **Marie-Jeanne**
wrote, and her husband signed, a most prescient letter to the king urging **Roland**
*him to support the revolution. When the revolution "began to eat its own
children" both were named in warrants. He, however, escaped arrest; Mme
Roland was jailed, released once, but then re-arrested and sentenced to
death. In her last days in prison she found no comfort in Rousseau but
turned to the classical historians, especially Tacitus. She faced her execution in the best philosophic tradition, nobly smiling. Her husband committed suicide soon after. So also did her lately acquired lover, another
revolutionary in hiding and also under threat of arrest.*

*It is not known how much Mme Roland wrote for she published nothing
before her death and much of her work was lost. Some work she did in
prison was published posthumously, in not very accurate collections. The
radical English publisher, Joseph Johnson, published an English Works in
1800. Her letters were published much later. Her prison Mémoires include
her comments on the events of the revolution, her husband's ministerial
work, her own childhood, intellectual development, and thoughts of death.
They record her desire, should she live, to write a history of France, to be
"the Macaulay of my country" (380).*

Recommended biographies: Gita May, Madame Roland and the Age of
Revolution; *Mary Patricia Willcocks,* Madame Roland; *I.A. Taylor,* Life of
Madame Roland; *in French, Gita May,* De Jean-Jacques Rousseau à
Madame Roland; *introduction to* Mémoires de Madame Roland; *Oct.
Gréard, "Mme Roland."*

Madame Roland's place in history comes more from the dramatic
events of her life and her tragic death than her writing. At the age of
thirty-nine she went to the guillotine, declaring at the scaffold, "O
Liberty, what crimes are committed in your name!" Unlike the other
women contributors discussed here she had published nothing in her
lifetime. Her prison memoirs were published soon after her death, her
political theory and methodological papers and letters later. Unlike the
other women writers she was, thanks to the influence of Rousseau, no
advocate for her sex. But she was passionately committed to democratic ideals and well understood the role of knowledge in achieving
reform. Her political observations are remarkably astute and well
written.

Roland's methodology rejected both the extreme materialism of
some Encyclopedists, notably Helvétius, and the Leibnizian solution

to the problem of relating matter and mind. She accepted an independent role for the mind/soul, giving it a capacity to act not possessed by mere matter. Yet with the materialists she saw the processing of sensation as the normal source of knowledge. A paper written in 1771, translated in the English *Works* as "On the Soul," sets out this intermediate position:

> The soul is considered as a substance distinct from matter because it has the power of performing actions which are not the properties of matter. It perceives, feels, compares, reflects, reasons, foresees, and judges: nothing, of all that we know of matter, permits us to ascribe to it these faculties ... Closely united to the body, the soul receives from it the impression of external objects, but it does not depend on the body in such a way that it cannot consult itself and act according to its own knowledge, without always attending to the impulse conveyed by the senses. (1-2)

The understanding, memory, imagination, and will were simply the names given to the different faculties of the soul. The understanding constituted the essence of the soul, the power of perceiving objects and of forming ideas of them. The senses were nothing but the understanding modified, making use of the organs of the body to perceive objects.

Roland described the anatomy of sensation from the fibres of our nerves, distributed as so many small nets to their central meeting place in the brain.

> When anything strikes them externally, the impression is communicated to the brain, and according to the different modifications which it experiences, the soul perceives and judges of the object that is the cause of them. But to explain how the soul sees these things, how ideas are formed in it, how a spiritual substance distinct from the body perceives what passes in another substance, these are things above our efforts, and which probably we can hope to know only in another state. (2-3)

Roland rejected the Leibnizian theory of a pre-established harmony between the soul and the body. This theory was "to convey no certain information, and even none at all," for the laws relating the two domains were unknown to us. "We are not better informed respecting the manner in which this is effected, and we must modestly acquiesce in an invincible ignorance, which has continued to the present day" (3).

Essay contests were popular in the eighteenth century and have served well since then as sources for writers' views on particular questions. Roland's entry to a contest on how the education of women could contribute to making "men" better is a case in point. Her answer is typical of eighteenth-century advocates for women:

> It would be absurd to determine a mode of education that did not deal with morals in general, which depend on government; and there should be no pretence at reforming one sex by the other, but to improve both by good laws.[29]

A paper written in 1775, "Thoughts on Morality and Religion," expresses Roland's abhorrence for racism. She declared herself personally indifferent to race. Caribbean, African, and Japanese were all the same; she could feel the misfortunes that crushed them.[30]

"Political Reverie," written 1776, is a source of Roland's views on rights and obligations, equality and liberty. As well it gives a remarkably accurate and feeling account of the events leading up to the revolution:

> People in a free state are poor without being discontented. If they lead a hard and labourious life they are, and consider themselves to be, compensated by their participation in government. The taxes they pay are self-imposed and are, on that account, less odious. In addition, they see their benefit because private and public good are so inter-connected that anything they do for the public good also reaps them a private benefit.[31]

As a result taxes had to be much heavier in a republic than under absolute government. The French system was monarchical, with intermediate bodies (parliaments and the clergy) supposedly counterpoising the royal authority. Yet the equilibrium was not maintained, for parliaments and the clergy, in their reciprocal opposition, let the monarch play one off against the other, to remain master. Parliaments were mere servants of the crown, not a voice for the people. Spies and informers were used to extend the king's reign. When people were hungry troops were marched in.

It was too much to lose at once both our liberty and livelihood; "slaves ought not to pay for their bread; they purchase it by their condition." Roland's sombre prediction then follows:

> If this system last, if food and rent remain expensive and if the

---

29 Roland, "Comment l'éducation des femmes pouvoit contribuer à rendre les hommes meilleurs?" in *Œuvres*, 1: 272.
30 Roland, "Pensées sur la morale et la religion," in *Œuvres*, 2: 56.
31 Roland, "Political Reverie," *Works*, 107-08. I have edited this and the following awkward translation.

people continue to suffer, there will either be a violent crisis which
may overturn the throne and give us another form of government,
or a lethargy similar to death. How sad it is to foresee such a
future! (109)

Roland's essay on liberty, written in 1778, expresses similar views
to those of Condorcet and the Declaration of the Right of Man:

Political liberty, for each individual of a society, consists in doing
everything that he judges proper for his own happiness, in what
does not injure others. It is the power of being happy without doing
harm to anyone.[32]

Happiness gives the human soul all the energy it can use.

Slavery and virtue are incompatible. Slavery breaks all the ties that
connect man with his fellow-creatures ... Tyranny equally debases
him who exercises it and those whom it enslaves; with it all lose the
sentiment of truth, the idea of justice and the taste of good. It is to
him who knows the extent and the limits of his rights that we may
look for a respect for those of others, a generous intrepidity in their
defence, and the noble care of their preservation. (133)

True courage belongs only to the free. Those under the will of a
master are capable of nothing except what that will determines. The
essence of liberty consists in the right to personal safety and property,
with the power of recourse in case of accidental injury. Yet "so many
things prevent [liberty's] being carried into execution, or counteract
its being brought to perfection and concur in its ruin, that very seldom
is it seen to subsist even for a short time, unimpaired. All nations are
not capable of enjoying liberty; the same nation cannot support it equally
at all times." The climate, soil and mode of production either paved the
way to liberty or estranged it from its inhabitants. Liberty usually accompanied poverty, for a country's fertility led to superfluities, which in
turn stifled liberty. "Indeed it is pretty generally true, that the finest
countries are those which have the worst government" (134).

The Roland letter to Louis XVI, June 1792, is a succinct statement
of the current state of the revolution and the king's remaining opportunity to avert disaster as well as a thoroughly accurate prediction of
what would happen if he did not support the revolution. Mme Roland
wrote the letter — it echoes much of her reverie on political liberty —
which her husband signed and submitted as his parting gesture on
handing over office. He had taken on the burden of a ministry only "for

---

[32] Roland, "On Liberty," *Works*, 132.

the good of the state" and owed the king, for his confidence, a full and truthful account of his views. Because he owed the same to public opinion and to the National Assembly it was read out to the members, who interrupted with applause.

> Sire:
> The present state of France cannot long continue; there is a state
> of crisis with violence reaching to the highest degree; it will neces-
> sarily finish in an outburst which will concern your majesty as much
> as the whole empire.[33]

The letter then explained that the French had given themselves a constitution, which the majority wanted to maintain and were sworn to defend with their lives. A minority opposed it and slandered the new regime. No one was indifferent; all acted either to support or alter the constitution. It was natural for the king to want to preserve his prerogatives of power, but this sentiment was used by the enemies of the revolution. The choice before the king was to cede to the habit of power, hardening the rebels in their resistance, or "to make the sacrifices dictated by philosophy, required by necessity" and unite with the nation, making peace with it. "Your majesty can today ally yourself openly with those who pretend to reform the Constitution, or, should you not generously devote yourself to making it triumph?" (41)

The question was not a metaphysical query concerning the French nation's readiness for liberty; it was not where the country would be in a century, but what this generation could do.

> What has happened in the agitation in which we have lived for four
> years? — privileges that were onerous for the people have been
> abolished; ideas of justice and equality have become universal, pene-
> trating everywhere; the yearning for rights has become justified in
> opinion; the recognition of rights, solemnly made, has become a
> sacred doctrine. Hatred of the feudal nobility has taken deep root,
> exacerbated by the manifest opposition of the majority of nobles to
> the Constitution that destroys them.
> In the first year of the revolution the people saw these nobles to be
> odious men, oppressing them with the privileges they enjoyed. But
> they would have stopped hating them if, after the destruction of
> those privileges, the conduct of the nobility in this period had not
> given them more reasons to dread them and want to combat them as
> an irreconcilable enemy. (41-42)

[33] "Lettre de M. Roland," 40.

The people became even more attached to the constitution, owing many benefits to it and expecting further still.

> The declaration of rights has become a political gospel and the
> Constitution a religion for which the people are willing to die. (42)

Roland's warning could not have been more clear:

> Fermentation is extreme in all parties; it will burst out in a terri-
> ble manner unless reasoned confidence in your majesty's inten-
> tions finally calms it. But this confidence will not be established
> by protestation; it must have its basis in fact.
>
> It is evident to the French nation that its Constitution can func-
> tion; the government will have all the force it needs the moment
> your majesty, desiring the victory of this Constitution, will support
> the legislative body with executive powers, thus removing all
> pretext for the people's anxiety, and all hope to the malcontents.
> (42-43)

The Assembly had passed two important decrees which Roland urged the king to accept. "Delay in sanctioning them inspires defiance; if it is prolonged it will cause discontent and, I must say, in the present turbulence of spirits, discontent can lead to anything." The letter counselled that it was too late to draw back or even to temporize. The revolution had now been established in people's minds; it would be accomplished at the price of blood. That is, if wisdom did not stop it, for it was still possible for the king to avert disaster. The letter warned against trying extreme measures to contain the revolution.

> All of France would rise in indignation and, tearing itself apart in
> the horrors of civil war, would develop this dark energy, mother of
> virtues and crimes, always deadly to those who provoke it. (43)

It was both reasonable and in the king's interest to join with the legislature and respond to the wishes of the nation. In closing Roland returned to the obligation of truthfulness. The "austere language of the truth" was rarely welcomed at the throne; "I know also that it is because it almost never makes itself heard that revolutions become necessary" (45).

The Roland letter is noteworthy for its stirring language, noble sentiments, and painfully correct prognosis. On any of these grounds it deserves recognition, yet in fact it has been overlooked in the history of the French Revolution and omitted as a contribution to political theory. It was known to have been Mme Roland's work but was not included in her works.

Probability, Quantification, and Social Science

The two most enthusiastic advocates of a probability-based, quantified, social science were Jean-Antoine Caritat de Condorcet and Germaine de Staël (see below). Condorcet was a skilled mathematician who made an original contribution to probability theory and "social mathematics." De Staël was not herself a mathematician but wrote on the use of a quantified political and social science. Condorcet clearly was her source on probability theory, much as she disagreed with him on political matters, especially when he criticized her father, Louis XVI's Minister of Finance. Paradoxically, Condorcet was a champion of women's equality, while de Staël was not. His own theory of morality was developed with his wife, Sophie Grouchy de Condorcet, translator of Adam Smith's *Theory of Moral Sentiments*, and author of her own commentary on it. She also was more radical than he when the Revolution broke out, taking part in street demonstrations.

Jean-Antoine Caritat (marquis) de Condorcet (1743-1794) and Sophie Grouchy (marquise) de Condorcet (1764-1822)

Condorcet's mother, a rich bourgeoise, dedicated him to the Virgin Mary and dressed him in girl's clothes for the first eight years of his life. Male biographers claim disastrous results, including stooping posture and an inability to play sports. Psychologically, it seems, he thrived. Certainly he was productive professionally, he married happily, and fathered a daughter. He rebelled against his family's plans that he become a cavalry officer and instead became a mathematician. (The aristocratic Condorcet family had lost some of its wealth.) He was admitted to the Academy of Sciences and wrote on natural science for the Encyclopédie. Voltaire then persuaded him to turn to social questions. He wrote on economics, was an assistant to Turgot, and worked a while for the French Mint.

Condorcet was involved in the revolution as a journalist, municipal councillor, and member of the Constituent Assembly. He belonged to no political faction and was a poor speaker. His proposals for a new system of education, which would include the social sciences, were not accepted. He was a slow convert to republicanism, raising abstruse, legalistic objections to the trial of the king. He opposed capital punishment in principle and voted against it for Louis XVI. He chaired the committee that prepared the first draft constitution, which omitted the vote for women but was otherwise a fairly liberal document. He publicly criticized the next, less liberal, version and was condemned to death for treason as a result. His status as

Condorcet *the last of the philosophes no longer sufficed to protect him. He wrote his movingly optimistic* Historical Sketch on the Progress of the Human Mind *while in hiding in Paris in the neighbourhood, in fact, of the guillotine. A law was then adopted stipulating the death penalty for anyone harbouring a proscribed person. Warned that his hideout had been discovered, Condorcet promptly left, poorly disguised. After wandering in the suburbs of Paris for several days he was captured. He died in prison that same night, whether by suicide or of exposure is not known.*

After his death Mme Condorcet earned her living by the ghoulish occupation of painting miniatures of people condemned to death. Her one known publication is a translation of Adam Smith's Theory of Moral Sentiments *with her own commentary. The Condorcet daughter saw to the posthumous publication of much of her father's unpublished work.*

The best biography is Keith Michael Baker, Condorcet; *see also Frank E. Manuel,* The Prophets of Paris; *in French, Elisabeth Badinter and Robert Badinter,* Condorcet; *on Sophie de Grouchy Condorcet see Antoine Guillois,* La Marquise de Condorcet.

As well as writing on the mathematics of probability theory Condorcet dealt with some of the practical problems of data organization and the application of the theory in actual hypothesis testing. He proposed innovations in both the collection and coding of social science data. He distinguished carefully between ethical and empirical components in his writing long before this became common. To avoid incorrect sense impressions he urged that objective measures be developed. In comparing men and women he argued for controls for education, to see how the advantages men had were not a product of nature but of social institutions.[34] Certain, deduced judgments, he maintained, would never be possible, but precise calculations of probability would be. Our grounds for believing something would not then be certain, but we could know how firm they were. Condorcet admitted that almost all opinion and judgments which direct our conduct rest on probability, more or less strong, but are always evaluated according to a vague, almost unconscious sentiment or uncertain and rough glimpses.[35] Yet by limiting oneself to reasoning without calculation, one risks falling into errors, even prejudices, either by according false generality to maxims or by deducing consequences from these generalizations which

---

[34] Condorcet, *Eléments du calcul des probabilités*, 99. See also Gilles-Gaston Granger, *La mathématique sociale du Marquis de Condorcet.*
[35] Condorcet, *Eléments*, 173-74.

do not follow from them. We would soon arrive at the state where progress in the social and political sciences, as in the physical, would be impossible without rigorous methods of calculation (174). Condorcet advocated the establishment of a data bank, based on mortality statistics, with information on occupation and marital status added as it became available.

Condorcet used the term "mathématique sociale" in the singular to imply that social science was but one branch of mathematics (172). He preferred "social" over "political" or "moral" for its greater generality and precision. In his "Report on the General Organization of Public Instruction" (1792), he included social science on the proposed curriculum. Universal education would provide opportunities for the children of poorer citizens to develop their talents. The truths of social science would be taught before their application (328). People's enthusiasm for the constitution and Declaration of Rights would not be based on prejudice or habit, but on what they had learned from their earliest years. This would include not only what rights they had to demand from society but what they owed it.

Condorcet's support for women's equality first appeared in a paper comparing American democratic institutions with French.[36] Because of their functions in pregnancy and lactation, women were little adapted to going to war, but Condorcet believed other differences between the sexes to be the result of education. He neatly answered the usual arguments for male supremacy, stressing the similarities between the sexes. Another essay called for political and legal rights for women. Men's rights, he argued, arise solely from the fact that they are sensible beings, capable of moral ideas and reason. So are women. Either everybody has rights or nobody does.[37] Where women have different interests, as in child bearing, they should not be deprived of their rights. Women are incapacitated by pregnancy, but are men disfranchised for getting the gout? Condorcet further argued for a role for women in scientific research. With education to overcome their present disabilities they could achieve as much as men. He praised Macaulay's ability in politics and Châtelet's in science. In an essay on Baconian science Condorcet also affirmed women's potential for scientific work.[38]

Sketch for a Historical Picture of the Progress of the Human Mind, written in hiding under sentence of death, is a remarkably optimistic and generous work, free of recriminations, bitterness, and even second

---

[36] Condorcet, "Lettres d'un bourgeois de New Haven," *Œuvres*, vol. 9, Letter 2.
[37] Condorcet, "Sur l'admission des femmes au droit de la cité," *Œuvres*, 10: 122.
[38] Condorcet, "Fragment sur l'Atlantide," *Œuvres*, 6: 630-5.

thoughts. There are factual errors and inconsistencies, for Condorcet was working without books or notes. There is much more confidence about solving problems, including methodological ones, than this otherwise most Lockean writer had ever elsewhere shown. Condorcet divided history into nine periods, plus a tenth for the future. His purpose was to explain the why and how, not just the what of events. The rise and fall of ideas, theories, and whole schools of thought were chronicled. Fundamental to the analysis was a belief in the unity of method. Natural science assumed necessary and constant laws. So also did the development of the intellectual and moral faculties of human beings. The last, future, stage of history could be better than all preceding ones. People made their social institutions and so could make them better. Condorcet had practical advice to give here, including a suggestion about the need for population control (189). He recommended a system of social insurance based on probability theory (181).

Like a number of the women contributors, Condorcet held strong views against war. In the tenth and best stage of human existence people would gradually learn "to regard war as the most dreadful of scourges, the most terrible of crimes." Evidently he had some vision of a United Nations:

> Nations will learn that they cannot conquer other nations without losing their own liberty; that permanent confederations are their only means of preserving their independence; and that they should seek not power but security.

Gradually the false sense of commercial interest would lose its fearful power. Nations would come to agree on principles of politics and morality and invite foreigners to share equally in all benefits (194).

Germaine Necker (baronne) de Staël-Holstein (1766-1817)

Germaine Necker was born in Geneva, the only daughter of the wealthy financier and Minister of Finance for Louis XVI. Her mother, the daughter of a poor Swiss clergyman, had been a school teacher. Mme Necker subsequently ran a distinguished literary salon and published herself. The young Germaine Necker was given an excellent education at home. She met the great men of France at her mother's salon, travelled to England with her parents, and made the pilgrimage to meet Voltaire. She early began to write, including verse, drama, and the customary letters. Letters on Rousseau at age seventeen includes criticism of his views on women. She then went on to contemporary history and her social science works proper. In 1786 she married the Baron de Staël, a Swedish Protestant, ambassador to France,

Germaine de Staël, miniature, 1816

Germaine and political liberal. He all too quickly spent her dowry, whereupon she
de Staël obtained a legal separation. She had one daughter by him, three by other
partners, the last of whom she married secretly (her husband was by then
deceased) to make the child legitimate.

De Staël witnessed the removal of the king to Paris and his swearing of
allegiance to the new constitution. She took part in the attempted escape of
the royal family, hid refugees, and organized the emigration of others. Her
salon was a meeting place for moderate revolutionary leaders. While herself
trying to escape, in disguise, she was stopped by a crowd. Later she got
away and spent most of the years of the Terror in England and Switzerland.
In 1793 she published a polemical defence of the queen arguing that she had
not been responsible for the mistakes made by the king. She returned to
France in 1795 but was banished by Napoleon in 1802.

De Staël's best-known work in social science, Influence of the Passions,
was published in 1796. She began Literature and Social Institutions that
same year. It was published anonymously in 1800 but was well known to
be her work. She wrote Circonstances actuelles probably in the period
1796-98, but it was not published until 1906. She wrote several novels
which have recently attracted attention for their sensitivity to women. In
1803 she learned German, visited Germany, and began her book, Germany.
She thought that by not mentioning Napoleon, and using a literary disguise,
she would be safe. Not to praise him, however, was unacceptable, and she
compounded the crime by praising the institutions of the country he had
just beaten. The police arrived, confiscated the manuscript, and gave her
twenty-four hours to leave the country. Naturally she had a spare copy and
published the work in England.

After Napoleon's defeat de Staël corresponded with the Duke of Wellington to urge an early end to the occupation. It was in fact ended before the
full payment of reparations, and her pressure may have helped. De Staël
took the opportunity of the peace negotiations to plead for another of her
long-standing causes: abolition of the slave trade. She had met Wilberforce
in England, then translated, and helped to circulate his ideas in France. She
published a short Reflections on Suicide in 1813. Her three-volume history
of the French Revolution was published in 1818, the year after she died.
Her chateau near Geneva now houses the World Council of Churches.

Recommended biographies in English are: J. Christopher Herold, Mistress to
an Age; in French: Simone Balayé, Madame de Staël; Ghislain de Diesbach,
Madame de Staël; David Glass Larg, Madame de Staël; G.E. Gwynne,
Madame de Staël et la révolution française.

That Germaine de Staël has been treated in intellectual history as a literary figure rather than a political scientist could be said to be partly her own doing. It is true that she defined herself as a woman of letters, but the reasons for this are so obvious that no one, least of all today's politically conscious feminists, should be fooled. Exiled by the Terror and then Napoleon, de Staël learned caution. She hoped that by packaging her ideas as literary commentary she would be allowed to publish. But even her *Literature and Social Institutions* (1800) is laced with political sociology, as is her *Germany* (1813). She wrote novels and literary criticism, both of which merit discussion in those fields. Here, though, she must be recognized as a political scientist. Two of her books consist almost entirely of political analysis: *Circonstances actuelles* and *Principal Events of the French Revolution* (1818). *The Influence of the Passions* (1796) is more general sociology, although the name had not yet come into use. De Staël was herself an early user of political science terminology, including "public opinion," "established facts," and the "moral and political sciences."[39] She was always a committed empiricist, as keen on quantification as her contemporary and her father's political opponent, Condorcet.

A feminist has more than the usual complaints about biographers in the case of de Staël. One of the best biographers, Diesbach, apart from not discussing de Staël's methodology, was thoroughly sexist. One chapter bears the title "On the influence of the passions on the life of the author." Another biographer, without Diesbach's redeeming scholarship, called de Staël "a perpetual child," which presumably justified his use of her first name in the title of his book.[40] (She would have been called "Madame la Baronne" by virtually everyone and signed her letters "Necker de Staël," with no first name at all.) Paradoxically, the author of *Mistress to an Age* regarded his subject as "above all a political thinker, moralist and philosopher of history." He gave considerable attention to that work, as well noting the growing literature on her "labyrinthine and astonishing love life."[41]

---

[39] On de Staël's political analysis see Forsberg and Nixon, "Madame de Staël and Freedom Today"; B. Munteaud, *Les idées politiques de Madame de Staël*; Walter Mönch, "Mme de Staël à la recherche d'un avenir de la société moderne." For excerpts in English of her political writing see Morroe Berger, *Madame de Staël on Politics, Art, Literature and National Character.*

[40] Wayne Andrews, *Germaine: A Portrait of Madame de Staël.*

[41] J. Christopher Herold, *Mistress to an Age: A Life of Madame de Staël*, 189.

As early as 1792 de Staël was trying to use public opinion to find peaceful resolution to the divisions of France, hence the title of her article, "By what Signs can the Opinion of the Majority of the Nation be Known?"[42] She would later argue that the only way to achieve peace was to establish a new, republican form of government, but at that time she considered that a constitutional monarchy was still possible. More to the point, she considered that the monarchy had popular support. As throughout her political writing, public opinion was key. However much public opinion would come to appear as the means of manipulation, for de Staël it signified empowerment of the people, basing government on the known desires of the nation.

The Influence of the Passions is a considered statement of the possibilities of rigorous, quantified, probabilistic, social sciences. De Staël would develop this approach further in *Circonstances actuelles*, to which we shall shortly turn. Not until Quetelet, in the 1830s, would there be any significant development of the rationale for the social sciences. De Staël noted the stability of the numbers of divorces in Berne and assassinations in Italy during the preceding decade. Events occurred in fixed proportions when numbers were large. "This is what must lead us to believe that political science can one day acquire the force of geometrical evidence."[43] The prediction of moral or social matters concerning a particular person could be entirely wrong, but in large numbers the results were always predictable. The organization of a constitution is based on fixed facts because great numbers of each fact were similar and predictable. Nations, ancient and modern, had the character of a person and could be studied with regard to the causes of their birth, history, destruction, and influences.

De Staël here also used the term "human sciences." Positive sources were Montesquieu on the role of constitutions in a nation's development, and Adam Smith on the theory of moral sentiments, two key themes throughout her political writing. "Kindess is the primitive virtue, which exists by a spontaneous movement; it alone is truly necessary for the general good and it alone is engraved in the heart" (167). To this duty and sentiment, in its largest meaning, is owed everything that is esteemed. "One sole sentiment can serve as guide in all situations, and can be applied to all circumstances: that is pity." Pity was then described as an "inexhaustible" resource. Yet Smith was only partially

---

[42] In *Œuvres complètes de Mme de Staël* (1821), vol. 17.
[43] De Staël, *Influence des passions*, in *Œuvres complètes* (1871), 108.

correct in deriving pity from our being able to "transport ourselves into the situation of another" (173). This was one cause of pity, but pity could also be independent of this self regard. It was important that people be moved spontaneously by misfortune, without thought or intervening steps.

De Staël's purpose in *Literature and Social Institutions* was to examine the influence of religion, manners, and laws on literature and, reciprocally, how literature affected them. She believed that thorough work was available on the art of composition and the principles of taste, but the attempt had not yet been made to analyze the moral and political causes which modify and mark literature. She considered also the influence of the French Revolution on the state of knowledge.

Here too de Staël used the "social art"[44] terminology of Condorcet, although she continued to use the terms "political and moral sciences" rather than the conglomerate "social science." The idea was the same, the need for a scientific base for the practical political work required to create a better society. She credited Montesquieu with starting the process toward attaining the certainty of a science for the "social art." Elsewhere she noted that the "social art" included the experience of political institutions in Britain and the United States.[45] Political science was needed by reformers and not wanted by despots.

Literature and Social Institutions includes some acute observations on the relationship of science and technology with other social institutions. De Staël mused as to how different social relations would be if aerial navigation became possible. She argued that progress in science made progress in morals essential:

> For, in increasing human power it becomes necessary to strengthen
> the brakes that prevent its abuse. Scientific progress also makes
> political progress necessary. We need more enlightened govern-
> ment, with greater respect for public opinion.[46]

The unsatisfactory relationship between natural scientists and government was described, giving credit to neither side. De Staël observed the lack of interest in politics among those in the "abstract sciences" — they easily yielded to obedience to the ruling authority, so keen were they to carry on their learned labours. The work these scientists pursued required that they wean their attention from the ordinary events of life. Nothing suited monarchs so well as men who

[44] De Staël, *Littérature*, in *Œuvres* (1871), 285.
[45] De Staël, *Circonstances actuelles*, 192.
[46] De Staël, *Littérature*, in *Œuvres* (1871), 199.

were so deeply engrossed in the physical laws of the world that they abandoned the care of its moral order to anyone who would take it on (204-05). Tyrants might be patrons of the arts and sciences, but they dreaded thinkers and philosophers.

Literature and Social Institutions also contains still-relevant observations on differences between French and English academic style. A chapter on "women who cultivate literature" has some acute observations on prejudice against women writers, the damned-if-you-do-and-damned-if-you-don't situation women still recognize. Ambition in women was treated as a crime, but women who remained slaves were persecuted and oppressed. "No sooner is a woman pointed out as a distinguished person, than the general public is warned against her" (304). Women belong neither in the order of nature nor in society; their good qualities are sometimes prejudicial to them, while they do well from their faults. She observed that women were readily allowed to sacrifice their domestic occupations to fashion or amusement, but any serious study they did was treated as pedantry. The cultivation of the female mind would be a rational object of the revolution, but men instead reduced it to the most absurd mediocrity.

> To enlighten, to instruct, to perfect the education of women as of
> men, of nations as of individuals; such is still the best secret for all
> reasonable ends. (303-04)

Literature and Social Institutions is of interest also for its treatment of emotions/passions as a source of morality. Morality, alone in human thought, could not be regulated by calculations of reason. Moral actions usually conform to people's self-interest, de Staël argued, but to depend wholly on such motives would be to remove the "necessary energy" to support sacrifices for virtuous conduct (319). The use of self-interest as a guide dried up the soul's source of good deeds. "Virtue is the daughter of creation, not of analysis." De Staël would not disavow all that philosophy contributed to morality, but "it would do injury to maternal love to believe it to be the result only of reason; we must conserve amongst the virtues those that are purely maternal" (320).

De Staël's *Principal Events of the French Revolution* (*FR*) had originally been intended as a defence of her father's policies. She then made it into a more general history, succeeding no less in being scrupulously fair to both her father and her old enemy Napoleon. The social science framework of the work, nonetheless, is clear from the beginning:

> The revolution of France is one of the grand eras of social order.
> Those who consider it as the result of accidental causes have

reflected neither on the past nor on the future; they have mistaken the actors for the drama; and, in seeking a solution agreeable to their prejudices, have attributed to the men of the day that which had been in a course of preparation for ages. (1: 1)

Like other liberals who wrote on the revolution she found excuses for its barbarity in the misery and ignorance which had preceded it. Unhappiness made the people of France cruel, for morality was absent without happiness. The analysis was full of causal links, in the last volume followed by more reflection and prescription. Still, the work bears an extra burden for its function of explaining her father's actions; this is another reason to turn instead to *Circonstances actuelles* for de Staël's views on the revolution and constitutional reform.

Circonstances actuelles was de Staël's second major work, a continuation and refinement of arguments in *Influence of the Passions*. To Simone Balayé, in a preface to the new critical edition, *Circonstances actuelles* was "a real treatise of political science," but one with few readers (ix). Any plans de Staël had to publish were abandoned; at the time of writing, 1796-98, it was not safe to publish, after that it was too late for the book to be relevant. Some of her analysis of what was wrong with the *ancien régime* appears also in *Principal Events. Circonstances actuelles* is the more political book and contains stronger analysis of institutions and structures. The title explains the rationale: the circumstances which could end the revolution and the principles required to found the republic. De Staël's political position offended for its moderation. By proposing that reformed monarchists be allowed to return to France from exile she alienated the radical Jacobins. Yet she was so thoroughly republican as to put off the royalists of her class. With the benefit of hindsight the staëlian view seems wise indeed.

De Staël would try to prove that the crimes of the revolution were not the consequence of a republican system, but that, on the contrary, republicanism was the real remedy to revolution. *Circonstances actuelles* requires a profound faith in rationalism, that there are principles of political organization that are "eternally true," and that they can be found and applied (5). There was great advantage in founding a state on principles capable of demonstration, that is, in sheltering the very basis of government from civil war. When once the principle on which the state rests is recognized without contest, a universal and powerful opinion is formed. One could yet ask if the passions, born of hope, recognize evidence. But recognized truths never become the object of unbridled passions. From infancy people become accustomed to knowledge within the compass of the possible and do not exercise their imagination outside it.

Just as Descartes applied algebra to geometry, de Staël maintained, it is now necessary to apply calculation to politics. Moreover, when this was achieved political quarrels would cease.

> Human passions are as susceptible to calculation as the movements of machines; given a certain number of cases the repetition of the same events is certain. The passions of a nation can then be calculated by a legislator, as are births, deaths and marriages, and the last stage of the perfecting of the human mind is the application of calculation to all branches of the moral system. There is a great advantage to the founding of government on geometrically true principles, to bring the peace of demonstration to the most terrible cause of war, which has torn human beings apart. It is to establish a principle of likeness among nations, which must triumph despite diversities, for all end by one day adopting the same theory of government, resembling each other in political associations, regardless of their diversity in development and their differences in individual morals. (27)

For de Staël social and natural science had the same foundations, and both sciences were intended for application. "Political theory without happy results is the most foolish of intellectual conceptions" (32). Note how she crosses easily from natural science to social science examples:

> The dreamer conceives a system and gives no material evidence for it; the practical man sees facts and does not link them to their cause. Newton discovered a theory which serves as a guide for experiments and which in turn confirms them. Montesquieu came to examine all the laws in all the combinations destiny brought; he explains the motives; he stated the historiography of chance and gives a reason for all chance happenings ... Theory without experience is nothing but a phrase; experience without theory is but prejudice. (31-32)

Like the British liberals who wrote in support of the French Revolution de Staël found excuses for its barbarity in the failings of the *ancien régime.*

> One can attribute the horrors of the Revolution to several principles, the chief of which are the obstacles it had to overturn: the character of the people resulting from the abuses of the old regime, the absolute lack of public morals ... finally the false application of the

sovereignty principle in representative government. None of these
causes was a product of the political theory that forms the doctrine
of enlightened republicans. So, then, in adopting this theory, far
from perpetuating the horrors of the Revolution, it contains the sole
efficacious remedy, that which is born of the very principle and
object of the Revolution. (33-34)

Developing these observations, de Staël blamed the horrors of the
revolution on the obstacles the revolutionaries faced. The republic
arrived in France before the understanding needed for it had developed. In 1789 the nation was a "tempered monarchy," but writers, under
absolute monarchy, lacked the time to prepare the republic. De Staël
argued that if a constitutional monarchy could have lasted ten years,
a republic would have been brought about by consent (35). Instead,
there was agitation, in which some of the boldest leaders forced the
revolution before its time. Abandoned by the better friends of equality
and liberty, those leaders resorted to criminal elements who later
assassinated them.

De Staël's analysis of the class structure in relation to the themes
of liberty and equality is interesting:

> One of the great disadvantages of a privileged class is that it and
> those close to it receive the preponderance of the resources for
> education and ensuing understanding. The intermediate class, which
> made the Revolution in France, armed the lowest ranks of society
> against the nobles, while with an absolute government the lowest
> ranks of a society are depraved by class inequality. (36-37)

The vengeance and ignorance found in the lowest ranks in turn
produced the most abominable ferocity.

> Finally there is a spirit of subordination in revolt, which differs
> entirely from a real love of equality. The man who, in such a situa-
> tion, ever believes himself to be subordinate cannot attain equality;
> he is a tyrant, despot, persecutor, never the equal of the one, in the
> bottom of his heart, he believes to have once been his master ... But
> this second cause of the horrors of the Revolution, far from arising
> from the equality principle, makes us realize the need for institu-
> tions to prevent the future establishment of the seeds of hatred
> between the two distinct parts of the human race. (37)

De Staël's faith in the Enlightenment was so great that she believed
that the scientific method could take partisan passions out of politics.
The idea seems naïve now, but we can appreciate the hope of peace it
permitted. De Staël advised people to base their political associations on

principles for which there were evident actions and natural sentiments.

> All that you submit to calculation you remove from the passions.
> When certitude has gained any point that was an object of dispute,
> discussion ceases, the passions abandon the post where reason is
> established and take their arms and furies to another question. (25)

Returning to the same theme later, she wrote:

> In applying all manner of geometrical methods to ideas one is sure
> to obtain certitude. All the political and moral sciences will be
> subjected successively to the geometric method. The calculation of
> probabilities applies to the human passions as much as to the throw
> of dice, when given a certain number of events. Arithmetic is applic-
> able to all complex knowledge. Chance is for the individual, never
> for the species, and all that is science, that is, general ideas, is
> indubitably susceptible to calculation. (281)

She pointed out that people no longer fought for slavery, religious
mysteries, or feudalism, but still fought over hereditary rights. In less
than a century hereditary rights, too, would be condemned and others
would take its place (25). In her day political science was the object of
war, in another morality would be that object. Philosophical writers
would end the battle over political science by bringing analysis and
understanding to bear. De Staël cited Condorcet and Godwin, among
others, for advancing the era when certitude would take hold of political science (281). Later she criticized Condorcet for his "party spirit,"
of being too close to the Jacobins (284).

De Staël was thoroughly committed to the merit principle and utterly
disdained inherited privileges. At the practical level she supported a
system of progress through the ranks for both the civil service and
elected office. A hierarchy based on merit would yield all the advantages and none of the disadvantages of the arbitrary distinctions based
on birth (183-84). Philosophically, she observed:

> Political equality is nothing but the re-establishment of natural
> inequality. All hereditary distinctions entail artificial inequality, some-
> times by agreement, but often in opposition to natural inequality.
> When all men are admitted to the competition for positions and free
> choice assured by good constitutional institutions, you will be sure
> that the people will call the most enlightened, honest, and esteemed
> to govern them. (10)

Instead, the Revolution had brought forward the most vile, limited,
and ferocious leaders. Terror replaced selection by the chance of birth
as the means of appointment. De Staël opposed both, favouring "natural

virtues," government by the most fit, democratically chosen:

> Political equality has as an immediate consequence the right of each
> man who fulfils the required conditions for citizenship to take part
> in the formation of laws and government. Since executive power
> occurs by delegation, it is the organization of legislative power that
> constitutes pure democracy or representative government. (13)

Napoleon had sought to establish the reforms of the French Revolution, or at least his selection from them, throughout Europe. De Staël opposed the very notion of exporting revolution. There were two means of propagating democratic principles: reason and arms. France's happiness and the writings of her philosophers would take political change to the rest of Europe by reason. These changes would come about voluntarily, by conviction, through knowledge, without a violent wrenching apart. Armed propaganda could only be conquest and a conquered people would lack the energy necessary for freedom (5-6). The beauty of the French Revolution was that it was *French*. The sentiment of liberty made people reject foreign influences.

De Staël even favoured some form of de-centralized government for France:

> The immensity of France makes something of a federal spirit neces-
> sary in regional administration. A government placed in the centre
> of such a large area cannot decide by itself or its direct representa-
> tives all the local interests of twenty-five square lieus and thirty
> million people. (182-83)

Legislators had to be paid, enough to ensure not only their independence but also to provide them the "consideration" due to riches. There should be no restrictions by age or marital status, but de Staël was too conventional to consider even the possibility of a vote for women (189). She knew and esteemed Godwin's political writing, but not, apparently, Wollstonecraft's. For executive positions there should be a ban on re-election after serving a term, given the enormous power and influence of high office (190).

> The object of a representative system is that the will of the people,
> otherwise stated the interests of the nation, be defended and
> protected as if the nation itself could be by bringing everyone
> together in one place. (171)

The proportion of representatives to people was not at issue. It was essential, rather, that the legislative body be organized to ensure independence of opinion and eliminate fear and factions. Both the conservative and the republican interests of a society had to be represented.

De Staël proposed a number of compromises to the republican ideal until the nation was ready for, meaning adequately educated for, full democracy. Elections in France were pitiful; people were unjustly disenfranchised and forced into exile. She had nothing good to say about the status quo, but neither did she become cynical:

> Equality exists no more than liberty in France. There are two completely distinct classes: one of authentic, known patriots, the other the rest of the nation. For the former a sort of liberty exists, temporary and conquered, which any division can destroy. For the rest of the nation, comprised of the unknown and the suspected ... their lot depends on whoever might attack them and accuse them of royalism. (203)

She was prepared to sacrifice liberty to give additional powers, for the time being, to property holders. Until public education had formed a new generation of voters certain old powers had to be prolonged. Given the choice between the dictatorship of institutions or persecution, de Staël preferred the former (160). The constitution could only be democratic as the public mind made progress. So she recommended the creation of intermediate institutions to share power, instead of the "annual revolution" which alternated royalists and terrorists. This she admitted to be an abrogation of revolutionary principles, but argued that they were violated in any event. Republicans did not themselves trust elections, banned their opponents, and kept others from voting to ensure that the majority was kept down by a minority (161). She observed that royalists used the methods of democracy: elections, newspapers, the speaker's platform, and attacks on executive power (164).

More generous treatment of those who had opposed the revolution would also be more politic, de Staël argued. Reaction would not end in France so long as persecution and misfortune continued. People could not believe than an intolerable existence would continue forever and this hope itself became a means of realizing their hopes. People would not believe the revolution over until justice and peace could be seen. Stability required justice, peace, happiness.

> This expression: it cannot continue, is the instinct of the unfortunate and becomes a sort of contagious opinion that inspires insubordination among the governed and false measures among the governors. (134)

She followed this explanation with an assertion about the nature of social science laws. Laws in the social world were similar to those of the physical. The small number of physical laws, so to speak, in the moral world, could never be reversed. Wrong comes to its own unhappy end as a stone falls by its own weight (134).

De Staël recommended that republicans learn to adapt some of the ideas of the aristocracy in order to establish democratic principles on a solid base. *Conservative* institutions were needed to protect the principles of the revolution and their authors from attack. And who better to learn them from than the aristocracy? "Place democratic principles under the protection of aristocratic forms and, as the partisans of prejudice have taken great precautions at all times to save themselves from being overthrown, you use their means of protection against them" (174). No one was happy in France, neither the powerful nor the obscure, the governed nor the governors, let alone the victims, the prescribed, the unjustly imprisoned, the innocent, and those excessively punished for their errors (205). Thus it was crucial to study the institutions that could result in the establishment of the principles of the French Revolution.

De Staël described the powerful impact of public opinion, despite its invisibility, in a republic. Like a person walking alone at night and afraid of the dark, a government would rather have a tangible foe.

> Governments must gather all their efforts to dominate it, for this opinion, so quiet, so submissive before the slightest demonstration of power, is at the same time the only invincible power. One cannot defeat it for it does not fight; one cannot destroy its influence because it is part of everything. (108)

One can forget about public opinion in war, but as soon as a government is founded it must rally this opinion to the republic, or government will not be established. In ancient times public opinion was won over by stirring up patriotism. For a long time the art of governing a republic was a military science, but the time had now come to consider public opinion, which was affected by people's real needs. Moral force had to be added to the "positive force." The objects of government had to be practical: protecting commerce, dealing with the national debt, and choosing knowledgeable officials — not military honour. Without public opinion in support of a government the only recourse was despotism (135).

As did so many women writers, de Staël disdained the military virtues. While she admitted admiration for "success at arms" and the "invincible valour of generals and soldiers,"

> Nothing is more contrary to liberty than the military spirit. A long

and violent war is scarcely compatible with the maintenance of any constitution and everything that assures triumph is subversive of the reign of law. (289)

The military spirit was all embracing, explaining everything and taking on everything by force. Liberty, on the other hand,

> does not exist except with the support of learning. The military spirit sacrifices men; liberty multiplies the ties between them; the military mind hates reason as the beginning of indiscipline; liberty bases its authority on conviction. (289-90)

It follows that intellectuals have a particularly important role to play in the kind of society de Staël favoured and that they would be feared by such a society's opponents.

> See how, in effect, thinkers have been feared by all partisans of despotism. Monarchs encourage poets, scientists, generals, all men of talent and rare knowledge, but they do not want thought. It alone is judge and expects the crown. Poets are susceptible to illusion, scientists are estranged from life, warriors belong to events; intellectuals, at the same time independent of circumstances and interested in them, bring enlightenment everywhere, and are feared by all institutions and men who depend on charlatanism. (292)

Intellectuals deserve the highest place in a society based on reason for they alone are adept at this "intellectual politics" (293).

An exchange of correspondence between Mme de Staël and Thomas Jefferson reveals profound differences in approach to international relations, despite their common commitment to liberty and democratic principle, and a personal link from Jefferson's stay in Paris. She initiated the correspondence in 1807 when in exile from Paris and considering moving to the United States, or at least facilitating her son's emigration. The exchange grew more heated in 1812 when the United States was at war with England — as the two described it, not mentioning Canada. De Staël argued frankly that Napoleon "makes use of you now against England," in his effort to establish a "universal monarchy," of which Germany, Italy, Holland, and Denmark were already provinces.[47] She reminded Jefferson that he had, in the early days of the French Revolution in her father's own house, warned the "exaggerated radicals" that their demagogic principles would lead to despotism in France, and that his prediction had been fulfilled (65-66).

---

[47] De Staël, "Unpublished Correspondence of Mme de Staël with Thomas Jefferson," 65.

If by a misfortune which would plunge all the world into mourning, England were to be subjected and her navy were to fall into the hands of the conqueror of the earth, it is against you that he would turn, for your principles are most in the world opposed to his and he would wish to efface from the very pages of history the time when men were not subjected to the despotism of one man ... You tell me that America has nothing to do with the continent of Europe. Has she nothing to do with the human race? Can you be indifferent to the cause of free nations, you the most republican of all? ... If you were to pass three months in France your generous blood would boil in your veins and you could not bear to serve Napoleon's projects, even though believing it for the good of your country. (66)

She admitted that England was guilty of many abuses — abuses justified by England's having for ten years been "the sole barrier against this singular despotism," a nation of twelve million struggling against the one hundred million under Napoleon's coercion. De Staël cited the basis for Anglo-American friendship in the two countries' mutual love of liberty and hatred of despotism:

All your old friends in Europe, all those who thought as you did when you upheld the independence of America, expect you to put an end to a war which seems to them a civil war, for free people are all of the same family. — Yes, the greatest misfortune which could come to the American people in the present war would be to do real damage to their enemies, for then the English would no longer be in a condition to serve you as a bulwark against the despotism of the Emperor of France or rather of Europe. When he shall have overthrown the liberty of England it will be yours that he will next attack. The Emperor, so versed in the art of dissimulation, does not even conceal his resolution of destroying every nation which desires to be independent. (66)

Jefferson countered that England was "the enemy of all maritime nations." Napoleon would die "and his tyrannies with him, but a Nation never dies." England's object was the "*permanent dominion of the ocean* and the *monopoly of the trade of the world*" (67). To that end she had to keep a larger fleet than she could afford with her own resources, so she usurped the resources of others. In her last letter, in 1816, de Staël informed Jefferson that she had upheld the American cause against a "noble adversary," the Duke of Wellington, conqueror of Napoleon. Jefferson was a slave owner, but this did not stop de Staël from making the plea: "If you should succeed in destroying slavery in the south there would be at least one government in the world as perfect as the human mind can conceive" (70). There is much more in this intense exchange. Jefferson's letters were published in a nine-volume set of his writings in 1854 but de Staël's even more sizzling ones were not published until 1918.

De Staël's *Reflections on Suicide* (1813) included social science observations and theory as well as the ethical discussion that is the book's main subject. She noted differences in rates of suicide by country, then sought to explain them. Here she drew on that old favourite, the influence of public opinion. Nearly a century before Durkheim published his famous *Suicide*, de Staël had a theory that the "empire" society held over the individual was an explanation for suicide. She rejected simplistic factors such as climate as causal explanations.

De Staël shared the aversion of so many women theorists for theories of the origins of society, or "metaphysical novels" as she put it in *Circonstances actuelles*. Research on the origin of society was "an idle study" lacking in interest, inventiveness, precision, and truth. Authors wandered at random in the imagination, losing themselves in chimerical abstraction, arid and futile imagination. "Society is founded in a thousand different ways. We know nothing from before the discovery of facts; moreover it is only since printing that each step already taken is assured, so that one can predict the next with certainty." With printing, assuming a free press, progress, even the "perfectibility of the human mind," was possible (280). Printing gave us the means of fixing the chain of ideas so that we could move from one to another, slowly, of course, but surely. If one missed a step or separated action from its evidence, theory from experience, one got off the track of truth.

The methodological stance de Staël took makes her an excellent bridge to the nineteenth century. No one was better grounded in the eighteenth-century Enlightenment than she, as a personal acquaintance of the *philosophes*, the hostess of a political salon herself, and the daughter of another *salonière*. With her mother she made the pilgrimage to Voltaire at Ferney; she cut her critical teeth on Rousseau. She has been justly called an "authentic disciple of Montesquieu."[48] Yet her vision of a probabilistic, quantified social science, which she shared with Condorcet and Lavoisier, was to become the great methodological project of the nineteenth century.

---

[48]   B. Munteaud, *Idées politiques de Madame de Staël*, 13.

The "Sterile Dogmatism" of the Enlightenment?

Before turning to the nineteenth century and the emergence of social science research as we know it today, let us return to the critique of the Enlightenment with which we began. Little evidence appeared to vindicate the view that the Enlightenment failed to help the cause of women and might have made it worse. No reforms were accomplished in the eighteenth century that actually improved the status of women, but that is only to blame the victims for their powerlessness. By the end of the century there at least existed detailed, sympathetic accounts of the disabilities from which women suffered, by both men and women writers. Some of the greatest figures in the period contributed to legitimating the cause of equality for women: Montesquieu, Holbach, Diderot, Condorcet, Hutcheson, Millar, among the men, compared with only the obscure Poullain de la Barre in the seventeenth century. Both the number of women and the vigour of their claims mark an advance over the preceding century: Wortley Montagu, Sophia, Macaulay, Wollstonecraft, and Hays after only the lesser-known Astell, Masham, and Drake in the seventeenth century. Many Enlightenment writers argued for equal education for girls, again both with more confidence and better documentation in support of the claim than before. The great advocates of reform asserted the moral equality of women. Even those who, like Diderot, made absurd statements about women offensive to today's feminists, at least served the cause with his sensitive treatment of the injustices women suffered.

By the end of the century the great manifestos for women's rights had been put forth, Wollstonecraft's in 1792 in England, Condorcet's the same year in France. Would these have been possible without the earlier work elucidating the problems? I doubt it. I doubt also that they would have been possible without the Enlightenment confidence that problems are challenges to be met with human ingenuity, that new and better social institutions can effect change. Instead of the "sterile dogmatism" conclusion of some critics of the Enlightenment we found empowering ideals. Belief in reason emboldened women and men to speak against established authorities which defended an oppressive regime. Far from Enlightenment rationalism's being "a distinctive *male* mode of thought" (see footnote 2) we saw women sharing its assumptions and using them to argue for the principles in which they believed. Mary Wortley Montagu used reason and experience to argue, against the medical establishment, for smallpox inoculation. Her beliefs and the confidence to act on them undoubtedly saved lives. Surely the

Enlightenment sense of self so decried by recent critics was in this instance an asset. Astell, frustrated in her attempt to establish a college for women yet opened and ran a school for girls. Hays had the perspicacity to publish a six-volume record of women's achievements as well as political tracts and journalism. Macaulay had enough sense of self to take on Hobbes, Hume, and Burke in the course of her struggle for liberty and equality.

Condorcet, a male and a great supporter of women's equality, advocated a quantitative probabilistic social mathematics. So did de Staël, who shared this vision, and who argued for a new order to end hereditary privileges, establish free elections and a merit system, and abolish the slave trade. That she had a sufficient sense of an autonomous self to say all this is a matter for rejoicing, not regret!

Those who would condemn the universal principles of the Enlightenment must remember that they dismiss the noble sentiments which enabled people like Wortley Montagu, Châtelet, Sophia, Roland, Condorcet, de Staël, Macaulay, Wollstonecraft, and Hays to act. In taking shot at their excesses it is too easy to hit the high ideals that inspired desperately needed reforms. Perhaps we can indulge their failures in foresight when we appreciate the strength of the forces they opposed, the weakness of the support they received, and the extent of the ignorance and prejudice which surrounded them.

Finally we must conclude that the Enlightenment for women (as well as for men) did indeed begin in the eighteenth century. Whether or not one believes that those who fail to learn from history are condemned to repeat it, we must at least give credit where it is due. There was a methodology of the Enlightenment which applied both to the social and the natural sciences. It built on the empiricism of the seventeenth century and was in turn refined and extended in the nineteenth century. It was accompanied by belief in the possibility of social reform and progress. Fewer women than men shared in this intellectual movement, for obvious reasons of lack of education and opportunity. But women did take part in the work of the Enlightenment, both in Britain and in France. Women, and some men, used those values to advance the claim for equality, liberty, and full participation in society. To assert that women generally or feminists specifically had to wait until the 1960s or 1970s for their own Enlightenment is do to a serious injustice to the people and the work discussed here, and to deny today's women their intellectual heritage.

Chapter 4

WOMEN
METHODOLOGISTS IN THE
NINETEENTH CENTURY

*T*he nineteenth century was the age of industrialization and, with it, urbanization, population growth, and social unrest. In western Europe, at least for the first half of the century, the rich got richer and the poor poorer. As in earlier periods social problems provoked social analysis and organization. The laissez-faire political economists explained how intervention in the economy would be unnatural and ineffective. In fact, there was no "social safety net" or welfare state when it was most needed. Millions of people lived in acute poverty; some starved. Others escaped by emigrating to the colonies. Some who stayed founded co-operatives, trade unions, schools, and reform organizations. Socialist movements emerged early in the century, socialist parties later. There were periodic uprisings in the cities.

The nineteenth century saw considerable movement on women's issues as the transition was made from the literary expression of problems to actual organization. Women's rights organizations were created in England, the United States, France, and other countries. Many of the people who organized to abolish slavery next made the connection to liberation for women. Both movements were ultimately successful, the abolition of slavery long before the achievement of legal rights for women. Women were involved in all these reform activities, analyzing and publishing on the problems, protesting and participating in organizations.

As it had been earlier, the need for knowledge was recognized: social sciences to ground the social art. Women took part in arguing the need for a new methodology and pioneering the new research methods. They contributed to the definition of assumptions and provided practical examples of their use in particular reform causes. Still, there were marked continuities with the eighteenth century. The framework for empirical social science had been specified by the end of that century, but it was not until the nineteenth century that research was undertaken in any systematic way. True, John Sinclair collected massive amounts of data for his *Statistical Account of Scotland* in the 1790s, but then he never tabulated, compared, or analyzed them comprehensively.[1] The establishment of censuses and centralized statistical offices was effectively an achievement of the early nineteenth century which in turn stimulated much social science research, especially of crime and social problems. The important methodological advances of the nineteenth century were made by people profoundly committed to social reform.[2]

The study of societies other than one's own was still fairly haphazard, relying, as earlier, on travellers' reports. The socialist women's advocate Flora Tristan published her observations of English society and numerous British women travelled to and reported on America. Harriet Martineau, on her trip to the United States, drafted the methodological rules she would use in collecting and analyzing her data. A year after publishing *Society in America* (1837) she published *How to Observe Morals and Manners* (1838), the first known book on how to conduct sociological research. A little later Harriet Taylor was collaborating with John Stuart Mill on the *Principles of Political Economy* (1848), bringing to his technical knowledge of logic the dynamic principle permitting the application of social science research to real social and economic problems.

The Belgian statistician Quetelet set out a number of the basic principles of empirical research in his *Physique Sociale*, demonstrating the use of statistical data in hypothesis testing, controlling for the "standard demographic variables." Florence Nightingale later in the century drew from Quetelet's approach for her own more ambitious espousal of applied research, especially evaluative studies. Although still concerned that unforeseen consequences could cause more harm than good, she was more optimistic than he on the potential for application. Nightin-

---

[1]   The technology for this of course emerged only later. Here the collaboration of Ada Byron Lovelace (1815-52) with Charles Babbage on the development of the "difference machine," or prototype computer, should be acknowledged.

[2]   On the early development of statistics, quantitative methods, and their relationship with reform activities see: Stephen P. Turner, *Search for a Methodology of Social Science*; Stephen M. Stigler, *History of Statistics*; Donald A. MacKenzie, *Statistics in Britain 1865-1930*; Helen M. Walker, *Studies in the History of Statistical Method*; M.J. Cullen, *Statistical Movement in Early Victorian Britain*; Theodore M. Porter, *Rise of Statistical Thinking 1820-1900*; Anthony Oberschall, *Establishment of Empirical Sociology*; Jean-Claude Perrot and Stuart J. Woolf, *State and Statistics in France 1789-1815*; G. Duncan Mitchell, *A Hundred Years of Sociology*; Philip Abrams, *Origins of British Sociology 1834-1914*; Jean M. Converse, *Survey Research in the United States*.

gale herself authored a statistical study on that most universal of subjects, childbirth. That her trail-breaking work on a question of such urgency — the high mortality of birthing mothers — should then promptly disappear is a tragedy on many levels.

The current terms "sociology" and "social science" came into common use in the nineteenth century. "Social science," with the "social art," had first been used in the French Revolution, but the older term "moral philosophy" lasted until roughly mid-century. A number of different terms were proposed. Quetelet used "social physics," Condorcet "social mathematics," both terms close to the seventeenth-century "political arithmetic." John Stuart Mill used "social economy" in his early years, Florence Nightingale "social or moral economy." Then Comte's "bastard" term sociology won out. The term "scientist" itself, for natural scientists, only came into use in the 1830s.

Late in the century the then Beatrice Potter both pioneered the method of participant observation and took part in the first recognizable social survey of all time, Charles Booth's *Life and Labour of the People in London*. Finally, in 1895, Jane Addams and her women colleagues at Hull House published the first work of the "Chicago School of Sociology," giving it its defining characteristics: urban, problem-oriented, and quantitative. That credit is normally given to two male sociologists, Burgess and Park, for work in the 1920s and 1930s, again underscores gaps in the history of methodology.

In the nineteenth century as well we begin to see the real beginnings of women's studies. Women, of course, had long been aware that they brought a different perspective to their research. Wortley Montagu was conscious that her observations of women's society in Turkey, in the early eighteenth century, yielded information no man could ever have found. Now there were explicit analyses of the distortions male bias had wrought, especially in theology. While earlier feminists had exposed particular instances of bias, in the nineteenth century whole books appeared accounting systematically for bias and arguing for a new approach.[3] There were even musings, if tentative ones, as to what

---

[3] See Rosalind Rosenberg, *Beyond Separate Spheres*; Constance Rover, *Love, Morals and the Feminists*; Dale Spender, *Women of Ideas* and *Feminist Theorists*; Janet Todd, *Dictionary of British Women Writers*; Jane Rendall, *The Origins of Modern Feminism*; Janet Horowitz Murray, *Strong-Minded Women*; Patricia Hollis, *Women in Public 1850-1900*; Diana Postlethwaite, *Making It Whole*; Terry R. Kandal, *The Woman Question in Classical Sociological Theory*; Claire Goldberg Moses, *French Feminism in the 19th Century*; Ivy Pinchbeck, *Women Workers and the Industrial Revolution*.

a distinctive women's culture might be like.

The radical American feminist, Matilda Joslyn Gage, demonstrated how much women had achieved in spite of all obstacles. She went beyond earlier witnesses to these facts to argue that they showed how men had stolen women's knowledge, either to suppress it entirely or use it for their own ends. Her *Woman, Church and State* was subtitled *The Original Exposé of Male Collaboration Against the Female Sex*. Her critique of the "patriarchate" was as devastating as any ever. Another American, Charlotte Perkins Gilman, also published work which challenged the preconceptions of male scholarship and posed alternatives.

The movement for women's suffrage and other political and economic rights began in earnest in the nineteenth century. Some of the same people were prominent in both the women's movement and the establishment of empiricism in the social sciences. The Mills, Martineau, and Addams are excellent examples. Tristan was a feminist, socialist, and union organizer as well as being a pioneer practitioner of the art of social observation. Gage first made public her arguments on women's achievements at a convention on women's suffrage, for which she worked for decades. She also worked to abolish slavery and to achieve respect for aboriginal treaty rights.

The contributors to empiricism in methodology continued to be the activists of their society. The British Martineau helped publicize the American abolitionist cause as well as supporting various women's rights. Tristan organized the Union ouvrière in France. Harriet Taylor died before the women's suffrage movement was organized, but J.S. Mill was a dedicated suffragist, as was Taylor's daughter Helen Taylor. Nightingale promoted her causes with articles and memos from her sickroom. Beatrice Webb was one of the founders of the British Labour Party and the modern welfare state. Jane Addams founded the settlement house movement in the United States, led in the struggle for the American welfare state, and helped establish the modern women's peace movement.

Public health measures continued to be an important area of concern. From the eighteenth-century interest in inoculation we now see a broad range of concerns, from Nightingale on sanitation and childbirth to Webb on state provision for health care. Contagious (venereal) disease was a big issue in the nineteenth century, when the British government brought in legislation to punish prostitutes and not trouble men with their part in spreading disease. Martineau and Nightingale joined in the early, unsuccessful, opposition to the Contagious Diseases Act.

Both challenged the prevalent male/medical model in favour of positive health promotion. Gage's history of the treatment of women also revealed the errors of male-dominated medicine, with historical examples of the safer and better practices of female-dominated medicine before its takeover.

Harriet Taylor Mill (1807-1858)

Born Harriet Hardy, Taylor Mill was the middle daughter of a respected obstetrician. She largely educated herself, at home. At age eighteen she married John Taylor, a successful merchant, Unitarian, and a decent if unexciting man. She confided her boredom to her Unitarian minister, who took J.S. Mill to meet her. The association between Mr. Mill and Mrs. Taylor initially caused scandal, but enough accommodation was made for it to become acceptable to the three parties most concerned. Bad feeling remained in Mill's family, with whom he continued to live.

Harriet Taylor and J.S. Mill spent a great deal of time together discussing ideas and drafting and redrafting Mill's manuscripts. He did most of the actual writing, but even her critics credit Taylor Mill with substantial input on ideas and editing. When the two were separated, drafts with detailed instructions for revision went back and forth by mail, the comments showing that Mill took her advice to the letter. Harriet Taylor was frequently ill and spent a great deal of time, as was the custom, travelling to more therapeutic climes for recuperation.

Harriet Taylor looked after her husband in his last illness and observed a two-year period of mourning after his death. He generously left her the life interest on his fortune, with no qualifications as to remarriage. When Harriet Taylor and J.S. Mill finally married in 1851 there was little time left for them. Mill used the occasion of their wedding to deplore the legal inequities suffered by women on marriage, renouncing the prerogatives he acquired over his wife. The two finished "The Enfranchisement of Women" on their honeymoon. They set up house in Blackheath, seeing little of friends and working hard. Together they revised Mill's Autobiography when they both had tuberculosis and thought they were dying. They recovered and went on to new editions of Principles of Political Economy and the laborious drafting and polishing of "On Liberty," which Mill published after Taylor Mill's death, making no further changes to the manuscript. On his retirement from the East India Company in 1858 the couple planned a lengthy stay in the south of France. Taylor Mill died en route, in Avignon, of congestion. Mill had her buried there and bought a cottage near her grave. He and Harriet Taylor's daughter, Helen Taylor, returned there regularly to spend time. Helen

Harriet Taylor Mill, miniature
The British Library of Political and Economic Science

Taylor, herself a feminist and writer, worked with Mill in the suffrage move- **Harriet**
ment and on other causes. Together they organized the Society for the **Taylor Mill**
Representation of Women.

Mill continued to work for suffrage. That was indeed the main reason he ran for Parliament, where, in 1867, he introduced an amendment to the Representation of the People Bill to give women the vote. He also spoke in Parliament on property law reform and violence against women. In 1871 he appeared before a royal commission to argue against the repressive Contagious Diseases Acts. His essay "The Subjection of Women" raised issues of a distinct women's culture, as well as the usual issues of rights. He contributed the first political economy examinations to Girton College, the first women's college at Cambridge University. In his will he left money for the first university in Britain or Ireland to open its doors to women and for scholarships to be held only by women.

On Harriet Taylor Mill see Alice Rossi, Essays on Sex Equality. *Biographies of J.S. Mill which are also a good source on Harriet Taylor are: Michael St. John Packe,* The Life of John Stuart Mill; *Karl Britton,* John Stuart Mill. *On the collaboration see F.A. Hayek,* John Stuart Mill and Harriet Taylor *and Josephine Kamm,* John Stuart Mill in Love.

Harriet Taylor Mill is one of the most-maligned women in the history of ideas. Not only has she been given little credit for her contribution as co-author with **John Stuart Mill (1806-1873)**, she has even been blamed for adversely affecting his work! Moreover, it is difficult to defend her, for it is impossible to ascertain exactly what her share of the collaboration was. When she met Mill, Harriet Taylor was a young woman of twenty-three, occupied as a wife, mother of two sons, and soon to bear a daughter. She published nothing in her own name after they began working together. Mill's own praise of her has to be taken with the proverbial grain of salt, although it need not be dismissed as mere chivalry or the result of lovesickness. There can be no serious doubt that she was the source of the couple's feminism. True, J.S. Mill had a sense of the injustices women suffered before he met her, but their earliest papers show that hers was the more radical analysis. The essay, "The Enfranchisement of Women," was first published in his name in 1851, but in his *Autobiography* he called it a "joint production," on which he had only acted as editor and amanuensis.[4] When Mill

---

[4]   *Autobiography, Collected Works of John Stuart Mill*, 1: 257. The essay appears in vol. 21, Appendix C, but the source used here is Alice Rossi, *Essays on Sex Equality*. All other citations from Mill and Taylor Mill are from the *Collected Works* (*CW*).

included the essay in his anthology, *Dissertations and Discussions*, Taylor Mill was listed as the sole author. Mill claimed that she was the joint author both of *Principles of Political Economy* and the famous essay "On Liberty." That her name never appeared as co-author does not disprove this claim, for her husband at the time of publication forbade such recognition. Mill dedicated a limited edition of *Principles of Political Economy* to her, but even this offended Mr. Taylor.

Mill acknowledged that Taylor Mill was the source of key elements of the methodology of *Principles of Political Economy*. He had already written *A System of Logic*, published in 1843, when the two met. The processes of verification and standards he set there for the construction of the "sciences" of politics and ethics were rigorous beyond hope. He himself was pessimistic about the possibility of ascertaining scientific laws on social matters given the number and complexity of interacting causal factors. The aim of *Principles of Political Economy* was accordingly more modest. Even where scientific laws could not be established practical advice on the social issues of the day was possible. The lot of humanity could be made better with the application of known principles.

J.S. Mill described the process of their collaboration in his *Autobiography*:

> When two persons have their thoughts and speculations completely in common ... when they set out from the same principles and arrive at the same conclusions by processes pursued jointly it is of little consequence in respect to the question of originality, which of them holds the pen; the one who contributes least to the composition may contribute most to the thought. (*CW*, 1: 240)

He claimed for himself authorship of only the "abstract and purely scientific" parts (1: 257), crediting Taylor Mill with the crucial insight of the book, the distinction between laws regulating the production of wealth and the modes of its distribution (1: 255). Most political economists, including Mill's own father, confused the two, subsuming economic practices into laws incapable of change by human effort. It was chiefly Taylor Mill's influence which gave the book its distinctive tone and usefulness:

> This tone consisted chiefly in making the proper distinction between the laws of the production of wealth, which are real laws of nature, dependent on the properties of objects, and the modes of its distribution, which, subject to certain conditions, depend on human will. The common run of political economists confuse these together,

under the designation of economic laws, which they deem incapable
of being defeated or modified by human effort, ascribing the same
necessity to things dependent on the unchangeable condition of our
earthly existence, and to those which, being but the necessary consequences of particular social arrangements, are merely coextensive
with them. (1: 255)

Instead the co-authors of *Principles of Political Economy* tried to understand social and economic causes, but not treat them as final:

> The economic generalizations which depend, not on necessities of
> nature but on those combined with the existing arrangements of
> society, it deals with only as provisional, and as liable to be much
> altered by the progress of social improvement.

The Saint-Simonians were Mill's first source for this principle, "but it
was made a living principle pervading and animating the book by my
wife's promptings." From her came the "properly human element."

> In all that concerned the application of philosophy to the exigencies
> of human society and progress I was her pupil. (1: 257)

She was "much more courageous and far-sighted" than Mill would have
been without her. This is high praise indeed, but is it credible?

Critics contest, for example, that "his extravagant laudations of her
genius rested on a very slender basis of fact."[5] By examining "The
Enfranchisement of Women," which was mainly her work, this same
critic gathered that "she was not the extraordinary genius so loudly
proclaimed by Mill" (ix). One biographer, H.O. Pappe, put his objection right into the title: *John Stuart Mill and the Harriet Taylor Myth*.
Hayek, who published a substantial work on the Mill/Taylor collaboration, and included a previously unpublished essay of Taylor's, nevertheless concluded that there was nothing "very remarkable" in her
work.[6] He credited her with great influence, strengthening the rationalist element in Mill's thought (17). John Robson, in *The Improvement
of Mankind*, conceded a positive contribution, describing her as the
artist to his scientist. Yet, "She was not, in any meaningful sense, the
'joint author' of his works" (68). Karl Britton gave mild credit to Taylor
Mill in his biography, *John Stuart Mill*, on the practical possibilities of
socialism. He conceded that "On Liberty" was their joint work, but not
the *Principles of Political Economy* (26). Stillinger is exceptional in treating Taylor Mill as joint author of Mill's *Autobiography*, pointing out the

---

[5] W.B. Columbine, introduction to *On Liberty*, viii.
[6] F.A. Hayek, *John Stuart Mill and Harriet Taylor*, 40.

pros and cons of the changes she introduced in editing. The revised text they produced together "is more graceful, more straightforward than the original, but also barer, starker."[7] Taylor Mill omitted details, corrected logic, and added style.

Feminists trying to correct the record still tend to omit Taylor Mill or negatively assess her work. Susan Moller Okin's *Women in Western Political Thought* is an example of the latter, arguing that it was "only Mill's distorted impression of her abilities that suggests that she was endowed with any qualities of genius" and not "the hardly startling quality of her own extant writings" (206). Gail Tulloch in her excellent coverage of J.S. Mill, *Mill and Sexual Equality*, gives Taylor Mill only passing mention, as "Harriet."

Since Taylor Mill's letters to Mill during their work on *Principles of Political Economy* were lost, we can only speculate about their collaboration. A number of her early essays and poems were published in the Unitarian *Monthly Repository* in 1832. Although these are without attribution, they are known to be hers and to predate the collaboration. Francis Mineka considered that her articles showed only "average ability."[8] My judgment is more favourable: I believe that they show both good judgment in social analysis and superb style. Taylor reviewed books on the French Revolution of 1830, the reformer Hampden, Mirabeau's Letters, Plato's mysticism, Australia, and Mrs. Trollope's book on American manners. Altogether I find it entirely credible that Harriet Taylor Mill was the joint author of *Principles of Political Economy* as well as of "On Liberty," and the major author of the "The Enfranchisement of Women."[9]

The Mills' methodology allowed for both economic/material factors and intellectual or other ideal factors. Both play a role in causation and both needed to be investigated:

> The creed and laws of a people act powerfully upon their economical
> condition, and this again, by its influence on their mental development
> and social relations, reacts upon their creed and laws. (*CW*, 2: 3)

How a society regulates its mode of conduct was "as much a subject for scientific enquiry as any of the physical laws of nature" (2: 21).

---

[7] Jack Stillinger, "Who Wrote J.S. Mill's *Autobiography*?" 22.

[8] Francis Mineka, *The Dissidence of Dissent*, 352. Exact references to these articles are given in this work.

[9] For authoritative attributions of joint authorship see Jean O'Grady, "Introduction," J.S. Mill, *Collected Works*, 33: vii-xxx.

Harriet Taylor is normally credited with shifting Mill to the left politically, which can be seen in successive editions of *Principles of Political Economy*. The first edition had been written before the uprisings
of 1848 and the social experiments they prompted. By the second
edition Mill was qualifying his apparent anti-socialism. By the third
edition there was further clarification, now a statement that the only
objection to socialism was lack of preparation for it among people in
general and the working classes in particular. The power of people to
determine their own future was affirmed and socialists described this
force as a principal means of improving human society (3: 987). French
producers' co-operatives had impressed them both. A chapter on the
future of the labouring classes, by Taylor Mill, gives examples of such
enterprises. She argued as well that co-operatives had beneficial results,
both moral and material.

In his *Autobiography* Mill stated that the "On Liberty" essay was
"more directly and literally our joint production than anything else
which bears my name" (1: 257). The whole mode of thinking was
"emphatically hers": the work would have been less radical and democratic without her. She had both led him to truths and rid him of errors
(1: 259). This was an essay with a single theme, "that the only purpose
for which power can be rightfully exercised over any member of a civilized community, against his will, is to prevent harm to others" (18:
223). The individual was sovereign over his own body and mind, and
subject to society only for that part of conduct that concerns others.
Exceptions occurred, however, in the case of children under the age
of fifteen and people in more primitive societies.

"On Liberty" shows the Mills at their most laissez-faire selves, but
even here they were far from classical liberalism. The state had a legitimate function in providing education (short of a state monopoly),
labour laws, public health, the protection of the young and animals,
and some welfare provisions, apart from the usual duties of national
defence and the administration of justice. Governments could also
undertake, on a voluntary basis, activities to stimulate individual efforts.

J.S. Mill had begun to struggle with the problem of sexist language
when writing *A System of Logic*, where he called the generic "he" a
"defect in language" (8: 837). Successive edits of later works show the
substitution of "one" for "man" and "person" or "people" for "men."[10]

---

[10] Gertrude Himmelfarb, *On Liberty and Liberalism*, 202.

The much-polished "On Liberty" essay shows the least sexist language, with "human being," "individuals," and "persons" for "man" and "men."

"The Enfranchisement of Women" was a comprehensive argument for the admission of women, "in law and in fact," to equal, political, civil, and social rights.[11] The discrimination women actually experienced in each of these areas was described. The effects of dividing society into two castes, one ruling and one ruled, were said to be no less than "perversion and demoralization, both to the favoured class and those at whose expense they are favoured" (97-98). There ought to be perfect equality between the sexes, permitting no "power or privilege" to the one side, or "disability" to the other (125). J.S. Mill would continue to make these same points, with other developments, in his Parliamentary speeches and in *The Subjection of Women*. He was one of the world's greatest advocates for women ever, as well as being a major contributor to the social sciences, both in methodology and content. To insist on a place for Harriet Taylor in all this in no way diminishes his status but redresses a major injustice to her — an injustice which ironically reflects precisely the discrimination which she and J.S. Mill so vigorously opposed.

Harriet Martineau (1802-1876)

Harriet Martineau was born in Norwich, the sixth of eight children of a prosperous manufacturing family. The family was Huguenot in origin, its religion Unitarian, its politics liberal. Martineau's childhood was unhappy. She became deaf young and had to use an ear trumpet for life. This she found to be an asset in social research, creating intimacy between interviewer and subject. She was educated at home with her brothers, becoming fluent in French and Latin. Her brothers went on to university while she stayed at home. She then began to write, publishing articles as early as 1822 and a devotional book in 1826. Her first earnings came from a book to convert Catholics, Jews, and Muslims to Unitarianism. Martineau herself later lost her faith and wrote, with some relief, about atheism. While still an adolescent she heard Wilberforce speak and became an instant convert to the abolitionist cause. She was once engaged, but her fiancé died and she remained single.

[11] J.S. Mill and H.T. Mill, "Enfranchisement of Women," in Rossi, *Essays on Sex Equality*, 93.

Harriet Martineau, an engraving
By permission of The British Library

Harriet   *The death of her father left the family with little money, so that Martineau,*
Martineau *who had wanted independence, at age twenty-four got her wish. She there-*
after earned her living as a writer and journalist — often an investigative
journalist — publishing more than fifty books and over 1600 feature articles
on an enormous range of issues. Her first success was a popular presenta-
tion of the principles of economics, Illustrations of Political Economy
(1832). In it she demonstrated major aspects of economic theory using
fictional characters and scenes, with summaries in a more conventional
form at the end of each chapter. Illustrations *long outsold the Mills'*
Principles of Political Economy.

In 1834, when Tocqueville was back in France writing up the notes from
his visit to the United States, Martineau left on her more extensive trip (two
years compared with his nine months). During the lengthy passage, by sail-
ing ship, she wrote the first draft of her methodology, which was published
in 1838 as How to Observe Morals and Manners. *Her* Society in America *was published in 1837, two years after Tocqueville's still better-known*
Democracy in America. *Her first work on methodology, "Essays on the*
Art of Thinking," *dating from 1829-32, appeared in an 1836 anthology.*
Her History of the Thirty Years' Peace *(1849), reflects an emphasis*
made often enough by women writers, seldom by men of the time. She
later supported Britain fighting in the Crimea, however, on the grounds that
the czarist tyranny in the region had to be stopped. She wrote a popular
history of the British Empire. After suffering a prolonged illness, which was
cured by "mesmerism" or hypnosis, Martineau turned the experience to
good account by writing about it in yet another book, Letters on Mesmerism
(1845).

Politically Martineau was a laissez-faire liberal, although not as extreme
as Herbert Spencer. She opposed certain, but not all, factory legislation, for
her liberalism was always qualified by a more basic Utilitarianism. She raised
money for Oberlin College, the first university to admit women and blacks.
At age forty she refused a government pension; she would not benefit from
a system of taxation she condemned in her own writing. With the proceeds
of her writing she was able to build a house and garden and settle comfort-
ably in Ambleside, in the Lake District. In 1853 she published a much
condensed English edition of Cours de philosophie positive, *which Comte*
liked so much he had it retranslated into French. She prepared a three-
volume Autobiography *for publication immediately after her death.*

Although they are little read now, Martineau's novels sold well at the
time. The hero of one is the black liberator of Haiti. Writers of the calibre of
George Eliot and Elizabeth Barrett Browning approved. Charlotte Brontë,

then still disguising herself as Currer Bell, sent an appreciative letter. **Harriet**
Martineau, not fooled, replied: "C. Bell, Esq., Dear Madam." **Martineau**

Recommended biographies are: Vera Wheatley, The Life and Work of
Harriet Martineau; *R.K. Webb,* Harriet Martineau: A Radical Victorian;
Valerie Kossew Pichanick, Harriet Martineau; *Susan Hoecker-Drysdale,*
Harriet Martineau: First Woman Sociologist; *Gayle Graham Yates,*
Harriet Martineau on Women; *John Cranstoun Nevill,* Harriet Martineau;
Gillian Thomas, Harriet Martineau; *Diana Postlethwaite, "Mothering and
Mesmerism in the Life of Harriet Martineau;" Seymour Martin Lipset,
"Harriet Martineau: A Pioneer Comparative Sociologist," a chapter in Deirdre
David,* Intellectual Women and Victorian Patriarchy; *and Michael R. Hill,
"Empiricism and Reason in Harriet Martineau's Sociology" in a new (1989)
edition of* How to Observe Morals and Manners. *See also Harriet
Martineau,* Selected Letters.

S.M. Lipset, in publishing a new edition of Martineau's *Society in
America* in 1962, described it as "one of the most important" of the
early accounts of American society and one "which played a major role
in forming English opinion, especially among the liberal left" (9-10).
Martineau was "one of the first to apply explicitly a sociological
approach to comparative analysis" (37). Her *How to Observe Morals
and Manners* was "perhaps, the first book on the methodology of social
research in the then still unborn disciplines of sociology and anthropology" (7). A number of good biographies have since been published
on Martineau's life, but she has yet to receive the credit she deserves,
even from feminists, for her work in the formation of the social sciences.
Alice Rossi lists her, in the table of contents of *The Feminist Papers*, as
"the first woman sociologist," but in the text names her only as "a fore-
runner of the discipline of sociology" (124). It is quite unfair that
Martineau should be more known as the translator of Comte's *Cours
de philosophie positive* than for her own, *earlier*, methodological work.
All three of her methodological books appeared before Comte had even
coined the term "sociology," in 1838, and used it in the *Cours* in 1839.

Martineau deserves her place in history also as an activist. She was
a strong supporter of the anti-slavery movement. She worked for the
vote for women and rights to education, divorce, and occupations. She
wrote on violence against women. She worked with Florence Nightingale to try to stop passage of the Contagious Diseases Act when it was
first proposed and continued in the struggle for repeal of the various

acts that were passed. She collaborated with Florence Nightingale in the promotion of public health and preventive medicine. It is difficult to find faults in this remarkable person except, perhaps, that she smoked cigars.

Martineau's first publication on methodology was her "Essays on the Art of Thinking," published in *Miscellanies* in 1836. This was effectively empiricism-for-all: how to think logically and bring appropriate evidence to bear on the problems of the day. This was methodology not just for scientific investigation but for decisions on legislation, running a household, and raising children. Still, it is hard-line empiricism, stressing unity of method between the social and natural sciences, observation of nature, induction, objectivity — the works. Martineau sought the causes of and best cures for such evils as deficient observation, perverted judgment, unchastened imagination, indolent attention, and treacherous memory (1: 57). She wondered how far the sciences would have advanced if there had been chemistry instead of alchemy. If physicians had known how to study disease scientifically plague might have been stopped. If legislators had hit upon the best modes of civil law and nations had supported them, we might have been saved from war.

Citing Francis Bacon, Martineau argued that the correct process was to form theories from facts. "To habituate the mind to follow the inductive method in all research is the general rule which lovers of truth should ever keep in view." Unfortunately, our minds had a tendency "to become too firmly attached to a theory deduced by ourselves" (1: 73). We should guard against stretching a theory beyond the class of objects to which it relates. We had to discipline our minds to receive new facts without prejudice. Nature was the wisest, the only infallible teacher:

> Books are but her interpreter, and, though valuable aids when she
> is silent, are never to be preferred to lessons of wisdom. (1: 91)

By ascertaining the relations of cause and effect we could make our experience useful. Present circumstances became conducive of future good in all forms of knowledge.

How to Observe Morals and Manners both addresses the complex issues of the acquisition of knowledge and gives practical advice on how to do research. There is no doubt that Martineau saw her subject as a science, with laws to be discovered, but it would be quite wrong to consider her empiricism simplistic. She was acutely aware that there were "two parties to the work of observation," the observer and the observed. "The mind of the observer — the instrument by which the work is done, is as essential as the material to be wrought. If the instrument be in bad order, it will furnish a bad product, be the material what it may" (11). Objectivity was crucial, for "every prejudice, every moral perversion, dims or distorts whatever the eye looks upon" (40). Observers must exclude prejudice and not allow themselves to be perplexed or disgusted. Along with the facts there must also be an understanding of their organizing principles. Social laws were possible because the human heart was the same everywhere, sympathy the key to understanding motives.

Part 2 of the book set out what should be observed in a new society, beginning with *things*. Religious institutions should be studied by visits to temples, marking their locality, number, diversity, and theological opinion (84). The type of religion — licentious, ascetic, or moderate — should be noted. In a young country the clergy were unusually influential, hence merited particular study. A society's saints, heroes, and sages showed the "moral taste" of a people (118). Every society had its idols — warriors, poets, artists, or philanthropists but rarely statesmen.

Patterns of suicide indicate prevalent sentiments and moral notions. There was no better place than the cemetery to learn what moral sentiments lie deepest in the hearts of most people. Are their values military, courtly, domestic, or commercial? The inscriptions on the monuments gave "instructive teaching" as to what was considered worth dying for. The "brief language of the dead will teach ... more than the longest discourses of the living" (105).

A society's treatment of its criminals reflects its own moral notions, or at least does so when people have a voice in these decisions. "The treatment of the guilty is one of the strongest evidences as to the general moral notions of society" (129). The observer should converse with a variety of offenders to find out the causes of crime, the views of society of the relative gravity of offences, and the condition of those who have broken the law. Knowledge of criminality would throw light on other disorders of a society, revealing its mistaken principles or weak organization. Martineau's Utilitarian approach to the subject is quite clear:

> To have criminals at all may in time come to be a disgrace to a community. (132)

The existence of a police force was a sure sign of liberty, definitely to be preferred to recourse to the army for law enforcement (185).

The observer had to consider a society's culture in its various manifestations. Songs reflected "the most truly popular part of a nation's poetry" and were the only poetry of the great body of the people (132). One had to examine both the new literature of a people and its preferences from the past. What kind of dramatic productions do they put on? It is also necessary to consider the "mental philosophy of the society," its general ideas, not so much because philosophy affects the national mind but because it emanates from it (142).

The occupational structure of the society had to be considered along with the characteristics of the people engaged in its various pursuits. The artisan population was prophetic of the society's future, for ideas of equal rights, the representation of people as well as property, and other democratic notions originated chiefly in manufacturing towns (145). Martineau predicted that Russia would be "despotically governed" so long as she lacked manufacturing (148). By contrast, England and the United States were saved from "retrograding" into feudalism by the strength of their manufacturing. There was a long and complicated causal chain from the nature of the soil, through the type of employment produced, to the mental and moral state of the society. Markets, the system of land tenure, prevalent mode of agriculture, manufacturing, and commerce had to be studied. The nature of the class system was important, whether there was a division into only two classes or a series of classes with gradations. Liberty was deficient where there were only two classes, proprietors and labourers (190). Martineau considered that gradations were becoming more frequent, an opposite conclusion to that made later by Marx and Engels, one in which she was correct, not they.

The health of a community was "an almost unfailing index" of its morals. The relationship went both ways, good and bad health as both cause and effect of morals (161). Again, burial grounds were a good source of data. The age of death indicated the state of health and comparative force of the various diseases (164). So also enlightened philanthropists needed "a faithful register of births, marriages, and deaths" as a test of national morals and national welfare (161). Wise laws had a "preventive influence." The extent of popular education was a fact "of the deepest significance," reflecting a nation's ideas of human dignity (199). Despotic governments permitted only the smallest amount of popular education. Freedom of the press was crucial; societies vary in the kind and degree of penalties for expressing contrary opinions (205).

On a practical level, Martineau advised the investigator to prepare a set of questions in advance, with every great class of facts connected with the condition of the people being studied, suitably divided and arranged (232). This list could be added to as new subjects arose. A journal was needed for reflecting on as well as remembering facts. A sketchbook would help to add to written notes. The work of generalization should be deferred until the investigator returned home. Still, she cautioned that "mechanical methods are nothing but in proportion to the power which uses them" (238). Without sympathy, intellectual and mechanical aids would not yield wisdom.

Tocqueville's *Democracy in America* is richer in quotable quotes than *Society in America*, but Martineau's book is in many respects wiser. Both authors give moving accounts of the misery caused by slavery. Both saw it as a fundamental violation of the American Constitution and thus destined to disappear. But Martineau was the more astute in recognizing the separate issue of racism, relating the discrimination freed blacks faced in the urban north. Generally speaking, where there are differences in findings between Tocqueville and Martineau she, with the benefit of hindsight, turns out to have been accurate. While, for example, the French aristocrat judged political participation to have been extensive, she saw apathy and indifference. She treated the high level of church attendance in America as a sign of conformity, from fear of dissent. Tocqueville was dead wrong on the status of women, a subject she discussed at length and with excellent judgment.[12]

Although Martineau had wanted to give her work a more academic title, *Theory and Practice of Society*, her publisher insisted on the simpler *Society in America*. She set out to compare the existing state of American society with the principles on which it had been founded, "thus testing institutions, morals, and manners by an indisputable, instead of an arbitrary standard." Both English and American readers would be served by having this fixed reference point. Martineau held that she had spared no pains to discover the truth and invited corrections "in all errors of fact" (48). She had prepared herself well by reading before leaving England. Her itinerary and access to political leaders were both impressive. She stayed with the Madisons at Montpelier, met the chief justice, professors, clergy, and native people, saw state legislatures, Congress, and the Supreme Court in session. She visited prisons, insane asylums, hospitals, literary and scientific institutions, factories, plantations north and south, western farms, palaces, and log cabins. She travelled by wagon, stage coach, horseback, and steamboat. She

---

[12] See Lipset's introduction to *Society in America* for a comparison of Martineau with both Tocqueville and Marx.

attended slave auctions, abolition meetings, July 4 celebrations, rural fairs, religious services, and weddings. As a woman she saw much more of domestic life than a man would have.

Martineau held herself to be an equal judge with others on matters of opinion. She declined the office of censor, however, to "put praise and blame as nearly as possible out of the question" that more might be learned. Her object was "a compound of philosophy and fact" (48). Readers would be able to judge for themselves the worth of her testimony. Her declaration of ethical neutrality, as Weber's later, must be taken as intention rather than achievement. Martineau went on to describe how she sought to be objective:

> I went with a mind, I believe, as nearly as possible unprejudiced about America. (50)

Yet she conceded her predisposition to democratic institutions.

Politics was a branch of "moral science," hence its principles could be studied much as other aspects of human behaviour. Martineau was here something of a functionalist, seeing a fairly well-articulated system of components in which changes in one sector influenced others. "Natural laws, which regulate communities, and the will of the majority may be trusted to preserve the good" (86). Slavery was an anomaly, which could not last. It had been an anomaly politically since the American Revolution and in time had become an economic one also (189).

> It requires no gift of prophecy to anticipate the fate of an anomaly among a self-governing people. Slavery was not always an anomaly but it has become one. Its doom is therefore sealed and its duration is now merely a question of time. (93)

Martineau forcefully pointed out the inconsistency between slavery and a constitution proclaiming equality and stipulating the consent of the governed. The cruelty of slavery itself was described in considerable detail. On anomalies in general, she wrote:

> The law in a republic is the embodiment of the will of the people. As long as the republic is in a natural and healthy state, containing no anomaly, and exhibiting no gross vices, the function of the law works easily ... If there be any anomaly among the institutions of a republic, the function of the law is certain to be disturbed sooner or later. (117)

Such a disturbance led usually to the detection of the anomaly and then its cure. This would happen not only with slavery but "with every institution inconsistent with the fundamental principles of democracy" (117). This could take time, for the worldly interests of the minority were bound up with the anomaly. "It takes some time to awaken the will of the majority, and until it awakes, the interest of the faction is active and overbears the law." The evils might be tremendous, but the eventual result was sure (118).

The same logic about anomalies led Martineau to see an analogy between the status of women and slaves and to predict the right to vote for women. A fundamental principle of the American Constitution was the consent of the governed, yet women were taxed, fined, imprisoned, and deprived of their property with no say. They needed laws to protect their own particular interests, which were not identical with those of their fathers and husbands.

> The principle of the equal rights of both halves of the human race
> is all we have to do with here. It is the true democratic principle
> which can never be seriously controverted, and only for a short time
> evaded. (128)

It would, of course, be more than a short time before American women won the vote and other rights. (Tocqueville, by comparison, wrote that American women were content with their purely domestic roles. In fact, the largest women's suffrage movement in the world was launched at the Convention on Women's Rights in Seneca Falls, New York, only fifteen years after his visit!) Society's exercise of the right of the strongest over the powerless was a test of its civilization (291). She described the limitations of marriage, problems in occupations, and implications for health. Martineau's observations on women in American society are still germane, the writing vigorous, even pithy.

Martineau continued to write on her two chief concerns: slavery and the status of women. *The Martyr Age of the United States of America* (1838) recounts the origins and growth of the abolition movement. She was invited to the Women's Rights Convention of 1851, declined, but sent a letter of encouragement. In newspaper articles she tackled such controversial subjects as wife beating, divorce, prostitution, and witchcraft as well as more conventional subjects like education and the vote.

In *Illustrations of Political Economy* Martineau noted the importance of the ways of procuring the necessaries and comforts of a society. Yet political economy had been less studied than perhaps any other science, "and not at all by those whom it most concerns — the mass of the people" (1: iv). She used fictional characters and events to show how a society produced, distributed, and consumed its wealth. As in other popular writing there was a moral: we must mend our ways, learn to do better; knowledge could be applied. The work shows Martineau at her most laissez-faire. Yet she also acknowledged that the utility principle was "the last and best principle" professed by the nation, if not acted on by its rulers: "the greatest happiness of the greatest number" (9: 144). John Stuart Mill, who always encouraged women writers, and chided them only gently when they were not feminist or radical enough, found "considerable merit" in the book. He saw it as less subject to the criticism of books with "far greater pretension," whose authors were liable to be slaves of their own hypotheses.[13] His one substantive criticism was of Martineau's unqualified condemnation of the Poor Laws, which he held to be right in principle, if not in application. Martineau's opinion of Mill was considerably less positive. She considered him "enormously overrated," and doubted if anything but his *System of Logic*, if that, would survive.[14]

In her preface to *The Positive Philosophy of Auguste Comte* Martineau described Comte's approach as a means of integrating a philosophy of life, or "anchorage" for people alienated and adrift (v). She understood the theological intolerance of Comte's positivism, which treated belief as a transient state of the human mind, destined to pass away (ix-x). She saw the "moral charm" of the philosophy of people controlling their own moral development:

> We find ourselves living, not under capricious and arbitrary conditions, unconnected with the constitution and movements of the whole, but under great, general, invariable laws, which operate on us as part of the whole. (x)

Our knowledge was small, but our faculties had great potential, if we used them. "Pride of intellect" made people insist on "belief without evidence and on a philosophy derived from their own intellectual action, without material and corroboration from without" (xi). Human progress was possible, including moral progress, the fostering of virtue.

Martineau published a substantial article on the 1851 British census, discussing the role of such a project in nation-building, especially democratic nation-building, as well as presenting main trends. She noted how the idea of a census was first rejected, in 1753, so that the Americans were the first to conduct one, in 1790. "It was soon found by a self governing people, that a Census ought to be a thorough survey and record of society, by which every sort of social experience might be

---

[13] J.S. Mill, "Miss Martineau's Summary of Political Economy," *CW*, 4: 227.
[14] Harriet Martineau, *Selected Letters*, 172.

embodied for social guidance."[15]

Martineau's original scholarly work peaked with *Society in America*. She continued to write extensively on a wide range of issues in addition to her early interests on women's equality and the abolition of slavery. Much of her journalism was policy oriented. In 1859 Florence Nightingale enticed her into a collaboration which used Martineau's journalistic skills and took her the next step to active lobbying on causes. This remarkable collaboration, prominent concerns of which were health promotion (with its corollary of rejection of the medical model) and the targeting of prostitutes for regulation under the Contagious Diseases Acts, is related as a separate section after discussion of Nightingale's own work.

Frances Wright (1795-1852)

Frances Wright was born in Dundee, Scotland, orphaned young, then raised by an aunt in England. Her father, a rich liberal, had sponsored a cheap edition of Thomas Paine's Rights of Man. *On her coming of age she returned to Scotland to live with a great uncle who was professor of moral philosophy at Glasgow University. He gave her instruction and access to his books and the university library. In 1818 she and a sister spent two years travelling in the United States. Her* Views of Society and Manners in America *(1821), reports observations from this trip. The book won Wright fame and a request from the elderly General Lafayette to visit him in France. In 1822 she wrote an essay/translation of Epicurus,* Few Days in Athens, *which she dedicated to Jeremy Bentham and in which she espoused pro-empiricist views. On her second trip to the United States, with the sister and Lafayette, she discovered the horrors of slavery. She became an abolitionist two decades before there was an organized anti-slavery movement. She set up a co-operative for slaves to prepare them for freedom. When this failed she provided for their move to Haiti. On her second American tour she also bought, with Robert Owen, a radical paper, renamed it* The Free Enquirer, *and moved it from New Harmony to New York City. It became a major outlet for the anti-slavery cause, public education, women's rights, and the Working Men's Party. She also bought a church and turned it into a "Hall of Science" for free adult education. Wright went on the public lecture circuit, speaking for a fee, at a time when women did not do such things.*

In Paris in 1831 she made a disastrous marriage with a Frenchman,

---

[15] Martineau, "Results of the Census of 1851," 182.

*Philquepal d'Arusmont. After they broke up he made protracted attempts
to gain control of an inheritance she had received. Their daughter sided
with him and otherwise rejected her mother's atheism and feminism for a
conventional religiosity, even rejecting the vote for women. The inheritance
allowed Wright to stop lecturing, but her last years were marked by bitter
legal battles and alienation from her daughter.*

On Wright's life see Celia Morris Eckhardt, Fanny Wright; *A.J.G. Perkins
and Theresa Wolfson,* Frances Wright Free Enquirer; *William Randall
Waterman,* Frances Wright; *Margaret Lane,* Frances Wright and the
"Great Experiment"; *Paul R. Baker, "Introduction" to Frances Wright,*
Views of Society and Manners in America; *Barbara Taylor, "Fanny Wright,"
in* Eve and the New Jerusalem; *Wright's own* Life, Letters and Lectures.

Martineau was not the only Englishwoman to make the journey to
America and write about it. She was preceded notably by Frances
Wright, a determined opponent of slavery and defender of women's
rights. Wright made no original contribution to empiricist methodology as such, but she showed how it could be put to use in her radical
causes. She is an excellent refutation of the contention that radical
beliefs and empiricism do not mix. In her journal she promoted
women's equality, co-operatives, free public education, birth control,
free love, divorce, property law reform, and atheism while opposing,
among other evils, slavery, capital punishment, and imprisonment for
debt. For her pains she was called "the red harlot of infidelity" and
required police protection at her public lectures.

Wright (as the doctoral student Karl Marx would be two decades
later) was attracted by the materialism and atheism of Epicurus. Her
translation of Epicurus sets out the ancient theory of materialism, of
the motions of particles producing all the causes and effects we
perceive. More precisely, "These particles produce or are followed by
certain other qualities and effects." *Few Days in Athens* continues:

> An analogous course of events, or chain of causes and effects, takes
> place in morals as in physics; that is to say, in examining those qual-
> ities, of the matter composing our own bodies, which we call mind,
> we can only trace a train of occurrences, in like manner as we do in
> the external world; that our sensations, thoughts, and emotions, are
> simply effects following causes, a series of consecutive phenomena,
> mutually producing and produced. (194-95)

When this view is taken abstruse questions disappear. As other animals
exercise their faculties, so people ought to trust their testimony, follow

their impulses, and enjoy happiness.

Three of Wright's surviving lectures on knowledge set out a similar unqualified empiricism, basing all real knowledge on positive sensations. One declared that "whatever we see, and feel, and attentively examine with *all* our sense, we *know*; and respecting the things thus investigated, we can afterwards form a correct opinion."[16] When we are in error we must refer back to the object itself. Regrettably, colleges taught words and signs, not facts, abstractions which inculcate credulity. Yet the growth of knowledge, and "the equal distribution of knowledge" was the best, even the only means for reforming the human condition (16). Wright believed that her sex and situation qualified her rather than incapacitated her for intellectual undertakings. A just system of education and a fearless spirit of inquiry were needed for progress. Fathers and husbands were also held back if their wives were bound by lack of education (21).

Wright collaborated with Robert Owen on tracts for republican government and national education. Not only were "the industrious classes ... the bone and marrow of the nation," but they were the nation itself. "The fruits of their industry are the nation's wealth." In a "Plan of Nation Education" she advocated:

> National, rational, republican education, free for all at the expense of all, conducted under the guardianship of the state, at the expense of the state, and for the honour, the happiness, the virtue, the salvation of the state. (15)

This system of education would be funded by taxes.

Flora Tristan (1803-1844)

Flora Tristan (Flora Célestine Thérèse Henriette Tristan Moscoso) was born and lived most of her life in Paris. Her father, who was of semi-noble Spanish descent, came from one of the oldest colonial families of Peru; her mother was French, but had lived in Spain. The family's circumstances were comfortable; such visitors as Simon Bolivar came to call. Her father died when she was a child. Because the marriage had not been properly registered and no will was left, her mother could not inherit and the family was left destitute. The older child in the family died in childhood. At age fifteen Flora Tristan went to work in a small factory, married the boss, and had three children.

In 1833 Tristan set off with her youngest child, daughter Aline, to Peru to try to claim her inheritance. There she was well received by her relatives, thoroughly enjoyed Lima society, witnessed a revolution, stopped in

---

[16] Frances Wright, "On the Nature of Knowledge," *Life, Letters and Lectures*, 10.

Flora Tristan
Phot. Bibl. Nat. Paris

England en route home, but returned to Paris without any capital. She next obtained a legal separation from her husband and succeeded in resuming use of her maiden name. Her husband then abducted the children and shot her, but she recovered. At his trial for attempted murder she successfully pleaded that his life be spared. She petitioned the Chamber of Deputies to abolish capital punishment; earlier she had petitioned it to reinstitute the right to divorce.

All this notoriety helped sales of Tristan's Pérégrinations d'une pariah, written after her Peru travels and published in 1838. Also in 1838 she published a two-volume "philosophical" novel, Méphis. Relentlessly melodramatic and now long out of print, it is still a good read. Its thesis is not so much the equality of women, or even maternal feminism, but the superiority of women through self-sacrifice. Women had a spiritual quality to contribute to society and civilization. All Tristan's writings show her rejecting the institutional church but not belief.

Tristan's work as a social observer and activist now began in earnest. She published her observations on English society in 1840 as Promenades dans Londres. An English translation, the London Journal of Flora Tristan, appeared only in 1980. Convinced that the industrial class was the most important in society, and that justice would not be attained without strong organization, Tristan began to found workers' unions. She financed publication of her Union ouvrière by subscription. Loosely organized, it set out workers' demands for reform with their rationale and advice on how to organize. Tristan was herself a powerful speaker, in her element rousing workers to join the cause. She was totally open in her intentions, advised the police of her whereabouts and, as a result, was frequently harassed.

Tristan was on a tour speaking and organizing in Bordeaux when she fell ill. She died suddenly at age forty-one and was buried there by her saddened comrades. Observations from this organizing tour were published in 1973 as Le tour de France. Her feminist manifesto, L'Emancipation de la femme, was published posthumously in 1846 from her notes. The Impressionist painter Paul Gaugin was proud to be her grandson.

Biographies in English are Laura S. Strumingher, The Odyssey of Flora Tristan; Dominique Desanti, A Woman in Revolt; the introduction to The London Journal of Flora Tristan; a chapter in Margaret Goldsmith, Seven Women Against the World; in French, Jules-L. Puech, La vie et l'oeuvre de Flora Tristan; Dominique Desanti, Flora Tristan; Jean Baelen, La vie de Flora Tristan. See also Flora Tristan, Lettres.

While British women were visiting America and writing up their observations a redoubtable Frenchwoman was making four trips to England, her account of which she would publish as *Promenades dans Londres*. The socialist feminist Flora Tristan was both a keen observer and a lively writer. A contemporary of Harriet Martineau, she knew Martineau's popular work on political economy but not that on methodology. The latter had only just appeared when Tristan was back in France writing up her own findings and otherwise coping with her husband's abduction of their children and attack on her life. Tristan's object was to study the English mind and customs, to understand causal determinants and dynamic relations as well as to describe what she saw. The spacing of her visits — between 1826 and 1839 — permitted her to note changes in social and economic conditions, from which she drew her own theoretical inferences. From the growing poverty she observed she predicted social upheavals, even revolution. Tristan moved on to the next phase, active organization of the working class. Since she had had little formal education, and none in philosophy, her contribution lies not in the development of methodology but its use. As well as being an early practitioner of social observation she was an early visionary of European union.

Tristan's one book of sociology, available in English as *The London Journal of Flora Tristan* (1840), includes observations on social and economic conditions, both for society at large and by class. At the time Tristan was making her observations, women were not even allowed in the galleries of the House of Commons. She accordingly made her visit disguised as a man. After a Tory MP had declined to assist her, she asked the aid of a Turkish diplomat, who not only loaned her the necessary clothes but even took her to Parliament in his carriage. There were chapters in the *London Journal* on the situation of women, causes of crime, treatment of criminals, prostitution, ethnic divisions (Irish, Jewish, and immigrants), and the Chartist movement. The introductory chapter includes discussion of the effects of climate on morals. Later the school system is described. The book reported that women were excluded from nearly all the professions. Starving women were forced into prostitution and theft. Mothers committed infanticide out of desperation. The chapter on the status of women pays homage to Mary Wollstonecraft, whose *Vindication of the Rights of Woman* Tristan termed an "*imperishable*" work," in existence for half a century, but of which nobody had ever heard (257). *London Journal* was dedicated to the working class, as was Tristan's *Union ouvrière*. She correctly observed the increasing misery of the ordinary people. She noted that in 1835 conditions were worsening even for the middle class. By 1839 the misery was deeper yet. Engels published his *Condition of the Working Class in England* in 1845, or five years later, with many similarities in findings.

Tristan reported on visits she made to three prisons. She saw the horrible conditions in which child prisoners were kept. Prisons did not achieve reform of their inmates but were purely places of repression. Released prisoners who could not live from their occupations fell back into crime. She witnessed a public execution and related the procedure. Tristan's brief discussion of the causes of crime relied largely on economic conditions. Absolute poverty, desperate need, prompted some people to commit crimes. She also cited relative deprivation, or discrepancies in the means people enjoyed — badly off people suffered further from seeing others with great wealth. In places Tristan also drew on the newly popular theory of physiognomy.

Tristan argued that the poverty of the English worker was worse than slavery and not to be appreciated without visiting the industrial cities of Birmingham, Manchester, Glasgow, and Sheffield. "When the division of labour is carried to extremes, industry makes enormous progress, but it dispenses with man's intelligence and reduces him to the function of a mere cog in the machine" (67). She described the extensive pollution caused by industry and dangers of on-the-job accidents.

Tristan related the great deprivation she saw to revolt as well as crime:

> Poverty on the scale that exists in England and Ireland can lead only
> to revolt and revolution. (112)

English law treated its workers more harshly than the aristocratic French treated black slaves.

> In my eyes slavery is no longer the greatest human misfortune since
> I have become acquainted with the English proletariat, for the slave
> knows he will get his daily bread all his life and be cared for when he
> falls ill, but there is no bond between the English worker and his
> master. (70)

The "slave" to English capitalism had to pay taxes as well as earn a living (67). Marx and Engels, whose collaboration had not yet begun, would soon make similar predictions of revolution and analyses of alienation.

A foreword Tristan wrote in 1842 in defence of her book explained that readers were accustomed to hearing England's prosperity extolled and thought that she had exaggerated the misery. She defended herself by citing the objective basis of her conclusions:

> In reply to these accusations I can only say that the facts set down here are taken from *authentic documents*, that they are generally acknowledged as a *public scandal*, and that my account is a truthful one. (9)

People in France in 1840 still believed in England's power, philanthropy, and strict moral code. "Today the mask has dropped" (10). Tristan cited two other authors who had recently published data documenting English poverty. She further argued humanitarian reasons for her negative assessment. Nationalism was the source of many evils.

> So if I have spoken out strongly against the system of privilege and tyranny which oppresses the English people, against the monopolies England *imposes on her subject races* and *her lack of consideration in commercial dealings with other nations*, it is because this system forms an insurmountable obstacle to that European unity which I pray may come one day as it is the only means of achieving world peace. (10)

When Marx lived in Paris in the early 1840s he was advised to meet Tristan, but declined. The spiritual dimension in her social thought has been cited as the reason he rejected her as an influence. Certainly Marxists later criticized her for this spirituality, but they could hardly say that she was not radical enough! Her book on England was too radical to be covered by the respectable press, yet it was largely ignored by the socialist press.

It is easy to see how both atheist Marxists and the conventionally religious would be scandalized by Tristan's *L'émancipation de la femme*. It denounced the inhumanity of priests relative to the misery of the people (14). Tristan claimed eternal justice as God. She called on women to be slaves no longer, to protest and die. They should protest against tyranny as had Christ, who was a man of the people. The Holy Spirit was the "maternal genius" of woman (36). She wanted women to have living faith and sustaining love, without losing their dignity by confessing to impious priests. Like so many Christian feminists, Tristan did not think much of sin. Evil was but ignorance and error, which people never chose (50). Love, on the other hand, was light, force, and liberty. Because women rose higher in the scale of love than men, the future belonged to them. Women unite the family and make harmony. The movement to regenerate the future needed women at its head (81).

Tristan declared her opposition both to materialism and atheism (68). She sought God not outside humanity but in it. She likened herself to Christ. God, she maintained, revealed himself in the development of our faculties of intelligence and love. Shame to "these pretended communists" who wanted to expropriate humanity from progress and God (70).

Despite her personal fame and the success of at least two of her books, Tristan soon dropped out of sight. G.D.H. Cole devoted a short chapter to her in his *History of Socialist Thought*, giving her credit as an observer and narrator but not as a theorist (1: 187). She deserved a place in socialist history, he said, for being the first person to have put forward a plan for an "all-inclusive proletarian International," the Union ouvrière (1: 188). The women's movement of the 1970s rediscovered her passionate defence of women. Her works, including letters, have been republished and new biographies have appeared. Yet she remains unacknowledged as a contributor to the social sciences, even by those who endorse *engaged* social research. In style Tristan belongs to the older tradition of social observation through travel, following Wortley Montagu and Martineau. In substance she was one of the earliest nineteenth-century socialists. Her feminism and faith informed everything she did so that the result was a unique blend that did not meet the approval of any school of thought.

Florence Nightingale (1820-1910)

Florence Nightingale was born in Florence to great wealth and high connections, both of which she put to good use. Her father gave her an excellent education at home in the classics. Apart from learning French, Latin, and German, her Greek was good enough to correct Benjamin Jowett's translations of Plato's dialogues. The family had been Unitarian and liberal on both sides, but Nightingale's mother moved them back to the Church of England, as more befitting the landed gentry. At age sixteen she experienced a call to service. She was still young when she wrote her religious philosophy of life, later privately published as Suggestions for Thoughts. *She travelled extensively in Europe with her family, visiting hospitals and nursing institutions as well as the usual places on the grand tour. As she turned down offers of marriage she found herself increasingly confined to a wholly useless role at home under her mother's thumb. An autobiographical essay, "Cassandra," relates this frustration. At length Nightingale persuaded her family to allow her to take training in nursing with a German order of sisters. (Nursing*

*Florence Nightingale, watercolour portrait from a photograph
taken shortly after her return from the Crimea*
The Florence Nightingale Museum Trust, London

was not then a profession but a low-paid occupation pursued in appalling **Florence**
conditions by working-class women, who were often said to drink too much.) **Nightingale**

In 1854, at age thirty-four, Nightingale set off for the Crimea to head
the nursing services for the British Army. There, apart from coping with all
the challenges of war, disease, and inadequate supplies, she had ongoing
battles with incompetent and complacent medical administrators. When
she returned to England a national heroine she became an unofficial consult-
ant to the War Office and later to other government departments as well.
She became an expert on hospital administration, public health, and many
other questions of public administration, especially in India. She was instrumental in getting a royal commission established on health conditions in the
army. She largely determined its composition and gave evidence to it which
then shaped its conclusions. She next succeeded in getting a similar commission established for India. She tried, unsuccessfully, to interest Queen Victoria
in the actual conditions in which the people of India lived.

Nightingale devoted the fund raised in her honour after Crimea to establish
a training school for nurses, the first in England without a religious affilia-
tion. She began the transformation of the ill-esteemed occupation of nursing
into a skilled profession, but herself balked at the establishment of a system
of registration for nurses. On prodding by John Stuart Mill Nightingale joined
the National Society for Women's Suffrage. She paid her dues and let her
name be used but never considered the vote a priority; she herself had
wielded great influence without it. She annoyed women's rights advocates
also by not fully supporting medical education for women, deeming it more
important to get them into nursing and midwifery. Later in life she softened
this stance and her last doctor was a woman.

Nightingale's Crimean work in turn inspired Henri Dunant to do similar
work in a war in Italy, which led to the founding of the Red Cross. He credited Nightingale with the idea of the "neutralization" of the wounded, that
is, that they be treated without regard to nationality. Nightingale herself
drafted the instructions for the British War Office, in 1864, for the international congress that framed the Geneva Convention. She helped launch
the British Red Cross in 1870.

Nightingale spent many years of her adult life confined to her sickroom,
possibly as a way to avoiding intrusions to her work for trivial reasons, especially from her family. She rose from her bed after her mother died and
lived to age ninety. All the while she received the experts and politicians
who could aid her various endeavours to bring good order and sound
management to government. Memoranda, briefs, and letters streamed back
and forth to ministries with her advice and pointed questions. She actually

Florence
Nightingale

published little of what she wrote but sometimes had essays privately printed for limited circulation. She contributed articles to the National Association for the Promotion of the Social Sciences, Fraser's Magazine, and the Nineteenth Century. Her classic study of mortality in childbirth appeared in 1871 as Introductory Notes on Lying-in Institutions. *It received scant circulation and is even now hard to find. In 1907, shortly before she died, Nightingale became the first woman to be awarded the Order of Merit. An offer of burial in Westminster Abbey was declined by the family.*

The best biography remains Edward Cook, The Life of Florence Nightingale; *see next Cecil Woodham-Smith's excellent* Florence Nightingale; *the chapter in Lytton Strachey,* Eminent Victorians *is refreshingly irreverent; F.B. Smith,* Florence Nightingale *is even more iconoclastic, even hostile; W.J. Bishop and Sue Goldie,* A Bio-Bibliography of Florence Nightingale *gives an overview of her scholarly contribution; a new edition of letters,* Ever Yours, Florence Nightingale, *also includes biographical material; Raymond G. Herbert,* Florence Nightingale: Saint, Reformer or Rebel? *covers a good range of her health promotion work.*

Queen Victoria wished that she had Florence Nightingale in the War Office. Nightingale indeed would have improved the management of any government department, for she had a method. After starring as "the lady with the lamp" in Crimea, she became the passionate statistician, convinced of the need for a rational approach to public administration based on evaluative statistics. She was committed to a determined, probabilistic social science as to a religion. Indeed, she described the laws of social science as God's laws for the right operation of the world. These features of Nightingale's life and work are still little known. Numerous biographies of her portray her as the romantic nurse, while more recently there has been speculation as to the "hysterical" nature of her lengthy illness. Yet she deserves a place in the history of the social sciences for her promotion of applied statistics and evaluative research. Her own statistical study of mortality in childbirth is a prime example of the application of empiricism to one of the great issues of the day. She had great facility for presenting data and pioneered the use of charts. She also used statistics to argue against the repressive (for women) Contagious Diseases Acts.

Soon after her return from the Crimea Nightingale worked behind the scenes to have a royal commission established to investigate the "sanitary condition" of the British Army. The evidence she gave to the commission, in the form of written answers to questions, summarizes in a very few words the immensity of her accomplishment in reducing mortality. It gives glimmerings of her later, more comprehensive, approach to the use of knowledge for application.

> We had, during the last six months of the war, a mortality among
> our *sick* not much more than among our *healthy* guards at home,
> and a mortality among our troops in the last five months two-thirds
> only of what it is among our troops at home.

The death rates from disease in the Crimea had been worse than those in the worst cholera epidemic. Nightingale showed how statistics ought to be collected and used in future. The exercise itself was "a complete example — history does not afford its equal — of an army, after a great disaster arising from neglects, having been brought into the highest state of health and efficiency. It is the whole experiment on a colossal scale."[17] Yet she warned:

> We cannot try this experiment over again for the benefit of inquirers
> at home, like a chemical experiment. It must be brought forward
> as a historical example. (362)

Nightingale acknowledged her debt to Dr. Farr for the mortality data themselves, but neither he nor any of the other contributors to the Royal Commission on the Sanitary Condition had her skill at statistical presentation. Nightingale's coloured area charts were more than the simple pie charts which still bedeck many a corporate prospectus and annual report of government ministries. Hers managed to compare data *both* cross-sectionally and over time. She gave mortality rates for soldiers in Crimea by preventible diseases separately from other causes, so as to facilitate comparison with mortality rates for a similar age group of men at home in Britain. Each wedge of the pie was for a different month, so that one could see the progressive reduction of deaths by disease, until the death rate declined below that for the comparable British population, men in Manchester.[18] Her further considerable efforts toward implementation of reform are part of the story of the collaboration with Martineau to be discussed shortly. Nightingale

---

[17] Nightingale, "Answers to Written Questions," *Report of the Sanitary Condition of the Army*, 361.

[18] Some of Nightingale's charts are reproduced in colour in I. Bernard Cohen, "Florence Nightingale." For another impressive use of charts see Nightingale, "Army Sanitation Administration and its Reform under the late Lord Herbert." The sophistication of her statistical analysis can also be seen in a book-length treatment, *Notes on Matters affecting the Health, Efficiency, and Hospital Administration of the British Army* (1858).

worked also to have a health promotion/preventive medicine approach applied in India, not only for the British Army there but the civilian population.

Nightingale later sought to have the improvements in mortality rates achieved in the army obtained also for ordinary civilians. In her letter to the International Statistical Congress, 1860, read by the Earl of Shaftesbury, she called on delegates to bring examples to the next congress of successful cases of the reduction of mortality and disease. She was undoubtedly correct that "there must be a large amount of statistical information bearing on the prevention of disease in possession of the Governments of different countries."[19] Nightingale then sought to allay concern over the cost of any reforms to be implemented from her proposal. It could be shown that the cost of crime, disease, and excess mortality was greater, she argued, than the cost of sanitary improvements. Showing this would remove one of the most legitimate objections in the minds of governments and nations against such measures.

Quetelet was Nightingale's major source for her conceptualization of the social sciences as a system of laws/regularities that could be ascertained and used as a basis for intervention for good. De Staël or Condorcet could equally well have been a source, but it seems that Nightingale did not know their work. She systematically annotated the 1869 edition of Quetelet's *Physique sociale*. She left extensive notes, which were published only in 1981, on the application of probability theory to social questions.[20] The two met when Quetelet was in London to attend the Congress of the International Statistical Association of 1860. Prince Albert, Quetelet's former pupil, opened the meeting with an enthusiastic speech of his own writing. On Quetelet's death in 1874 Nightingale wrote an "in memoriam" (Part 3 in the Diamond and Stone series). Late in life she tried to establish a chair or readership at Oxford University to teach Quetelet's probability theory and statistical approach, "social physics and their practical application." Her rationale was that since the ancient universities were the training places for England's public administrators, the new methodology should be taught there. She chose Francis Galton as her agent to arrange things with the university, offering to put up £2000 of her own money. Galton, alas, was not up to the charge. He was willing to squander the money on a

[19] "Letter from Miss Nightingale" to the International Statistical Congress, 1860.
[20] See the series by Marion Diamond and Mervyn Stone, "Nightingale on Quetelet."

statistical contest and essays. Nightingale withdrew, but her correspondence with Galton shows precisely the sort of questions she
believed could be dealt with:

> What education was retained and what wasted after schooling? from
> night schools and secondary schools particularly?
> What were the results of the various punishments for crime? what
> were the deterrent effects? what was the effect of education on crime?
> What were the effects of charity and workhouses? were children
> pauperized or de-pauperized by workhouses? what was the effect on
> girls?[21]

Concerning Britain's administration of India Nightingale asked
whether the people were better or worse fed and clothed; were they
healthier or more diseased, their crafts encouraged or ruined? She
sought, in effect, empirical study of the impact of imperial rule on the
lives of the subject peoples. She also asked Galton for his own ideas
about what could be studied statistically and "how to use these statistics
in order to legislate for and to administer our national life with more
precision and experience" (2: 417). She complained that the government did not use the statistics it had "except to 'deal damnation' across
the floor of the H of C at the Opposition and *vice versa*." Why were the
excellent available statistics not used? Though the great majority of
ministers and officials had received a university education, what had
it taught them of the practical application of statistics? (2: 418) Galton's
negative response shows how little he understood her proposal.

A letter to her friend Benjamin Jowett, Master of Balliol College, on
the proposed statistical professorship, makes a similar point about the
use of data by decision makers, that the "enormous amount of statistics at this moment available at their disposal (or in their pigeon holes
which means *not* at their disposal) is almost absolutely useless. Why?
Because the Cabinet Ministers ... their subordinates, the large majority
of whom have received an University education, have received no
education whatever on the point upon which all legislation and all
administration must — to be progressive ... ultimately be based. We
do *not* want a *great arithmetical law* — we want to know *what we are
doing* in things which must be tested by results. We want experience
and not experiment. We legislate *without knowing* what we are doing."[22]

---

21 Nightingale, letter to Galton, in Karl Pearson, *Life, Letters and Labours of Francis
   Galton*, 2: 417.
22 Nightingale Manuscripts, Add. Mss., 45785:f144 (January 3, 1891).

Nightingale's eulogy of Quetelet shows, apart from her appreciation of him, how she conceptualized his social physics.

> I cannot say how the death of our old friend touches me, the founder of the most important science in the whole world, for upon it depends the practical application of every other and of each art, the one science essential to all political and social administration, all education and organization based on experience, for it only gives exact results of our experiences.[23]

Nightingale sought to have the decennial census include questions on sickness and health, which apparently had been done in the Irish census of 1851. She and her colleague Dr. Farr had made representations to census authorities to no avail. A letter from 1860, when the 1861 questions were being chosen, set out the case:

> I feel so very strongly about this Census bill that I cannot help writing to you of how much importance it would be, as bearing on all questions of the public health, to have a column in the enumeration paper in which should be entered the number of sick people in each house with the diseases.
>
> In this way we should have a return of the whole sick and diseases in the United Kingdom for one spring day, which would give a good average idea of the sanitary state of all classes of the population.
>
> The Mortuary Returns take no cognizance of a large amount of disease which rarely proves fatal, but which nevertheless represents a vast loss of efficiency in the population. How important to bring this out for once.[24]

She asked why a compulsory sick return should be any more obnoxious for officials than a compulsory death return.

> The public benefit would infinitely outweigh any inconvenience in filling up these returns. And, when taken with the sick returns of hospitals, asylums, workhouses and so forth, they would afford insight into problems of great importance.

The government decided, however, that the question of health or sickness was "too indeterminate" to be made a question to each individual. The answers would not be based on a uniform principle and the results would be inaccurate. Nightingale tried to answer this objection but blamed bureaucratic inertia as the real reason: "Mr. Waddington does not like to take the trouble."[25]

---

[23] Add. Mss. 43400:f276.
[24] Add. Mss. 43398, letter April 21, 1860.
[25] Add. Mss. 43398, letter May 10, 1860.

Nightingale's social science was intimately connected with her religious philosophy. This departed from conventional Church of England Christianity in one respect of particular interest to feminists — its being more positive and less preoccupied with sin. Reforms in the world's morality would not be made "by confessions and bewailing our 'desperate wickedness,' but by practically growing the new moral world out of the discovery of what the laws are."[26] She asked when we would come to registers of virtues instead of vices and crimes, ideals and not failures? "When will the day come when we shall register not crimes and drunkenness as we do now but virtues and great deeds of heroism and endurance and self-sacrifice and love and faith?"[27]

> How will "original sin" be exchanged for "original goodness?" By discovering all the "laws" (God's thoughts) which register — we will not say subject — man's actions in the plans of God's moral government ... these are the details of his "vast scheme of universal order."[28]

Working without knowledge of these laws the best philanthropist could be doing more harm than good. A favourite example here was the foundling hospital, whose establishment resulted in increased numbers of infants being abandoned.

> Moral laws of God can be found by induction as physical laws. Indeed, God's moral, social and physical laws act and react on one another. By Quetelet's method moral laws can be stated in numerical results. If anything can be called a law, is not that the effects of which can be prophesied like an eclipse?[29]

We cannot modify the state of the solar system which produces the eclipse, but we *can* modify the social state.

Nightingale argued that the nation collectively had responsibilities. To fulfill them there should be a "Chancellor of the Exchequer and a Budget for morality and crime" as well as for finance. There were perfect regularities and correlations in God's mind. Here she referred to the "unintended tribute of positivism to God," that we *cannot but 'know God'* through the discovery of laws.[30] The existence of regular social laws pointed to the nation's collective responsibility. "Cannot the

[26] I use the original source in the Nightingale Papers, indicating the folio number, but have modernized the spelling and punctuation. Where possible I also give a reference to the printed source in the Diamond and Stone series, part 3; thus, Add. Mss. 45842:f143/Diamond and Stone, 333.

[27] Add. Mss. 45842:f167/Diamond and Stone, 345.

[28] Add. Mss. 45842:f144/Diamond and Stone, 333.

[29] Add. Mss. 45842:f51.

[30] Add. Mss. 45842:ff60-61.

'collective' nation be brought to such knowledge and sense as to be responsible for ... an ever increasing degree of *good*?"[31]

Nightingale's views on social welfare were complicated. On the one hand she opposed, with laissez-faire liberals, "indiscriminate alms giving," believing that it made paupers of people and discouraged their becoming independent. Misguided charity could do real harm, as the establishment of foundling hospitals and the accompanying *increase* in the number of abandoned infants demonstrated. Yet she was aware that the converse was not, as was often supposed, true: "If we do not give to the vagrant, he will not therefore find work." The suppression of the foundling hospital did not insure that some poor child would not die who might have been saved by one.[32]

"A Note on Pauperism" in *Fraser's Magazine* in 1869 reveals the complexities of Nightingale's position. On the one hand paupers who could move an arm or a leg could support themselves. The millions spent annually on Poor Law relief only increased the pauperism it was meant to relieve. Yet "every imbecile old woman or dirty child is a sort of treason against the Almighty" (281). According to the Poor Law there should not be a single orphan wandering the streets, but there were more than 100,000 stray children in London (283). She disagreed with the "old political economists" who would "simply give the go-by to the whole question, saying 'Let well alone,' which being interpreted means 'Let bad alone'" (282). She recommended that all the sick and incapable be removed from the workhouses and provision be made for their cure or care (281). We should not punish the hungry for being hungry, but teach them how to feed themselves. She referred to the "tyranny of trades' unions," which deprived individual workers of their rights, but declared unequivocally that "it is always cheaper to pay Labour its full value." Except in times of exceptional distress, the state should be able to give productive work at remunerative prices. The recent distress in East London was the result of the new liberal policies:

> Free trade, from which so much was expected, although it may have provided for many willing workers, has left a vast number without work. (282)

Nightingale's unpublished papers contain extensive discussion of the unforeseen consequences of intervention. The "social law" said only "that but for foundling hospitals so many illegitimate children will

---

[31]   Add. Mss. 45842:f184/Diamond and Stone, 346.
[32]   Add. Mss. 45842:f145/Diamond and Stone, 334.

not be deserted, perhaps will not be born, that foundling hospitals produce foundlings: produce, that is, an 'enormous increase in the number of exposed illegitimate children' and that to render it easy to abandon a child safely and secretly is to demoralize."[33] The "second law" meant

> that almsgiving and ... Poor Law relieving — "distribution of doles" by Poor Law or by individual, without system, enquiry or discrimination, without, above all, any plan for thereby setting the recipients on the way to maintaining themselves, or without practical judgment how to accomplish this, directly produces "idle and miserable" people, as well as maintains them at others' expense, directly diminishes industry, frugality, self-reliance. This is not to say that we are to exercise no "charity." It is the reverse: our "charity" is to do good and not harm.[34]

These two laws were more than proved by but were the actual result of facts and numbers.

> The discovery of these two laws has revolutionized or is in process of revolutionizing a whole Department of Social or Moral Economy — showing how essential it is, how it is indeed the "one thing needful" for us to know God's laws or thoughts if we are to do any good, if even we are not to do immense harm — showing too how the discovery of "law," or rather of *what* these moral, divine laws are, will make all the difference between the new and the old moral worlds.

People said that the great moral laws were well known. Yet a whole revolution had taken place in the meaning of such law: charity. "It did mean: *giving* to beggars. There is danger lest it should come to mean: *refusing* beggars. For people are always tumbling over the horse the other side."[35] Nightingale was acutely aware that well-meaning people, acting from the highest religious motives, could be doing great harm — "manufacturing" illegitimate children and even killing them. The mortality rate of foundling hospitals was "quite out of all proportion to that of the poorest homes," destroying more infants than infanticide.[36] The French practise of farming poor children out to nurse, she observed, was another form of infanticide.

Yet, if we did but once discover, understand, and apply the "laws,"

---

[33] Add. Mss. 45842:ff145-46/Diamond and Stone, 334.
[34] Add. Mss. 45842:f146/Diamond and Stone, 334.
[35] Add. Mss. 45842:ff146-47/Diamond and Stone, 334.
[36] Add. Mss. 45842:f148/Diamond and Stone, 335.

all this evil might be transmuted into good. Nightingale conceded the overwhelming, dreadful waste of evil's working out to no apparent good. "But, whenever we do find out the 'law,' and set our hands to the plough, the transformation of evil into good is as striking and often as rapid and complete as the growth of 'original' evil."[37] She wanted to show how, practically, when someone does the thing right, all the results come out right, both the foreseen and unforeseen sequences. "You made pauperism; you can make independence." We know which schools produce honest bread winners and which send people to the workhouse. These ideas are "as old as the hills," pre-Christian, Platonic. "But the discovery of law is new, almost of our generation. And is it not obvious that, if these laws exist at all, we can only work, so as to do anything, in accordance with these laws?"[38]

Nightingale speculated, from Quetelet's crime statistics, that education might result not in diminished crime, but only in more criminals getting away with their crimes. Moral and mental education should not be confused. Simply learning to read and write did not reduce crime, as was commonly supposed, but only put a new instrument into the criminal's hands.

> Is it not possible that 'education' prevents less the crime than the
> conviction? So as to suicide; we have the same exact data by which
> we can prophesy exactly how many will kill themselves every year
> — supposing always the same state of society to continue — and
> even by what instruments and at what hours of the 24.[39]

Rather than think that we are predestined to some fixed number of suicides we should use this information to shape our own fate. It is the same with "accidents" in the streets, which also can be regularly predicted despite the name. How can we tell when someone will make a foolish dart across the street just as a cab is tearing round the corner?

> Yet our friend the Registrar-General will tell us exactly the number
> of accidents that will happen next quarter; nay, were the number
> not made up on the last days of the quarter, we await (not with cool-
> ness, let us hope) the inexorable law or fate, which — always
> supposing the state of society not to be changed — always fills up
> its quota.[40]

So also with marriages, where we would expect people's fancies and

---

[37] Add. Mss. 45842:f151/Diamond and Stone, 336.
[38] Add. Mss. 45842:f152/Diamond and Stone, 336.
[39] Add. Mss. 45842:f153-55/Diamond and Stone, 337.
[40] Add. Mss. 45842:ff154-55/Diamond and Stone, 337.

uncontrollable feelings not to be amenable to anything like the regularity of laws. Yet the numbers who will marry and their ages can be
predicted with exact precision for each year.

Much of Nightingale's discussion was a paraphrase of Quetelet, done
for her own understanding and not for publication. She had, however,
begun her analysis earlier, in 1850-51. Publication of his 1869, expanded
edition of *Physique sociale,* disinterred the manuscript and gave her material for further work. She used, and recommended, this second French
edition, on occasion also citing Quetelet's *Système social* of 1848.

Nightingale accepted all of Quetelet's statements on the unity of
science. Laws of different types were co-ordinated, acting and reacting
on one another throughout the moral, social, and physical worlds. "We
can scarcely say where one ends and the other begins — or which
belongs to the physiological world, which to the moral world, and which
to political economy."[41] On the connection between material conditions
and moral actions, she wrote:

> Or in other words that the laws of the material world and the laws
> of the moral world, of the political world, or the action of govern-
> ment, of the economical world, or the conditions of trade, commerce,
> manufacture, agriculture, act and react on each other."[42]

Nightingale frequently made comparisons between the physical and
social sciences. She asked whether, if we studied the political and moral
world as we studied the solar system/material world, we would arrive
at the same certainty in predictions. Theoretically we should be able
to, for not even the most trifling actions and feeling were left to chance.
Anyone who could see into the mind of the Creator could predict
history, for it operated by the same laws that governed eclipses. Elsewhere she described "scientific experiments" in both the moral and
physical world:

> Advancing civilization increases the watchfulness and powers of
> induction and deduction, of every member of mankind, and thus
> effects arising and continuing under somewhat different conditions
> become as valuable as scientific experiments planned on purpose
> to find out the way of producing or discovering phenomena, moral
> or physical.[43]

Perhaps her Platonic training had prepared her for the mathemati-
zation of the universe. Certainly no one was more committed to that

[41] Add. Mss. 45842:f166.
[42] Add. Mss. 45842:f170/Diamond and Stone, 341.
[43] Add. Mss. 45842:f61.

conceptualization than she was. Again, from Quetelet, whom she likened to Plato:

> Let us glance as we pass at what is perhaps the most extraordinary feature of the whole subject, and which stamps it with the precision and force and truth of "law": namely that the series observed, and the series calculated beforehand, in all cases approximate so closely as to remind us of Newton and his observation of the apple falling.[44]

Newton was so agitated on the eve of discovery that he was obliged to call in someone to finish his calculations. So Quetelet calculated his curve or formula. She cited his "average man" concept, describing how it worked for height and weight, that is, how these measurements fit onto the normal curve. The same applied to other qualities, intellectual and moral. Nothing was accidental: "the observed facts of nature are reduced to numerical calculation." Again, this law did not mean fatalism or encourage resignation.

> A law does not "govern" or "subordinate," does not compel people to commit crime or suicide. On the contrary, it put means into our hands to prevent them, if we did but observe and use these means. It simply reduces to calculation observed facts; this is all that a law means.
>
> These laws or results change of course with the causes which give them birth; for example, civilization, sanitary and moral, changes the law of mortality by diminishing the death rate. So it is with the law of morality. The causes influencing the social system are to be recognized and modified. From the past we may predict the future.[45]

Consequently we should no longer act haphazardly in legislation, philanthropy, or government, but we should study and learn these laws. She hoped that this "all important science" might become a part of university education.

> Let us make it a subject of study in our schools and universities, and then apply the laws it discovers to us in our political and social institutions.[46]

To do this we must be able "to appreciate with exactness" the conditions of society which produce these observed facts.

> Great social, political, and scientific causes, when they were altered, change the course of events. The causes are human, but generally not

---

[44] Add. Mss. 45842:f156/Diamond and Stone, 337.
[45] Add. Mss. 45842:ff157-58/Diamond and Stone, 338.
[46] Add. Mss. 45842:f158/Diamond and Stone, 338.

the will of one individual. The point was that the social conditions that produce undesirable effects have to be known exactly. Nightingale clearly did not subscribe to the "great man" theory of history. Individuals had their place, but broad social circumstances and long-lasting customs were more influential. The laws were quantified and fixed, so long "as national laws and customs and individual circumstances remain the same. Many of these circumstances cannot be altered by persons; they can only be altered by nations and governments. How great the importance then of statesmen studying these laws — Parliaments or powers which can gradually change those conditions of society of which these laws are the product."[47] Among these powers was the press. She asked whether it represented society or led public opinion: "Does it only tell us what men say? Does it only 'give back to the world their own opinions?' "[48]

Nightingale insisted that social as well as individual conditions could be changed. She did not use terms like "reflexivity," or "dialectical relations," but she evidently understood the human capacity for creative action.

> It is only for society to will it. But society can only alter society.
> Mankind must create mankind; that is, government, legislation,
> institutions, churches, must bear a part in it.
> That individual characters are so largely influenced by circumstances
> is however a proof, if one were needed, that the national character
> may be so too. In other words, that there is no fatality in these laws.[49]

That so little was done to discover social laws was discouraging. People did not distinguish between the factitious and the essential. People judged from their own small circle and gave contradictory judgments. "We sometimes appear to know more about the social state of Rome or Athens some centuries before Christ than of the state of London in 1874."[50] Yet the very existence of statistical enquiries and interest in social laws might indicate that we are on our way to an exact estimate of conditions, that is, if such and such continue to be the antecedent circumstances, such and such a number of thefts, murders, suicides, foundlings, or pauper children and so forth will occur in future years. But we scarcely had even the method of the *moral* sciences yet. Quetelet had discovered something, both of method and facts, capable

---

[47] Add. Mss. 45842:ff160-61/Diamond and Stone, 339.
[48] Add. Mss. 45842:f161/Diamond and Stone, 339.
[49] Add. Mss. 45842:f162/Diamond and Stone, 339.
[50] Add. Mss. 45842:f163/Diamond and Stone 340.

of inexhaustible application: "a true conception and a certain inkling of facts. He is always on his guard against confounding probability with truth."[51]

"Free will" was the effect of the causes of a social system. Modify the system and you modify the causes, the person, "free will," and all.[52]

> If, from year to year, we must expect to see the same crimes, in the same proportions, punished in the same proportions, the same marriages, the same suicides, the same accidents and so forth, can there be any free will?
>
> But to say that we must expect to see the same crimes is merely saying ... that the same causes will have the same effects.[53]

Mortality tables do not tell us at what ages Mr. A or Mrs. B will die. Free will has its place. We can modify the causes, or some causes, which influence our own lives and actions or those of our nearest and dearest. "And if this were done on any great scale, by unity in purpose of a great many and, with knowledge and wisdom, we should of course be able to modify the national life and action."[54] It was not fatalism to acknowledge that the same effects follow from the same social causes.

The notion that history unfolds according to certain laws was entirely compatible with personal and national activism. An article in *Fraser's Magazine* opens with:

> Supposing us to study the laws under which the political and moral world is governed as we study those under which the solar system, the material world, is governed — could we arrive at something of the same certainty in predicting the future condition of human society? how it will be with Europe? how will it be with England? how it will be with any of our homes or institutions on August 11, 1999, at ten o'clock in the morning? (for I would not be particular to a minute.)

One thing was certain, that everything was determined down to the most trifling action or feeling:

> All will be order, not chance. But whether it be the order of disorder, so to speak, or the order of good order, depends upon us. And this is practically what we have to consider. What will this world be on August 11, 1999? What we have made it.[55]

---

[51] Add. Mss. 45842:f164/Diamond and Stone, 340.
[52] Add. Mss. 45842:f168/Diamond and Stone, 341.
[53] Add. Mss. 45842:f181/Diamond and Stone, 345.
[54] Add. Mss. 45842:f182/Diamond and Stone, 345.
[55] Nightingale, "A Sub-'Note of Interrogation,'" 25.

Nightingale speculated on the relationships among idiocy, madness, and social influences. The seasons influenced madness and suicide. Age, similarly, was a factor in all forms of mental alienation. She mused about the relation between the "increase of civilization" and madness, but again drunkenness bred madness. She merely glanced at these "curious relations," leaving it to others to work out. Social organization had a regular influence on suicide. Nightingale here explored patterns by sex and marital status. Again, she maintained that no results were accidental and all could be modified if their causes were changed.

> In this regularity and certainty, which makes our hair stand on end, lies in fact our best, our only hope for the future. For were results not certain, how could we foresee them? How could we modify, change them?

She noted the case of southern Italy's glaring civil and religious misgovernment by priests and despots. Yet improvements were being made in the form of roads, railways, schools, cultivation, marsh drainage, and capital investment. "Who shall say that we cannot cultivate and make man as we cultivate and make land?"[56]

> The great *sensitiveness* of statistics to acting causes is what strikes us, rather than the reverse. Statistics, that is, statistical facts, answer to the helm, that is to the modifying cause, or spur. We are always blundering ... as to free will and choice. Man's will is *determined* by the *acting causes* of his "social system." Alter these and his will is altered.[57]

Political science was the enquiry into the precise laws of politics. Yet "nothing has tended so much to stop the development of these sciences as the so-called free will theory."[58] No one seriously denied that the general will produced the causes that act on particular wills, and this general will could be modified. Nightingale stressed the interaction between physical and social factors.

> Man is born, grows up and dies according to certain laws, of which the whole or the mutual reactions have never been studied. The science of man gives us only researches on some of these laws, results of single observations, or *theories based on views*. Moral and intellectual man has not been studied in his development.
>
> Nor has it been studied how he is influenced by the physical man, which impresses its action at each age upon him, nor how the moral

[56] Add. Mss. 45842:f172/Diamond and Stone, 342.
[57] Add. Mss. 45842:f185/Diamond and Stone, 346.
[58] Add. Mss. 45842:f188/Diamond and Stone, 348.

> and intellectual man impresses *his* action on the physical man. That
> is, we have not studied these matters by the science of observation,
> observation of numbers and facts.[59]

Although she recognized that people found it repugnant to look upon
moral phenomena as subject to law, Nightingale considered that laws
registered relations rather than *determining* them. Nor was it possible
for anyone alone to undertake the work of observation.

For Nightingale the regularities, even of crime, meant not discouragement, but the reverse:

> Men can be improved by improving their institutions and all that
> influences their being — same causes: same effects. Alter the causes.
> Man can govern by laws moral, as he does by laws physical. For
> mankind can discover the laws and govern by their means.[60]

God alone set the limits, by setting the laws within and by which we
act. God acted by laws, and so do we when we have discovered them. "If
it were otherwise, we could not learn from the past for the future. This
reaction, or reflection of man upon himself is, as Quetelet says, one of
his noblest attributes, his finest field of activity. As a member of the
social body, he is subject to causes, but as a man he is their master."[61]

Nightingale saw a crucial role for public opinion in determining the
"national character" which in turn shapes patterns of social life. These
regularities were fixed laws never to be broken.

> Individuals cannot alter these except by carrying what is called
> "public opinion," which makes governments with them.[62]

Even a despotic prince was not an exception, for a despot could do
mischief only as far as the nation would let him.

Time and again Nightingale made clear that, however fixed and
certain social laws were, this did not mean an unyielding determinism.
Governments could alter social conditions through legislation, hence the
importance of studying the determining laws. The inexorable Treasury, the budget of customs and needs, could be drawn up beforehand
with even more certainty than that which the Chancellor of the Exchequer estimates national revenues and expenditures. These, the nonmon-
etary rates and taxes, were paid in more regularly than the nation, especially Italy, paid its taxes.[63] Human actions, more than the actions of

---

[59] Add. Mss. 45842:f186/Diamond and Stone, 346.
[60] Add. Mss. 45842:f187/Diamond and Stone, 347.
[61] Add. Mss. 45842:f188/Diamond and Stone, 347.
[62] Add. Mss. 45842:f192/Diamond and Stone, 349.
[63] Add. Mss. 45842:f194/Diamond and Stone, 349.

other creatures, were reducible to laws, but humans were at once the register and keeper of the register, unlike other creatures. This was our safety, that we can alter ourselves and, through political and religious institutions, the nation.

> The influence of civilization, of political and religious institutions, on the moral and physical nature of man is at present little known as an exact science, still less as an art by which to do perfectly that which we now do gropingly and in the dark.
>
> We know ... that civilization lengthens life by sanitary measures, by extending commerce and improving agriculture, by liberalizing institutions. We know vaguely that certain crimes disappear in civilization but, on the other hand, other crimes increase. We know that some populations increase, others remain stationary, others actually decrease. And this appears to coincide with the increase or decrease of prosperity.[64]

We know generally that morals and religious and political institutions influence vital statistics. The number of stillborn children increases with illegitimacy, as does the death rate of living children. Among political institutions, conscription and war, which fall upon the strongest and most valuable part of the population, are causes that enfeeble successive generations.

> But above all it is governments which dispose of life. Is it not then the first, the most essential step to have a political science — to raise it, if it is a science at all, into an *exact* science — to determine the actual results of legislative measures, and political institutions in figures, not to go in this blind way, changing laws almost at random, at the caprice of party, but to make that an art which is the most essential of all arts?[65]

Despotism in general stops the development of the race. With slavery, we see the extreme effects. Slaves not only do not multiply but die in an immensely greater proportion than their masters. Freedom favours individual effort and industry.

In making her plea for evaluative statistics Nightingale was acutely aware of the complexity of social life and the power of unintended consequences. Individuals and governments should act and intervene on the basis of social science laws but, with imperfect understanding of those laws, could often do the wrong thing. Hence the need for careful

---

[64] Add. Mss. 45842:f195/Diamond and Stone, 349.
[65] Add. Mss. 45842:f197/Diamond and Stone, 350.

evaluation of actions taken. Nightingale had herself experienced well-intended efforts (a training institution for midwives) resulting in harm (deaths from puerperal fever). The results could sometimes be the reverse of what was intended.

> We cut our pattern so badly that our coat fits no one. We create institutions expressly for our protection; we have calculated so ill that some reproduce the same evils from year to year which they were meant to cure; others show results so blurred that we hardly know whether in remedying one evil we have not created another; others seem to produce exactly the opposite effects to what was expected.[66]

Nightingale examined the impact of smallpox vaccination as an example. Its introduction diminished the rates of death and blindness, but might have unintended harmful consequences. By concentrating on vaccination and neglecting sanitary measures, for example, other diseases from foul air might not be checked and could make up the number of deaths formerly caused by smallpox.

Nightingale dedicated her *Introductory Notes on Lying-in Institutions* to Socrates' mother, who had been a midwife. Herself a Greek scholar, Nightingale was doing the most difficult statistical analysis of her life and found inspiration for it in Socratic scepticism:

> If I may dedicate, without "permission," these small "Notes" to the shade of Socrates' mother, may I likewise, without presumption, call to my help the questioning shade of her son, that I who write may have the spirit of questioning aright, and that those who read may learn not of me but of themselves? And, further, has he not said: "The midwives are respectable women, and have a character to lose"?

The problem arose when Nightingale discovered unacceptably high death rates among women in an institution she had established for training midwives. She closed the institution, although her analysis later showed higher rates in continental midwifery wards. The question remained as to how midwives could be trained. Nightingale had effectively to establish what a normal mortality rate was and then consider whether a training institution could be devised that would not exceed it. As this is exemplary analysis on a question of literally vital importance, sufficient excerpts will be given to show the logic. Nightingale's exasperation with the abysmal state of available data comes through with her customary wit:

[66] Add. Mss. 45842:f198/Diamond and Stone, 350.

The first step to be taken in the discussion is to enquire, what is the real normal death-rate of lying-in women? And, having ascertained this to the extent which existing data may enable us to do, we must compare this death-rate with the rates occurring in establishments into which parturition cases are received in numbers. We have then to classify the causes of death, so far as we can, from the data, with the view of ascertaining whether any particular cause of death predominates in lying-in institutions; and, if so, why so? And finally, seeing that everybody must be born, that every birth in civilized countries is as a rule attended by somebody, and ought to be by a skilled attendant; since, therefore, the attendance upon lying-in women is the widest practice in the world, and these attendants should be trained; we must decide the great question as to whether a training-school for midwifery nurses can be safely conducted in any building receiving a number of parturition cases, or whether such nurses must be only trained at the bedside in the patient's own home, with far more difficulty and far less chance of success. (1-2)

Obtaining the necessary data had been extremely difficult for there was no centralized agency for collection. There was no uniform system for recording causes of death and no common period within which deaths were to be counted as due to puerperal fever. There were defects in records of home births as well. Still:

With all their defects, midwifery statistics point to one truth; namely, that there is a large amount of preventible mortality in midwifery practice, and that, as a general rule, the mortality is far, far greater in lying-in hospitals than among women lying-in at home. (3)

Nightingale noted the "secondary influences" that affected the results, such as the age of the mother, number of pregnancies, and duration of labour. Other relevant conditions were the general state of the place of delivery, social class of the patient, health and stamina before delivery, and time kept in midwifery wards before and after delivery. Nightingale then went on to ascertain the (necessarily approximate) death rate for women delivering at home.

It would be expected that women in workhouses, because of their poverty and generally worse health, would have higher mortality rates than women giving birth in regular midwifery institutions. In fact, despite their obvious disadvantages, their death rates were lower (58). After making a number of such comparisons Nightingale concluded that the effect of the institution was greater than that of social conditions (65).

The data showed higher mortality rates where doctors and their students were in contact with birthing mothers, and Nightingale did not shrink from drawing inferences from the association (48). She wanted as little medical involvement as possible and would ban medical students entirely from attendance at births (69). Since giving birth "is not an illness, and lying-in cases are not *sick* cases, it would be well ... to get rid of the word 'hospital' altogether, and never use the word in juxtaposition with lying-in women, as lying-in women should never be in juxtaposition with any infirmary cases" (73). All midwifery wards connected to general hospitals should be closed at once. Home deliveries were to be preferred, and where midwifery was practised in small training institutions, conditions should emulate those at home as much as possible.

> If we are to have a training school at all, we must, before all things, make it as safe for lying-in women to enter it as to be delivered at home; and having made up our minds what is necessary for this purpose we must pay for it.

Otherwise, we would "ensure killing a certain number of mothers for the sake of training a certain number of midwives" (71). Nightingale continued to work on the problem and was planning a second issue of her book. She needed more information on private practice, especially to compare mortality rates by social class. We do not know why she did not proceed or whether she was discouraged by negative reviews of her book.

Women today trying to reclaim childbirth from the medical profession would find an ally in Nightingale. Although she was not in any conscious sense a feminist — and would probably have bristled at the suggestion — Nightingale brought a distinctive woman's perspective to the practise of childbirth. The medical profession noticed the difference and disapproved. The *British Medical Journal*'s review was prompt, sarcastic, and sexist.[67] Nightingale's findings were not summarized nor her rationale explained. Instead the reviewer gave his own views of the statistical debate. The "authoress" was "a great woman truly, and yet a woman; for we think we can perceive her sex even in her way of settling this knotty point," that is, of establishing a normal mortality rate for childbirth. Her analysis was "free and easy ... perfunctory," assuming a "sublime simplicity." The reviewer even jested that she "throws herself into the arms of Dr. Farr, the well-known English statistician," in fact her long-time collaborator. "But the weakest argument,

----

[67] Anonymous review, *British Medical Journal*, November 11, 1871: 559.

yet one highly creditable to the kind womanly heart," turns out to be Nightingale's non-medical treatment of the subject, that childbirth was not a disease but an entirely natural condition, and that the high death rate at births attended by medical professionals needed enquiry. Her argument was "purely sentimental ... yet ingenuously urged as if it were a logical thunderbolt." Her detailed proposals for hospital construction and management were dismissed as "hints" the book "throws out."

This, of course, is the male medical establishment, but neither has Nightingale been given her due by women. *Introductory Notes on Lying-in Institutions* effectively disappeared from the literature. Nightingale's anti-woman statements still circulate, but few know of her radical, pro-woman work on childbirth.

Unpublished correspondence shows how Nightingale dealt with another aspect of the issue: access of unmarried women to services. According to the evidence, some unmarried women were excluded from maternity hospitals in England but not in France, a variant which complicated the comparison of mortality statistics. The French expert, Dr. Lefort, "like every other Frenchman," expended "a great deal of wrath upon the total or partial exclusion of unmarried mothers from our lying-in hospitals — which (though I agree with him as to its being queer morality) is rather ill-timed wrath, considering that poor mothers go to lying-in hospitals to die, but to workhouses to live — at least in much greater numbers."[68]

The last Nightingale contribution to be discussed here consists of a two-part article on Indian famine relief.[69] This is vintage Nightingale in describing the callousness and ineptitude of colonial administration, while celebrating the achievements of the few able and effective exceptions. The analysis is remarkable also in the integration of issues of public administration with observations on class, caste, religion, and ethnicity. Nightingale here used her health promotion/prevention of disease principles to deal with a new issue: environmental degradation. She explained how deforestation caused famine while irrigation was a "present necessity," whose limitations she recognized. She decried the stupidity of cutting down wood without replacing it. The result was that for the long dry season the whole country was like a hard road. Then the rains came, destroying everything and resulting in scarcity. Irregular rainfall was also related to rates of death by fever and cholera.

---

[68] Wellcome Institute, letter to Dr. Farr, August 7, 1869.
[69] Nightingale, "A Missionary Health Officer in India."

"Tree-planting would do much both to bring rainfall and to arrest floods" (638).

The Nightingale-Martineau Collaboration

It is astonishing how little is known of the collaboration between Florence Nightingale and Harriet Martineau, despite the resurgence of interest and recent scholarly publication on both. In fact the two women worked together from 1858 on into the 1870s (Martineau died in 1876) on health promotion and preventive medicine, both generally and with reference to the army, and in opposition to the Contagious Diseases Acts, legislation which in effect scapegoated women/ suspected prostitutes as the means to control venereal disease.[70] Martineau tried unsuccessfully to interest Nightingale in psychiatric nursing. Nor did Nightingale respond to her colleague's advice on hospital design — to line up beds north/south, in order to take advantage of the reputed therapeutic effects of magnetic fields.

The initiative for collaboration came from Nightingale, who saw Martineau's journalism and methodological sophistication as an effective means of getting her reform message out. Apart from health promotion they pursued such related issues as army organization, the appointment of the Secretary of State for War, and lobbying tactics. The women presumably never met but developed a warm and mutually supportive relationship, exchanging presents, commiserating about illnesses, and complimenting each other on their publications. A correspondence that began with "Dear Madam" moved on to "Dear friend." Nightingale's closing went from "yours faithfully" to "yours truly and gratefully" when Martineau agreed to work with her. Although eighteen years younger than Martineau, Nightingale was clearly the leader throughout the collaboration. She was fastidious in acknowledging assistance, sometimes thanking Martineau in the name of a wider team.

In her opening letter, in November 1858, Nightingale enclosed confidential documents on the Royal Commission on the Sanitary

---

[70] The few pages in Cook, *Life of Florence Nightingale*, are still the best source on the collaboration with Martineau; see 1: 385-87 and 2: 74-76 respectively on preventive medicine in the army and the Contagious Diseases Acts. The brief coverage in F. B. Smith's biography deprecates Nightingale's work, as the book does generally. Curiously, biographies of Martineau, even recent ones, neglect this most interesting aspect of her professional life. Gayle Graham Yates's *Harriet Martineau on Women* (239-67) discusses and reprints Martineau's letters for the repeal of the Contagious Diseases Acts and gives one excerpt from the campaign against their introduction, but does not cover the collaboration with Nightingale.

Condition of the British Army, suggesting that Martineau might be able to use them. The terms of collaboration were soon agreed on: Nightingale supplied the documents and vetted everything for accuracy, but Martineau had full discretion and her name only would appear. Martineau promptly produced a feature story and Nightingale urged more. Indeed in their first month of collaboration, she sent Martineau her own draft feature on the failure of the British government to act on the recommendations of the royal commission report. This article carefully reviewed the commission's proposals for reform and their rationale:

> Are the deliberate recommendations of a Royal Commission of experts to be adopted and future armies saved or has the whole plan so carefully considered and so intelligently framed been shelved by the genius of dulness and stupidity in the War Office to which Great Britain from time immemorial has committed the destinies of her soldiers, in peace and in war?
>
> Why this delay? Or rather has not the time arrived when the nation should call for a Royal Commission of Enquiry into the manner in which the interests of the Army are neglected through the ignorance of a set of obscure paid officials who in all probability would never have been able to earn their salt in any other walk of life?

Appropriating the voice of the journalist Nightingale's draft concluded: "Our columns show from time to time the progress which is made. Let them also tell the War Office that unless other equally necessary reforms are carried out it is quite possible that better men may be found to attend to the health and efficiency of the Army."[71] It seems that Martineau used the substance of Nightingale's material but not the actual wording (her own was much tamer). Or, possibly, the editor of the *Daily News* found the criticism of the government too pointed and refused to print it.

The main result of this early collaboration was a full-length book, *England and her Soldiers*, published by Martineau in 1859. It is probably the best current source of Nightingale's views as well as Martineau's, for her own reports are buried in government documents and privately circulated limited editions. Martineau, as author, acknowledged Nightingale at key points. Accompanying the text was a series of fold-out coloured graphs depicting the causes of mortality in the army, reprints of Nightingale's pie charts. Martineau had quickly seen

---

[71] Add. Mss. 45788:ff29-31 enclosure in letter January 23, 1859.

the merit of the diagrams and requested their use. Nightingale provided her with the printer's blocks, although pointing out that she had had to have them renewed four times in the printing of her own work on the subject.[72] Nightingale gave practical advice on the sale price: better to sell 5000 copies at 2s.6d or 3s than 1000 at 7s.[73] She also paid Martineau £55 out of her own pocket, to add to the £45 the publisher had paid her; sales had been expected to bring in £100 and Martineau had to earn her living.

England and her Soldiers proposed a whole new system of preventive health measures, complete with an office for the collection and evaluation of health statistics. The argument begins with the devastating fact that casualties in actual combat were a "mere trifle" compared with those from preventible diseases (vi).

> More armies have ... been lost by disease than by any kind of sudden
> accident, or by ill-fortune in warfare. (3)

Martineau/Nightingale blamed, in part, the medical approach to the problem. It was the function of doctors to treat illness and injury, while the study of health required not only a different, but an opposite, mind to that of a good physician. Physicians counselled individuals as to what was bad for them with regard to cholera, but:

> When the question is of instituting such conditions as shall promote
> and protect the health of a whole society, physicians are not prepared
> with either principles, facts, or methods. (21)

The most enlightened civil officers of health realized how little progress had yet been made in either the science or the art of hygiene. The best results of their inquiries were "merely provisional," because the very bases of classification were subject to correction and change (22). The War Office needed a statistical bureau to keep track of diseases and their treatment. Examples were given of terrible epidemics for which a remedy was known and available, but the data had not been kept in such a way that the epidemic could be recognized (232). Statistics showed that better diet and sanitary measures were successful in fighting disease. At Scutari, in the Crimea, mortality was reduced to one-nineteenth of the initial rate (258). Instead of the "gratuitous mortality" troops suffered, rates were reduced to below those for comparable populations in England. Empiricists had long argued that knowledge could be applied for the betterment of society. This work by Martineau and Nightingale is a landmark example of the application of the new methodology.

---

[72] Add. Mss. 45788:f29, January 16, 1859.
[73] Add. Mss. 45788:f35, March 3, 1859.

Nightingale not only gave Martineau a great deal of help behind the scenes on *England and her Soldiers*, but she tried to get the work disseminated to those who most needed to read it: the soldiers themselves. She planned to purchase a copy each to be sent to every regiment but the War Office refused to accept the books. They would make the men "discontented."[74] Nightingale instead paid to have a book chain distribute £20 worth of copies to reading rooms across the country.

Nightingale had seen her causes suffer by poor appointments in high places. The minister who succeeded her friend Sidney Herbert was evidently an idiot, a "muff": "The reign of intelligence at the War Office is over. The reign of muffs has begun."[75] She advocated the appointment of Lord de Grey when it came time to replace the muff. Nightingale wrote Queen Victoria to that effect and prevailed on Martineau for help. A telegram urges: "Agitate, agitate for Ld de Grey to succeed Sir George Lewis."[76] Martineau evidently complied, for a note a week later expresses "great relief that Lord de Grey is War Minister ... A thousand thanks for all you have done for us."[77]

That Harriet Martineau took a prominent part in the campaign to repeal the Contagious Diseases Acts is well known. She was instrumental in founding the Ladies' National Association for the Repeal of the Contagious Diseases Acts in 1869. (The acts were first suspended in 1883 and then finally repealed in 1886 after a lengthy campaign led by Josephine Butler.) It is little known that Nightingale was active on the issue behind the scenes right from the beginning, indeed she sought to prevent the legislation's enactment in the first place. According to Josephine Butler, in *Personal Reminiscences of a Great Crusade*, Nightingale was active as early as 1860, giving evidence before a committee of the House of Lords considering the introduction of acts for the "regulation of vice" in India (4). It was evidently a difficult issue for Nightingale, as a single woman of high rank; she had her friend and co-militant Dr. Sutherland sign one clandestine paper for her. Apparently she was subjected to "vulgar abuse" — we would call it sexual harassment — in an anonymous letter sent her by an Army Medical Department official.[78]

[74] Add. Mss. 45788:f57, August 21, 1859.
[75] Add. Mss. 45788:ff133, September 24, 1861.
[76] Add. Mss. 45788:f174, April 16, 1863.
[77] Add. Mss. 45788:f175, April 23, 1863.
[78] Cook, *Nightingale*, 2: 75. In correspondence with Martineau August 25, 1863, Nightingale referred to having received a "threatening anonymous" letter, whether the same or another is not known (Add. Mss 45788:f210).

Nightingale was instrumental in recruiting Martineau to the cause. Again the *modus operandi* was a letter with pertinent facts. In August 1863, prompted by coverage in *The Times* arguing the need for regulatory legislation, Nightingale wrote to Martineau with alternative information.[79] In September she forwarded further material to contradict a *Saturday Review* article on venereal diseases: "Please show up the Sat. Rev. Please use the facts in the Report and return it to me."[80] In March 1864, Nightingale sent material on syphilis in the army, bemoaning the wholly medical approach to the problem and failure to consider prevention. "Medical *opinion* is absolutely worthless — except as to the treatment. As to prevention, that is another thing. About that, they have given us no evidence at all."[81] Nightingale's approach to the issue was coloured by her rejection of the germ theory. She saw better general sanitary conditions and healthy recreation as key to control. The women's campaign was unsuccessful: the House of Commons passed the first law in July, 1864; even more repressive measures against prostitutes (and suspected prostitutes) followed in subsequent amendments.

Nightingale took her losses, as she did her wins, much to heart: "Dear friend, This is only to tell you (what you know already) that we have lost, and the House of Commons have gained, the "Contagious Disease" Bill (amended).[82] She returned an article "for which we were deeply grateful," that she had lent to committee members, all but two of whom (one being her sister's husband) were for the bill. Nightingale was particularly furious about a remark of a War Office official, Lord Hartingdon, who had suggested as a means of containing venereal disease "*The only way* would be to attach a certain number of these women to each regiment *and to put them under religious instruction* (sic)"! Nightingale was occupied at the same time with a campaign to improve health conditions in India, so she regretted that she had not been able to do so much with the parliamentary committee as she could have wished:

> Though I cannot reproach myself with having neglected to answer any of their questions. All in vain. I feel a kind of hopeless despair.

---

[79] Add. Mss. 45788:f208, August 25, 1863.
[80] Add. Mss. 45788, September 17, 1863. This report seems to have disappeared. It may have been based on the evidence Josephine Butler described Nightingale as having given to a House of Lords committee in 1860.
[81] Add. Mss. 45788:ff253-54, March 14, 1864.
[82] Add. Mss. 45788, July 22, 1864.

She observed that the War Office was "utterly demoralized," accused an official of not speaking the truth, and declared that "the Horse Guards deserve the V.C. for their cool intrepidity in the face of facts." Nightingale presumably did not totally give up, for she ventured to remind Martineau of a planned pamphlet. They had to counter the contention that the French had succeeded in banishing venereal disease with their methods of regulation. (The French had pioneered the system of state-organized prostitution for the armed forces; Britain was the last European country to adopt it.) Nightingale proposed to demonstrate the French failure in another paper. "Now we have the facts: the French admissions (in the Army) are *exactly the same* as the English (in the Army): — the French inefficiency (or length of time in hospital) is *one-tenth more* than the English.[83]

Martineau, soon to be joined by Josephine Butler, became a prominent spokesperson in the next phase of the struggle against the Contagious Diseases Acts. Her three letters in the *Daily News*, December, 1869, after adoption of the fourth and most repressive law, launched the public movement for repeal. On December 31, 1869 the *Daily News* printed the women's declaration, which was signed, ultimately, by 2000 women. Martineau and Nightingale led the list, followed by Josephine Butler. Apart from the futility of the French system in controlling disease, the women argued against the contention that men could not be chaste, and therefore that prostitution was required. They denounced the loss of liberty women suffered by measures being directed only aginst prostitutes (women) and suspected prostitutes (also women). A Ladies' National Association was organized which, with a National Association and numerous regional, local, and affiliated religious organizations, eventually succeeded in repeal. Nightingale continued to support the cause behind the scenes but her main research focus had by then moved on to the high mortality rates of women in childbirth.

Beatrice (Potter) Webb, baroness Passfield (1858-1943)

Beatrice Potter was the eighth of nine daughters (the only son died) of a prosperous business family, upwardly mobile on both sides. Her mother, a religious woman, was well educated. Her businessman father held numerous company directorships and was president of the Grand Trunk Railway of Canada. He left behind the dissenting religion and radical politics of his father for the Conservative Party and the Church of England. As an adult

[83] Add. Mss. 45788, July 22, 1864.

Beatrice Webb, photo, 1892

Beatrice Potter met her working-class cousins, who still had jobs in the textile **Beatrice** mills of Lancashire and Yorkshire, attended chapel, and supported unions **Webb** and co-operatives.

The Webb diaries record years of anguish as she searched for a craft and a creed. Deeply religious as a child, she came to reject certain doctrines and conventional practice, blaming Herbert Spencer especially for a loss she later regretted. She read the French Encyclopedists, Mill, Comte, and the social novelists. She became a visitor/rent collector for the Charity Organization Society. This brought her into contact with the poor people of London and made her sceptical of the possibility of distinguishing the "deserving" from the "undeserving" poor.

Beatrice Potter did her first participant observation partly to find out how ordinary poor people lived and partly in search of her own roots. Her own family was very wealthy; her charity work took her to the very poor. Her Lancashire weaver cousins belonged to the group between, employed at modest wages, with small cottages and some savings. In order not to intimidate them she presented herself as "Miss Jones," a farmer's daughter, later revealing the hoax. From the experience she learned the worth of co-operative and collective institutions which are derided in liberal, laissez-faire doctrine.

In 1887 Potter began work with her cousin's husband, Charles Booth, on his massive survey of poverty in East London. Her first project was on the East End docks. For her second project she again used participant observation, now on the tailoring trades, a "sweating" industry. She took classes on tailoring and got herself a job as a "plain trouser hand." She was not much good at the job, but her organizing ability won her an offer of promotion. She quit, by then having enough understanding of how the industry worked to write up her findings. Again, she learned from the experience, reaching conclusions she would not have expected from her preconceptions. The papers reporting both experiences were published first in the Nineteenth Century and then in the Life and Labour series. Potter also collected information, at Booth's suggestion, by going around with an agent of the Singer Sewing Machine Company, ostensibly to check their books. She was not proud of this part of her work, nor did she find it very useful, and she did not include it in her autobiography, My Apprenticeship (it is reported in an interview with her, by Sarah A Tooley, "The Growth of a Socialist," in 1895.) Potter gave evidence to a committee of the House of Lords on the sweating industries and helped several of its members to write their minority report. Booth continued years more on the East London study, but Potter went on to other things.

Her next study was of the co-operative movement, which convinced her that the only way out of the recurring crises of inflation and depression was

Beatrice socialism. She met Sidney Webb about the time of her political conversion and
Webb married him in 1892. It was not, initially at least, a love match. Potter was
much attracted to a man with different political convictions and conventional expectations of a wife. Webb was an extremely able man of lower
middle class origins. He eventually became a London city councillor, member
of Parliament, and cabinet minister in the House of the Lords as Baron
Passfield. He joined the Fabian Society before she and was a contributor to
the first Fabian Essays; she was instrumental in the founding of the Fabian
Research Department. Both wrote pamphlets. Their partnership included,
as well as their publications, the founding of the London School of Economics. Beatrice Webb played a lesser role on the political scene, but helped
"get out the vote" for her husband and shared in the back room work,
entertaining influential people, and coalition building.

One important example of their collaboration was the famous Minority
Report of the Royal Commission on the Poor Laws. Beatrice Webb was the
member of the commission, although Sidney did most of the writing. The
report took Britain a significant step toward the establishment of a welfare
state, arguing that the state had the obligation not only to relieve distress
but deal with its causes.

Beatrice Webb was a late bloomer as a supporter of women's equality
but some of her studies contributed to the cause. In My Apprenticeship
she explained the "false step" she had taken in initially opposing the vote
for women. She had herself not been disadvantaged as a woman, growing
up in a household of girls and encouraged by a father who believed in the
superiority of women! On her mother's death she became, at age twenty-four,
the effective manager of her father's household. Later she supported the
vote for women, protective labour laws, and equal pay. Her Fabian pamphlet,
"Women and the Factory Acts" (1896), makes the case for protective labour
legislation for women.

The last of the Webbs' many travels was to the Soviet Union in 1932,
when they were given a carefully controlled tour. They wrote on the experience without applying any of their rules for verification. The result is a
naïve and superficial account, which Webb's Diary shows later troubled
them. The Diary itself is a splendid document, full of tantalizing entries,
like one for December 1926: "Lunched with the Oswald Mosleys to meet
Mackenzie King" (4: 108). My Apprenticeship, published 1926, is effectively
an autobiography up to her marriage, based on the diary. Its frankness and
verve made some people reverse their opinion of the deadly dry social
scientist; Beatrice Webb was human after all. She died in 1943, Sidney
Webb in 1947. Their ashes were buried in Westminster Abbey in 1947 in
a ceremony organized by the first majority Labour government.

Recommended biographies are: Deborah Epstein Nord, The Apprenticeship **Beatrice** of Beatrice Webb; *Lisanne Radice,* Beatrice and Sidney Webb; *Margaret* **Webb** *Cole,* The Webbs and their Work; *R.H. Tawney, "Beatrice Webb"; Carole Seymour-Jones,* Beatrice Webb: Woman of Conflict; *Barbara E. Nolan,* Political Theory of Beatrice Webb; *Shirley Robin Letwin,* The Pursuit of Certainty; *a chapter in Timothy Raison,* The Founding Fathers of Social Science; *Royden Harrison, "Sidney and Beatrice Webb," in Carl Levy,* Socialism and the Intelligentsia. *As well as Beatrice Webb's own* My Apprenticeship, Our Partnership *was published posthumously from her text; it covers the early years of their marriage. There is also a four-volume edition of* The Diary of Beatrice Webb.

Unlike the other women methodologists discussed, Beatrice Webb is occasionally mentioned among the founders of the social sciences, normally with her husband **Sidney Webb (1859-1947)**. Both appear in Raison's *Founding Fathers of Social Science* (along with twenty-nine other men). Even the joint listing is unfair for, if Sidney was the better socialist, Beatrice was the methodologist of the two. She had already done her first participant observation and worked on Booth's survey of East London before she met Webb; the application of the Webb method was a joint enterprise. Together the two produced some twenty books on the crucial social questions of the day, collaborating on the whole process from the initial stage of conceptualization through data collection to writing and editing. That Sidney Webb did most of the final writing is a mixed blessing. Undoubtedly more was produced in good time, but what Beatrice Webb wrote on her own is more engaging and intimate, for most people the better read.

Ironically the first person to have encouraged Beatrice Potter to become a sociologist was the social Darwinist, arch-conservative Herbert Spencer. He was, strictly speaking, a laissez-faire liberal, who opposed all government intervention. Spencer was a family friend and, in his younger years, a believer in women's rights. He not only encouraged Potter to read sociology but had her do library research for his own books. He helped her publish her first article, when she still shared his, and her family's, "individualist bias." Beatrice Potter served her apprenticeship with Charles Booth on what she called his "grand inquest," a survey of poverty in East London. Within a few years she had left behind the laissez-faire ideology of her upbringing for socialism. The socialist conversion is so connected with her methodology that neither can be discussed without the other.

Charles Booth had taken on the task, at his own expense and eventually resulting in seventeen volumes over two decades of work, to refute the social democrat contention that one quarter of the population of East London lived in poverty. Booth even called on the Social Democrat leader, H.M. Hyndman, to tell him he was wrong! But Booth had come under the influence of Comte and believed in the positive method. His painstaking work, all supported with the research assistance of his wife, Mary Booth, eventually documented the proportion of the population living in poverty at 30 percent, which fact he published. Never a socialist, he did become a red Tory, advocating medicare for the young, old, and those unable to work, a noncontributory old age pension, a compulsory public school system, and social assistance for those unable to work. Webb pointed out the scale of the collectivism Booth came to support: social assistance for over 300,000 in London alone.[84] Like Booth, Webb had embarked on the survey "with a desire to explode the socialistic fallacies and sensational accounts of London misery."[85] The experience had the opposite effect.

Herself influenced by what she saw and felt, Webb believed that others would be, too. Working with Booth convinced her "that social sentiment was formed by these descriptions, giving rise to a cry for political action," or venting itself, as in her own case earlier, in voluntary effort.[86] The fact that over 30 percent of the population were destitute, over one million people in the richest city of the world, had a profound effect on public opinion. Coming from a study by a captain of industry and a Conservative, it powerfully documented the futility both of private charity and the old Poor Law (298). Booth's work gave an impetus to "guaranteeism" or the "national minimum," the policy of securing a prescribed minimum to every individual, the foundation of the welfare state (304).

Yet Booth's principal contribution was not the discovery of these facts, "but his elaboration of an adequate technique" to obtain a vision of the condition of the whole population at a given point of time. Only with this static account would it be possible to discover the relative proportions of any problem and make sure that particular instances of good or evil "are not merely sensational exceptions" (292). Here Booth showed for the first time how "to combine the qualitative with the

[84] Webb, *My Apprenticeship,* (*MA*) 302.
[85] Sarah A. Tooley, "The Growth of a Socialist: An Interview with Mrs. Sidney Webb," 147.
[86] Webb, *MA*, 336.

quantitative examination of social structure."

> Charles Booth was much more than a statistician. He was the bold-
> est pioneer, in my judgement, and the achiever of the greatest
> results, in the methodology of the social sciences of the nineteenth
> century. (294)

Still, he was lax in explaining his own method, and it is only thanks to
Webb's diary entries and essays, published only much later in *My
Apprenticeship*, that we have any adequate account of how this
watershed study was achieved.

Webb's method was standard empiricism: an orientation to a real,
external world, diligent efforts to observe it objectively, and a common
framework with the natural sciences. There is nothing original here in
the conceptualization, but the concrete examples and practical advice
constitute a major contribution to the emerging methodology of the
social sciences.

Participant observation was obviously a means of obtaining data on
contentious and complicated matters. In Webb's first study, on the
tailoring industry, employers had every reason not to reveal the abysmal
working conditions and pitiful rates of pay. Nor could the workers themselves provide the necessary information, for as home workers they
saw only limited parts of the operation and were isolated from each
other. In *My Apprenticeship* Webb recounted that she learned more
about dock workers when meeting them as a rent collector that she
ever did touring the docks or visiting them for scheduled interviews.
"Observation is, in fact, vitiated *if the persons know that they are being
observed*" (387).

Webb included several short appendices on method in *My Apprenticeship*. These use "we" and "us" instead of "I" for, by the time of publication, 1926, the "working comradeship" was then thirty-four years old.
The writing was Beatrice Webb's, from the late 1880s when she was
working on Booth's survey. The papers were written, in other words,
before Weber and Durkheim's work on methodology. In *My Apprenticeship* she downplayed these early papers as reflecting "the zest of
the amateur," noting also their omissions, especially the failure to
discuss the use of historical records.[87]

"Personal Observation and Statistical Enquiry," the first appendix,
begins with a tribute to *facts*. The country was abandoning the theory

---

[87] Sidney Webb republished these papers in *Methods of Social Study* (1932), in both
their names, but the source used here is *My Apprenticeship*.

of laissez-faire thanks to people looking at particular facts over general principle. The narration of facts, such as medical reports of raging disease, brought about the first factory legislation:

> All the reforms of Lord Shaftesbury and his followers, constituting the principal constructive legislation of the last fifty years, were carried over the heads of political economists and interested opponents through the indignation evoked by detailed accounts of misery and crime. (464)

A body of students was needed who would "seek truth for its own sake," if possible with an explanation of social life:

> And the first step must be to ascertain a method of enquiry which will lead to a verified statement of fact, and which will aid us to break through the outer crust of events and to discover those hidden social forces which we must either submit to or control. (464-65)

Two methods were open to the student of society, the statistical or "*quantitative observation of aggregates*" and personal observation, or the "*qualitative observation of units*" (465). As in all other sciences, the quantitative and qualitative must go hand in hand. In the former the units were all equal and could conceivably be counted mechanically. In the latter different characteristics of people or events were the subject.

> Statistical enquiry without personal observation lacks all sure foundation; while personal observation unless followed by statistical enquiry leads to no verified conclusion. The two methods are in reality two equally essential acts in all scientific investigation of the structure and growth of existing societies. (466)

Webb then gave examples of statistics without personal experience and sensationalist pictures with no exact numbers.

> We must apply to these vivid pictures the hard and fast test of statistical enquiry. We must force those who present these striking statements to enumerate exactly the number of persons possessing the characteristics or living within the conditions described; we must compel them to compare this number with that of the whole population. And until the artist consents to bring his picture within a statistical framework, we may admire it as a work of art, but we cannot accept it as a verified statement of fact. (469)

The second appendix gave instruction on how to prepare for an interview, including the advice not to show off or argue, and not to take notes before rapport has been established. Listen, accept what is offered, take the tour. Then, "when you have got upon confidential terms, your new friend may cite private statistics or mention confidential documents; this should be met by an off-hand plea for permission to see them" (471). Any offer to produce and explain the documents should be followed up on the spot. The interview must be pleasing and agreeable to the persons interviewed. Webb recounted that she had once told fortunes to relax her interviewees:

> Without this atmosphere of relaxation, of amused interest on both sides, it will often be impracticable to get at those intimate details of daily experience which are the most valuable data of the sociologist. Hence a spirit of adventure, a delight in watching human beings as human beings quite apart from what you can get out of their minds, an enjoyment of the play of your own personality with that of another, are gifts of rare value in the art of interviewing. (472)

Webb added her view that these gifts were more characteristic of the woman than the man. Once the interview was over every separate fact or hypothesis should be promptly recorded.

In "The Art of Note-taking" (Appendix C) Webb explained how recorded observations become "an instrument of discovery," the process itself serving a similar purpose to that of an electroscope or prism in physics. "That is to say, it enables the scientific worker to break up his subject matter, so as to isolate and examine at his leisure its various component parts, and to recombine them in new and experimental groupings in order to discover which sequences of events have a causal significance" (473). Paradoxically, by exercising one's reason on the individual facts one might discover which of a series of hypotheses best explains the process underlying the rise, growth, change, or decay of a social institution.

Separate pieces of paper instead of a book should be used to facilitate the indefinite shuffling and reshuffling of the notes according to the various hypotheses being examined.

> It is vitally important to be set free from the particular category in which you have found any particular set of facts, whether of time or place, sequence or co-existence. In sociology, as in mineralogy, "conglomerates" have always to be broken up, and the ingredients separately dealt with. (474)

Specifically, each sheet of paper should contain only one date, place, source of information, and fact. A precise system had to be worked out so that others could go through and reassemble the same material. Webb gave actual examples of how they had used the method in their own studies, particularly how invaluable they found the later phases of sorting and resorting. She realized that it was difficult to convince students, especially those with literary rather than scientific training, that "it is by just this use of such a mechanical device as the shuffling of sheets of notes, and just at this stage, that the process of investigation often becomes fertile in actual discoveries" (479). Again she gave examples of how themes not discerned in the original observation only emerged later.

To become a sociologist herself Beatrice Webb had had to go through the process of understanding the failings of Herbert Spencer's method and political beliefs. Working as his research assistant she discovered that he was unsceptical as to any material she showed him. He was not a social investigator, she concluded, but sought out social facts to fit his theory, rather as a lawyer would look up cases to document a brief (45). Later Webb discovered a "deep-rooted fallacy" underlying his extreme liberalism or "administrative nihilism" (388). Spencer, who would have found a kindred spirit in Margaret Thatcher, opposed any role for the state beyond national defence and the administration of justice; all else was oppression and the road to slavery. He had assumed, Webb argued, that the for-profit enterprise belonged to the natural order of things. Actions by the state or municipality, by contrast, were artificial contrivances. Thus, to Spencer and other capitalists the Factory Acts, minimum wage, and public health measures were "clumsy mechanisms" bound to fail because they were against nature. To Webb no such distinction could be made, but every development of social structure was "artificial," the product of human intervention (389).

Webb, like so many of the women methodologists, took a broad approach to public health. In a lecture, "Public Health Administration" (1910), she related failings in health care to the great social problem of destitution. She held that there were three obligations on the part of individuals and the community.

> The first obligation is so to act as not to cause death or disease to other persons. The second, so to act as to keep your dependents in good health. The last is so to act as not to impair your usefulness to the community through bad health. Arising out of these there is the social obligation to alter the environment in such a way as to enable these obligations to be fulfilled by the individual. The whole of the work of public health administration consists in enforcing these obligations. (515)

An address Webb gave to the Sociological Society at the London School of Economics in 1906 is a good, succinct source of her method. "Methods of Investigation" reflects what Webb had to say to colleagues in the then young discipline. Social science was a science like any other, with numerous possibilities for experiment even if they could not be properly planned:

> What we have to do in social science is to apply the scientific method to the facts of social life. There is only one scientific method — that used in physical science. It consists of three parts — observation, conjecture as to the cause and effect of the facts observed, and afterwards verification by renewed observation.

The application of the method was a technical matter, involving telescopes in astronomy, other scientific instruments in chemistry and biology. "And so in the case of sociology, which is the science of men in combination, the application of scientific method needs the use of certain technical instruments" (345). Observation and experiment were methods held in common with all the other sciences. Statistics was a third, "necessary in nearly all observation, at any rate of present facts, to prevent falling into the fallacy of the individual instance" (349). If in a certain slum five babies died in the course of the summer, that will not tell accurately the effect of slum life on babies unless verified by the statistics of infant mortality in all slums. Webb cited a maxim that "the statistical method never discovers a truth, but it often prevents an error" (350).

Two methods were unique to the subject matter of "men in combination," the use of literature and the interview. Webb here warned against too much reliance on written sources; personal observation was also needed (347). She gave examples of how governments function differently from their descriptions on paper. Where human nature plays a part, personal observation is important, but it, too, must constantly be verified. The care Booth had taken to verify information in his survey was an example. Interview data presented their own problems, as instanced in the isolated facts and hearsay evidence turned up by commissions of inquiry. The great advantage of these data lay not in the provision of facts, but as sources for later corroboration. Such data were also a source for suggestions concerning cause and effect relations, which had to be verified.

Although it was said that experiments could not be applied to social facts, Webb pointed out examples to the contrary. County councils were perpetually making experiments and examining the results. So were businesses, railways, schools, and other public services. There was nothing wrong with this per se; the point was to safeguard the community against callousness and carelessness in experiments.

Webb distinguished between documents written to influence action and literature written to influence thought. A minute book, wage sheet, and the House of Commons Journal had to be more or less precise and correct, because decisions depended on them. "Documents are, therefore, likely to be much more precise than literature; they are unconscious testimony to the truth of the fact" (349). Literature, on the contrary, whether books, newspaper reports, or pamphlets, was intended to influence thought. Here, too, there were distinctions between "first-hand literature," like Hansard's Debates, and "second-hand literature," like a history.

Along with the statistical checks there had also to be qualitative methods, not as an alternative but as complementary:

> I might end my discussion of the methods of investigation by suggesting that it is the qualitative methods of observation — experiment and use of documents and literature — which enables one to discover the processes of society, and it is the statistical method which enables one to check these observations, to see that they apply to a large number of instances instead of to one only. (350)

Webb was cautious and sceptical in claiming validity. No amount of current knowledge enabled us to predict the course of future events. "We cannot foresee what will be the course of history a hundred years hence, for the reason that social facts are determined to some extent by others altogether outside the science we have in hand." Changes in climate, the influence of new inventions, and the appearance of a "great man" were "facts which may radically alter the course of society, but which do not belong to our science at all. No knowledge will ever enable us to foretell those facts" (350). Still she believed, as had the ancient constructive sceptics and more recent empiricists, that knowledge of society could be applied to predicting events. As the post office employed additional staff before Christmas, "We can ascertain, with sufficient certainty to base action upon it, what the conduct of the average man will be under ordinary circumstances." Successful government was based on this kind of knowledge.

> Though it will never help us to foretell the course of history, because of other facts intervening, yet it does help us to organize our own society. (351)

Interestingly, Webb was criticized in the ensuing discussion on this point. Other sociologists participating in the session were more optimistic about "sociological prevision": that inventions or a great man might quicken or retard the "laws of development" of a society, but that these could be ascertained in general (352).

Webb ended "Methods of Investigation" with her firm conviction that science could deal only with means or process, not purpose or end. An economist could only predict whether a *desired* result could be attained by a specified process, like cheaper commodities through free trade. But the economist could not tell whether that result *was* desirable.

> Medical science could perhaps tell you how to kill or cure a man, but it could not tell you whether you want to kill or cure him. The matter of ends or aims has nothing to do with science, but generally falls within the field of religion. (351)

She would continue to make this fact/value distinction whenever she engaged in methodological discussion.

The best joint source on the Webb method is the preface to *Industrial Democracy* (1897), a two-volume work on trade unions, which followed the Webbs' first collaborative project, published in 1894 as *The History of Trade Unionism*. The partnership included collecting data on unions on the couple's honeymoon in Dublin. Some six years' work went into the research, which encompassed the origin and growth of the trade union movement, as a whole and by industry, a statistical account of the distribution of unions by trade and location, and the methods and regulations of the unions. The object was to provide "a sketch from nature of trade union life and character ... a picture of these external characteristics of trade unionism, past and present, which — borrowing a term from the study of animal life — we may call its natural history." The external characteristics were insufficient for any scientific generalization as to purpose and effects. Nor could useful conclusions be arrived at by arguing from "common notions," nor by refining these into an abstract definition. "Sociology, like all other sciences, can advance only upon the basis of a precise observation of actual facts" (v).

The Webbs explained that they had done their best to be both accurate and exhaustive, giving statistics wherever they could be obtained. Only then did they venture into the domain of theory (viii). In the final chapter they even ventured into precept and prophecy. They hoped that their description of fact and structure would have "its own permanent value in sociology as an analytic record of trade unionism in a particular country at a particular date" (ix). Their economic generalizations could be no more than stepping stones for others to begin

where they had left off. They admitted that their moral judgments on
the place of trade unions in a democratic future would be shared only
by those who also shared their view of a desirable state of society.

The preface to *Industrial Democracy*, as does the preface to the trade
union history, makes clear that the observation and dissection of facts
does not require a mind free from preconceived ideas:

> If such a person existed, he would be able to make no observations
> at all. The student ought, on the contrary, to cherish all the hypothe-
> ses he can lay his hands on, however far-fetched they may seem. (x)

One must be on guard against being biased by authority, "as an instrument for the discovery of new truth, the wildest suggestion of a crank
or a fanatic, or the most casual conclusion of the practical man may
well prove more fertile than verified generalizations which have already
yielded their full fruit." Almost any preconceived idea could be helpful, so long as it was sufficiently limited and definite to be capable of
comparison with facts.

> What is dangerous is to have only a single hypothesis, for this
> inevitably biasses the selection of facts, or nothing but far-reaching
> theories as to ultimate causes and general results, for these cannot
> be tested by any fact that a single student can unravel. (x)

The Webbs considered royal commission and select committee reports
invaluable as sources of unintentional hypotheses, although they were
seldom of use "in any theoretic judgment or practical conclusion of
scientific value" (xi).

Documents, personal observations, and interviews were of different
and unequal value in qualitative and quantitative analysis or verification. The most indispensable was the document, as a kind of "mechanical memory, registering facts with a minimum of personal bias" (xi).
The comparison of confidential and public documents would show what
their authors desired to conceal. The investigator must accordingly
collect every document possible, however unimportant it might seem,
making copious extracts of the actual words.

> In this use of the document, sociology possesses a method of inves-
> tigation which to some extent compensates it for inability to use the
> method of deliberate experiment. We venture to think that collec-
> tions of documents will be to the sociologist of the future, what
> collections of fossils or skeletons are to the zoologist; and libraries
> will be his museums. (xii)

Personal observation meant "a continued watching, from inside the
machine, of the actual decisions of the human agents concerned, and

the play of motives from which these spring." The difficulty for the investigator was to get into a "post of observation" without altering the normal course of events. This was the only place "that personal participation in the work of any social organization is of advantage to scientific enquiry" (xii). This could be done by adopting the social class, practising the occupation, or joining the organization in question, all of which both Webbs had done in various ways. They added that "the woman" was especially well adapted to this passive form of enquiry, because she is accustomed to watch motives silently and is able to gain access and confidence instinctively refused to possible male competitors or opponents (xiii). They warned against the temptation to give undue importance to the particular facts and connections between them gained from this kind of observation.

The interview, as an instrument of sociological inquiry, meant more than the preliminary talks and social friendliness needed to gain access, but was "the skilled interrogation of a competent witness as to facts within his personal experience." One had to listen sympathetically to opinions, tradition, and hearsay reports, which might be useful in suggesting sources and revealing bias. "But the real business of the interview is to ascertain facts actually seen by the person interviewed" (xiii). One should make friends with the head of any organization, but actual information was better obtained from subordinates who were personally occupied with the facts in detail.

> But in no case can any interview be taken as conclusive evidence,
> even in matters of fact. It must never be forgotten that every man
> is biassed by his creed or his self-interest, his class or his views of
> what is socially expedient. If the investigator fails to detect this bias,
> it may be assumed that it coincides with his own! (xiv)

The interview was most useful in later stages of an enquiry, when the investigator knew what to ask.

The Webbs' term for what came to be known as the social survey was "wholesale interviewing." It enabled giving a quantitative value to a qualitative analysis. Once the significant attributes had been discovered, their distribution could also be ascertained. Booth's survey of the London East End was "one of the most brilliant and successful applications" of this method. The census itself was "only a gigantic and somewhat unscientific system of wholesale interviewing" (xiv).

Finally the Webbs recommended collaborative work: pooling stocks of preconceived ideas, provisional hypotheses, personal experience, sources, opportunities for interviewing, and access to documents. "They can do much by constant criticism to save each other from bias, crudities of observation, mistaken inferences, and confusion of thought." Their method, with intelligent, conscientious hard work, would certainly yield "monographs of scientific value" (xv). Whether any new generalization applicable to other facts would be discovered was still a question:

> Whether ... they will discover any new scientific law will depend on the possession of a somewhat rare combination of insight and inventiveness, with the capacity for prolonged and intense reasoning. When such a generalization is arrived at, it provides a new field of work for the ensuing generation, whose task it is, by an incessant testing of this "order of thought" by comparison with the "order of things," to extend, limit, and qualify the first imperfect statement of the law. By these means alone, whether in sociology or any other sphere of human inquiry, does mankind enter into possession of that body of organized knowledge which is termed science. (xv-xvi)

The preface made the traditional plea for practical application. "A knowledge of social facts and laws is indispensable for any intelligent and deliberate human action. The whole of social life, the entire structure and functioning of society, consists of human intervention" (xvi). Whether we like it or not, success or failure in political decisions depends on scientific knowledge of the facts of a problem and their causal connections.

> Perfect wisdom we can never attain, in sociology or in any other science; but this does not absolve us from using, in our action, the most authoritative exposition, for the time being, of what is known. (xvii)

Yet without better funding it was impossible to make progress. The total money available for sociological investigation in London, then the wealthiest city in the world, was less than £100 per year; more was needed.

The papers included in *Methods of Social Study* deal with particular, practical aspects of doing sociology. Beginners at social investigation often fail to make discoveries because they do not "realize that a good half of most research work consists in an attempt to prove yourself wrong" (33-34). Intellectual honesty was the "hardest and most essential of the habits" required (34). Intellectual curiosity and minute scrutiny would to the greatest possible extent put one's own bias "out of gear" (42). One must be eager to transcend orthodoxy. Yet "the human mind is terribly apt to perceive what it looks for" and to be blind to what it does not want to see (61). While eliminating bias it was essential to have a sympathetic understanding of other people. A "sensitive mind and broad human sympathies, coupled with width and variety of experience" were all needed (48).

While Karl Marx in 1880 devised a questionnaire for French workers, with 101 hopelessly complex questions, and had twenty-five thousand copies printed, Beatrice and Sidney Webb made their questionnaire mistake on a more modest scale. They had a thousand copies printed, of 120 impossible questions, which they sent to trade union officials. The report of this fiasco confides that they had tried to save themselves trouble. But it was "too frontal an attack," too many questions putting officials on the spot (68). The result was massive nonresponse. The Webbs, however, unlike Marx, were at the beginning of their research careers and did learn from the experience. They conducted interviews of officials for material which could be related verbally, attended meetings to see how decisions were made, and went through the written documents themselves. They learned how to combine historical records with personal observation.

Contrary to the contention that a hard-nosed methodology limited subjects of study to trivial questions, the Webb team took on questions as large as the welfare state, local government, and the need for socialism. They believed that though complete prediction of the future was impossible, enough could be learned for purposes of practical application. Conceptually, they were careful in their claims. "The more modest sociological investigator does not find himself talking about laws of nature, and he is cautious even about making sweeping generalizations" (219). They held that the demonstration of probability was all that was possible.

> Few and far between or at least very tentative and general, are the generalizations which the sociologist is yet warranted in dogmatically making as to causation. (233)

Sociologists were limited to tendencies with only a low order of predictability. Yet in these respects sociologists were no worse off than were biologists a century earlier (219).

The Webbs were thoroughly committed to empiricism in all the senses of unity of method with natural science, objectivity as a goal, despite all the pressures of bias, and the impossibility of deriving the "ought" from the "is." Beatrice Webb had early become committed to quantification as an essential check on being carried away by unusual cases. Both Webbs insisted on the integration of qualitative with quantitative methods. Their vision of sociology was of a collective enterprise. All the while their concern was with the great social questions of their day, and with research for application. All of this they taught to the next generation of social scientists in Britain, especially through the London School of Economics.

Beatrice Webb provides in her own life an excellent example of the results of holding to the principle of objectivity and learning from external results. She began her work as a social investigator with the biases of the individualistic, laissez-faire ethic. Her first publication, in 1886, even refers to the "unemployed" in quotation marks, with sarcasm.[88] Yet she learned from data, as did her cousin Charlie (Booth) in *Life and Labour of the People in London*. He became only a red Tory, she became a life-long socialist. She remained adamantly convinced of the need for ethical neutrality in scientific work, yet she devoted her life to the socialist cause, consistent with her values.

Jane Addams (1860-1935)

Jane Addams was born in Cedarville, Illinois, to a wealthy family, inheritance from whom later helped to found Hull House. She was one of the first American women to obtain a university degree. She then studied medicine for a year while still unsure of her vocation. Like so many of the women in this series, she spent some time and more anguish finding a useful place in society. She read, travelled, and struggled over religious belief. At school she resisted pressure for evangelical conversion. Her father's background was Quaker, but he did not practise. Eventually she figured out, as she put it, how to express the spirit of Jesus, share the lives of the poor, and do real social service without propaganda. A visit to Toynbee Hall in London in 1888 helped resolve things. Addams opened Hull House the following year in an immigrant area of Chicago. She remained there for the rest of her life with a core group of women residents, many volunteer helpers, and a constant stream of visitors, from the destitute and desperate to the prominent and powerful.

Hull House gave classes in all kinds of practical matters. The women residents put on cultural evenings, inviting the neighbours. They encouraged and assisted in union organization. As well as the popular Plato Club at Hull House there was a social science club. A branch of the American Socialist

[88] Beatrice Potter, "A Lady's View of the Unemployed," *Pall Mall Gazette*, February 18, 1886, 11.

Jane Addams, from a centennial edition of Peace and Bread in Time of War

Jane
Addams
Party held its meetings there. The first lobbying the women of the settlement did was for legislation banning child labour, on which they were successful. Addams herself was a much-sought speaker. She went on the Chautauqua circuit as well as speaking for the Progressive Party and for women's suffrage. She published a great deal on social policy, a selection of which is available in The Social Thought of Jane Addams, edited by Christopher Lasch. She published on juvenile delinquency (Philanthropy and Social Progress) and on prostitution (A New Conscience and an Ancient Evil). She was elected to the Chicago school board. Addams did some teaching in the Department of Sociology at the University of Chicago but declined the offer of a regular position. The head of that department, Albion Small, who was also the founding editor of the American Journal of Sociology, was a Hull House supporter. Addams wrote for the journal, then an outlet for radical social policy discussion as well as sociology proper. She continued to travel and learn from it. She visited Tolstoy, who reproached her both for her dress style and for being an absentee land owner.

Addams served as the president of the Women's International League for Peace and Freedom from its founding in 1915 until her death in 1935. She led the American delegation to the International Women's Congress at the Hague in 1915, then delivered its resolutions to President Woodrow Wilson upon her return. The resolutions (reprinted as an appendix in Women at the Hague) set out detailed recommendations for negotiation and conciliation as means of dispute resolution, and include many measures that went unimplemented until the United Nations was established after World War II. Addams also attended the second great women's peace conference, in 1919 in Zurich, held at the same time as the official Paris Peace Conference. She published Newer Ideals of Peace in 1906 and Peace and Bread in Time of War in 1922. Addams received many honourary degrees as well as the Nobel Peace Prize (1931). She gave her share of the Nobel Prize to the league for its international work. At her request her grave is inscribed "Jane Addams of Hull-House and the Women's International League for Peace and Freedom."

On Addams see Mary Jo Deegan, Jane Addams and the Men of the Chicago School and Women in Sociology; Daniel Levine, Jane Addams and the Liberal Tradition; John C. Farrell, Beloved Lady; Allen F. Davis, American Heroine; and Addams's own memoirs, Twenty Years at Hull House and The Second Twenty Years at Hull-House.

Jane Addams has for years been known as "Saint Jane," founder of the American settlement house movement and the profession of social work, and winner of the Nobel Peace Prize. She is recognized for her leadership of the women's peace movement, support for organized labour, and advocacy of the American welfare state. That she and her women colleagues at Hull House pioneered the quantitative methods of the "Chicago school of sociology" remains little known. Mary Jo Deegan in *Jane Addams and the Men of the Chicago School* gives her subject her rightful place in methodological history. Regarding *Hull-House Maps and Papers*, edited by Addams in 1895, Deegan concluded:

> Despite its preeminence, this scholarly classic has been erased from the annals of sociology. (55)

Hull-House Maps and Papers is in the direct line of succession from Booth's survey of poverty in East London, the first results of which had just been published when Addams was visiting England. Hull House was a feminist version of the English, male, university settlements, more practical and less religious, more co-operative and less hierarchical in style. It served as a base for many other women social scientists and activists in the various reform causes of the time.

Addams organized the settlement house's first research project a few years after its opening. The approach drew on the quantitative work of the Booth survey but included a more radical interpretation and considerable concern for remedy. While there is little practical advice in the many volumes of *Life and Labour of the People in London*, the single volume of *Hull-House Maps and Papers* gave advice in nearly every article. The title page describes the work as "a presentation of nationalities and wages in a congested district of Chicago together with comments and essays on problems growing out of the social conditions." It was the work of "Residents of Hull-House, a social settlement." Addams wrote a brief preface, which modestly stated the study's goals. The women offered no "exhaustive treatises, but recorded observations which may possibly be of value, because they are immediate, and the result of long acquaintance" (1). All the writers themselves lived in the area. An article on the method described the procedures for data collection, which took place in 1893. The work was part of a special investigation of slums undertaken by the United States government. The authors hoped that Chicago would take warning from their findings, "helping toward an improvement in the sanitation of the neighborhood, and toward an introduction of some degree of comfort."[89]

Similarity in aim with Booth's study was acknowledged, but the women claimed "greater minuteness" for their work, "a photographic reproduction of Chicago's poorest quarters." Their study was "an illustration of a method of research," painstaking in its method of inquiry (11). Houses were visited and reports on conditions corroborated by others. The "impertinence" of the questions would have been unpardonable:

> were it not for the conviction that the public conscience when roused
> must demand better surroundings for the most inert and long-suffer-
> ing citizens of the commonwealth. Merely to state symptoms and
> go no farther would be idle; but to state symptoms in order to ascer-
> tain the nature of disease, and apply, it may be, its cure, is not only
> scientific, but in the highest sense humanitarian. (14)

Coloured maps were included to show the nationalities of the residents, wages, and employment. Inclusion of the maps was costly, and Addams in the end waived royalties rather than let the publisher cut them. The book itself quickly sold out and was not reprinted until 1970.

Florence Kelley (1859-1932), a Marxist, translator of Engels, and government factory inspector, wrote the chapter on the "sweating system." Her article on child workers, co-authored with Alzina Stevens, was one of the most sophisticated in method. Graphs documented the health implications of bad working conditions. Charts compared the size and weight of children who worked in factories with those who did not. A male contributor, Charles Zeublin, described the Chicago ghetto. Julia Lathrop's article, "Cook County Charities," revealed corruption and inefficiency in the management of municipal charitable work, neither the first nor the last exposé of this subject. Addams later wrote a biography of Lathrop, first head of the United States Children's Bureau. An article by Ellen Gates Starr, "Art and Labor," drew on John Ruskin and William Morris to argue for the broader cultural needs of ordinary people.

Addams's chapter on unions related them to the settlement house philosophy. In order both to understand and to better the life of the poor it was necessary to share that life, by living in the area. She conceded the English origins of the settlement house concept but rejected the *noblesse oblige* component. Instead of the rich protecting

---

[89] Agnes Sinclair Holbrook, "Map Notes and Comments," in Addams, *Hull-House Maps and Papers*, 11.

the poor, as in the vision of Thomas Carlyle, workers' rights had to be recognized (192). Hull House itself lent its premises for union organizing meetings.

Addams's first article in the *American Journal of Sociology*, in its first volume, was a comparison of women's experience in domestic service and factory jobs. Short and anecdotal, "A Belated Industry" was based on interviews with women on return from work assignments from the Women's Labor Bureau. The observations are interesting, indicating an effort to understand conditions of work broadly as well as the specifics of wages and hours. The piece ends with a series of questions about the organization of work, the isolation of women working in the home — their own or someone else's — and the hope that women will themselves design better alternatives.

Women's Studies

The origin of women's studies is too large a topic to be treated here except to show the overlap and parallel trends with the development of empiricist methods in the social sciences generally. In both cases the origins date back much earlier than is normally thought. The early contributors to women's studies themselves used empirical methods, citing facts and arguing their objectivity against the biases and prejudice of the prevailing male literature. The enormous increase in the amount of ethnological data in the latter part of the nineteenth century gave them material with which to work. A number of historians and anthropologists were publishing new theories and interpretations of early human society. Some posited an original "matriarchy" or "mother-right" which preceded patriarchy. J.J. Bachofen's *Mother Right* dates back to 1861. Lewis Morgan's *Ancient Society* (1877), Friedrich Engels's *Origin of the Family, Private Property, and the State* (1884), and August Bebel's *Woman under Socialism* (1893) all challenged the reigning orthodoxy of the patriarchal family as the norm. Women were now to learn that the period before patriarchy not only was *not* one of savagery from which the patriarchal family rescued them, but was a time of superior power and respect.

Antoinette Brown Blackwell (1825-1921) published her influential *The Sexes throughout Nature* in 1875. It argued the equal overall contribution of the female in all species, conceding differences in specifics.

> It is the central theory of the present volume that the sexes in each
> species of beings compared upon the same plane, from the lowest

to the highest, are always true equivalents — equals but not identicals
in development and in relative amounts of all normal force. (11)

Thus sex and gender differences could be admitted without any accompanying concession of inferiority, a necessary element for the emergence of women's studies.

Matilda Joslyn Gage (1826-1898), as well as being a leader in and historian of the American suffrage movement, was prominent in the rethinking we can now identify as women's studies. In her first speech at a women's rights convention, in 1851, she cited the impressive accomplishments of women against all obstacles. She was only twenty-six at the time, but waited until she was, as Mary Daly put it in a recent foreword, a "crone" of sixty-seven when she published her research as *Woman, Church and State* in 1893. Gage took part in the anti-slavery movement as well, harbouring fugitives in her home. She supported rights for native people and condemned the breaking of treaties with them.

Gage was scathing in her analysis of institutional religion as the means of depriving women of their liberty. Original sin was not a Biblical concept, she argued, but had been invented by Augustine centuries later. She documented the horrors of witch burnings, noting the confiscation of the victim's wealth on her death. She described the male/female relation in marriage as that of capitalist/labourer. She pointed out the sex-determined differences in medicine and health care, blaming male medicine for high rates of mortality and crediting women with a superior approach. She discussed the crime of rape.

Woman, Church and State was dedicated to "all Christian women and men of whatever creed or name who, bound by Church or State, have not dared to think for themselves." She promised an exposé of how Christianity restricted women from the greater respect and power they had enjoyed in ancient nations.

> If in so doing it helps to show man's unwarranted usurpation over woman's religious and civil rights, and the very great difference between true religion and theology, this book will not have been written in vain. (11-12)

The Christian teaching that woman was not created equal with man was the "most grievous wrong" ever inflicted upon woman and led to her being denied her rightful place in both church and state.

> The most stupendous system of organized robbery has been that of the church towards woman, a robbery that has not only taken

her self-respect but all rights of person, the fruits of her own industry, her opportunities of education, the exercise of her own judgement, her own conscience, her own will. (327)

(Elizabeth Cady Stanton continued the attack with her own decidedly feminist interpretation of Scripture, *The Woman's Bible*, published in 1895.)

British historian **Lina Eckenstein**, in *Woman under Monasticism* (1896), not only argued the independence of women before the patriarchal family was established but showed how early convents were holdovers from that period. The early nuns were women wanting to avoid marriage and the control of a man. Only after some centuries of struggle were convents subjected to the control of the male hierarchy. Classical anthropologist Jane Harrison's *Prolegomena to the Study of Greek Religion* (1903) is another excellent example of a new consciousness being brought to bear on an old subject. Olive Schreiner's *Woman and Labor* (1911) offered a radical analysis of the division of labour by sex and provoked thought and action on women's issues.

Charlotte Perkins Gilman (1860-1935) as well as her influential *Women and Economics* (1898), published poetry, a utopian novel, *Herland* (1915), other fiction, an autobiography, and a semi-fictional account of her nervous breakdown, *The Yellow Wallpaper* (1892). The chief focus of analysis in her widely read and translated book on economics was the division of labour by sex. Gilman's *His Religion and Hers* (1923), is yet another feminist critique of male-dominated religion, although much more timid than Gage's *Woman, Church and State*.

Herland was a feminist, egalitarian, socialist utopia, inhabited only by women, who enjoyed a high standard of living, suffered no crime or illness, reproduced by parthenogenesis, and controlled population growth through will power. There was no nuclear family but all women acted collectively as mothers. Better than "a room of one's own," each woman had two rooms for her use. Herlanders were vegetarians, for they had discovered that cattle and other animals required too much food-growing space. The description of the country gave Gilman the opportunity to explore whether the basis for sex differences was biological or social, to consider which traits were truly human and which the product of a male-dominated culture. *Herland* was not the first feminist utopian novel — Sarah Scott's *Millennium Hall* preceded it by a century and a half. But its contrasts were more radical and it made greater use of the utopian form.

The German feminist leader and writer, **Marianne Weber (1870-**

1954), published several books on women's rights, including *Ehefrau und Mutter in der Rechtsentwicklung* (1907) on the period prior to the establishment of the patriarchal family. Max Weber cited this work in his *General Economic History* as a good source on "the present state of knowledge, and in general free from bias" (372). This is high praise from the high priest of objectivity in the social sciences. And he should know, for he helped proof read the manuscript. Marianne Weber also published on the participation of women in science.[90] She argued for the incorporation of women's particular gifts in the historical, cultural sciences, pointing out the omissions which resulted when cultural development is seen exclusively through the eyes of one half of humanity (5).

By the beginning of the twentieth century women's issues and consciousness were appearing in regular sociology texts and journals by major authors. Lester Ward's *Pure Sociology* (1903) included a chapter on "gynaecocentric theory." Thorstein Veblen wrote on women's issues. The *American Journal of Sociology* often covered women's issues, as it did other causes.[91] Durkheim's *Année Sociologique* frequently reviewed books both on the status of women and the challenge to the theory of original patriarchy. Durkheim himself reviewed Marianne Weber's book, in somewhat condescending terms, but with respect for her knowledge of the literature.[92] This literature cannot be reviewed here, but its impressive size, scope, and quality, must be acknowledged.[93]

Both the quantity of women's early work in the social sciences and its distinctiveness raise disturbing questions as we arrive at the next and last chapter. I will leave the questions as to why and how it was lost for so long to the sociologists of knowledge to explore. Instead we will return to the methodological debate of the first chapter, ponder the impact of the recovery of these women's work, and consider the prospects of either another disappearance or incorporation of the women founders of the social sciences into the permanent literature.

---

[90] Marianne Weber, "Die Beteiligung der Frau an der Wissenschaft" (1904), is included in her collection, *Frauenfragen und Frauengedanken*.

[91] The *American Journal of Sociology* in 1899 published the early work of the Canadian-born Annie Marion MacLean, "Factory Legislation for Women in Canada." MacLean (c. 1870-1934) did an American doctorate—the first at the University of Chicago by a woman—and made her career in the United States. See Mary Jo Deegan, *Women in Sociology*, on MacLean.

[92] Durkheim, review, *Ehefrau und Mutter*, *Année Sociologique*, 1906-09: 363-69.

[93] See Mary Jo Deegan, *Women in Sociology*, and Beverly E. Golemba, *Lesser-Known Women*, for other late nineteenth-century contributions.

Conclusions

It should be clear from the examples discussed that the contribution
of nineteenth-century women to the developing methodology of the
social sciences was prodigious. From the earlier, more ancillary roles
of women — defending the ideas of male methodologists and applying
their ideas — now we see major original works by women. Martineau's
How to Observe Morals and Manners was the first book on the practicalities of conducting social science research. Florence Nightingale's
study of mortality in childbirth was a powerful example of the application of the new statistical techniques to social data on one of the great
social problems of the day. Beatrice Webb pioneered participant observation research in sociology, showing how it can be integrated with
quantitative methods. Her methodological innovations, quite apart from
the substantive social analysis, predate the work of Durkheim and
Weber. Jane Addams demonstrated the quantitative methods later identified as those of the Chicago School. There were highly original, feminist challenges to Biblical interpretation. Women theorists joined with
men to overturn the theory of an original, ubiquitous patriarchy.

The numerous examples above refute assertions of a necessary
connection between empiricism and political conservatism. Radical
women as extreme as Frances Wright and Flora Tristan deliberately
chose empiricist methodology. Beatrice Webb became a socialist *after*
and *through* her empirical research. The progressive Jane Addams was
equally committed to empiricist methodology in general, with quantification as a component part. Harriet Martineau and Florence Nightingale were not at the progressive end of the political spectrum, but they
qualified their laissez-faire liberalism in significant ways. Both supported
a significant role for government in the running of society. Harriet
Taylor Mill similarly rejected much of the conventional political economy of the day. As well she moved John Stuart Mill to the left in his
political convictions. All of these examples make mockery of the charge
of a necessary connection between empiricism and support for the
status quo either in general or for traditional sex roles more particularly.

These nineteenth-century women methodologists continued to
support the Enlightenment ideals of rationalism and the sense of self.
They also had a strong sense of autonomy and, if this is a fault, they
must be judged guilty. Nightingale, quite apart from saving lives in the
Crimea, saw many of the reforms she proposed actually implemented.
Martineau could also look back to real accomplishments from acting
on her belief in an autonomous self. Flora Tristan chose a different

road, the organization of workers to press their claims, and she died too early to judge her success. Yet can we criticize her for acting on a "false doctrine" of the Enlightenment? Harriet Taylor Mill's work — both her own papers on women and the larger joint work with her husband — also deserves credit. She never lived to see women's suffrage or access to education and jobs, but she helped make all of these things eventually happen. Instead of condemning these women for their naïveté for reflecting their own times, let us consider their achievements in advancing the causes of women, workers, humanity in general and, as a means to all those ends, the methodology of the social sciences.

Chapter 5

WOMEN
AS MISSING PERSONS
IN METHODOLOGY

he three preceding chapters have demonstrated the important and sometimes even central contributions of women to the development of the methodology of the social sciences, its defence against opposition, application in actual research, and the evolution of key concepts. Women's significant contributions appeared as early as the rediscovery of scepticism in the late sixteenth century, and continued through the emergence of empiricism in the seventeenth century, the eighteenth-century Enlightenment, and the nineteenth-century development of rigorous techniques of data collection and analysis. Indeed, although that is not our subject here, women took part in the ancient Greek schools and in medieval learning. Thanks to recent women's studies at universities and colleges, many of these pioneer contributors have been rediscovered. Critical editions of their works have appeared, in some cases for the first time. Collected works and letters have been published. New biographies, some of high standard, are now available. At the very least reprints have made long out-of-print works accessible.

Welcome as the recovery of this lost or ignored material is, the question naturally arises as to whether or not it will all again disappear. We owe great thanks to the scholars responsible for the recovery and to the women's studies programs, centres, and networks which prompted it. Without them, it seems perfectly obvious, little of this recovery would have happened. Yet it is less clear that these institutions will suffice to prevent another disappearance. News of the recovery has not travelled far and some feminists, as evidenced in the ongoing attack on empiricism, do not want it to. It would be convenient for many scholars of both sexes to have the women founders of the social sciences remain on the missing persons' list.

Still Missing

This new scholarship and publication has had, in fact, scant impact on the mainstream history of ideas. Little of the material presented in *The Women Founders* has yet made it into regular university teaching. Despite more than two decades of courses and colloquia, programs and publications, university courses and texts on the foundations of sociology remain histories of male contributions. David Westby's *Growth of Sociological Theory*, published as recently as 1991, for example, lists not one woman in the table of contents, although precursors are named dating back to the Roman period. The men discussed, in alphabetical order, are Augustine, Cooley, Comte, Durkheim, Engels, Feuerbach, Hegel, Herder, Hobbes, Marx, G.H. Mead, Rousseau, Saint-Simon, Thomas, Weber, Znaniecki. Jane Addams is mentioned in relation to Hull House, but the fact that she and her women colleagues did research and wrote on methodological issues is not. Harriet Martineau appears only as the translator of Comte.

Irving Zeitlin in the fourth edition of his *Ideology and the Development of Sociological Theory* (1990), includes seven pages, out of a total 324, on Mary Wollstonecraft. This denotes progress, since the first edition of the same work, in 1968, discussed no women at all. Still, the analysis leaves much to be desired. Catharine Macaulay (both names misspelled) is described as having "anticipated and most directly influenced Wollstonecraft's *Rights of Woman*." The author allows that "most of the principles" expounded in the *Rights of Woman* are to be found in Macauley's work" which, nonetheless, is not discussed (40). Neither Wollstonecraft nor Macaulay is mentioned as a contributor to methodology or social and political theory generally. Zeitlin's text is not atypical, except perhaps that it is better than most in that it includes *one* woman on *one* aspect of theory rather than none at all. By comparison, the first edition of Raison's *Founding Fathers of Social Science*, in 1969, had twenty-three men along with Beatrice and Sidney Webb, while the second edition, of 1979, added six more men and no women.

Another text has a new section on feminism in its second edition, 1988. George Ritzer's *Sociological Theory* accords forty-three pages to feminist theory, recognizing the work of Jessie Bernard and other contemporary writers. Men only, however, appear in the coverage of the entire period up to the present! It would seem that no women contributed to the early development of theory. Four men and no women rate whole chapters, twenty-one men but only two women brief biographies. None of the women discussed in *The Women Founders of the Social Sciences* is analyzed in *Sociological Theory*.

Nor have women writers on the discipline been keen to include women contributors. R.A. Sydie's *Natural Women, Cultured Men* proclaims, in its subtitle, to *A Feminist Perspective on Sociological Theory*. It contains an excellent discussion of the issues of patriarchy and ideology, delivering on its promise. Yet, while much space is given to Durkheim, Weber, Marx, and Engels, no space is given to their women contemporaries and predecessors. The reader might conclude that only men had written on the subject. Anna Yeatman's "Women, Domestic Life and Sociology" sets out three phases of sociology: classical, the "great founding fathers" (Weber, Durkheim, Simmel, and Tönnies), and post-Parsonian.[1] The ruling paradigms of social science are accused of having a "masculinist bias" for excluding domestic life from analysis. The author, however, entirely omits women contributors to sociology, even those who incorporated domestic issues in their work.

Roslyn Bologh's analysis of Weber, *Love or Greatness: Max Weber and Masculine Thinking — A Feminist Inquiry*, fails to consider the intellectual contribution of relevant women. Marianne Weber is mentioned only in relation to her husband's work, on which she had much to say. That she also shared his interest in methodology is nowhere stated. (She had published a book on the relationship between Marxism and German idealism in 1900, before Max Weber published his famous papers on methodology in 1903-04.) Nor would one realize that Marianne Weber had published on such a central issue of feminist inquiry as early matriarchy. She dedicated her *Ehefrau und Mutter in der Rechtsentwicklung* to her mother-in-law, Helene Weber, whom Bologh also treats negatively.

Women theorists still discuss Rousseau with little or no recognition of the women critics who immediately perceived and denounced his sexism. J.S. Mill is commonly referred to, by women commentators as by men, as if he had worked alone. He deserves the deepest appreciation of feminists, scholars or not, but so does Harriet Taylor, the joint author of his most enduring works and the person who turned his youthful sentimental concern about injustices to women into a life-long and intelligent commitment.

James Terry, in a 1983 article, "Bringing Women ... in" argued for the inclusion of women in courses on classical sociological theory. He explained how he incorporated two in his own courses: Harriet

---

[1] In Carole Pateman and Elizabeth Gross, *Feminist Challenges*.

Martineau and Charlotte Perkins Gilman. Yet it seems that his advice, which was accompanied with information on available sources and references, has not been acted on.

The attack on empiricism in the name of feminism, discussed in chapter 1, continues in full force. Courses on women and knowledge treat the feminist critique of empiricism, but not women's positive contribution to its theory and practice. This raises the prospect of new generations of feminist scholars' rejecting empiricism, unaware that it was, for centuries, the chosen methodology of leaders of the women's movement. Young scholars continue to be warned off quantified methods as inconsistent with feminist principles, an approach which excludes the use of such methods as a check on qualitative findings, as argued by Beatrice Webb.

More recent experience only confirms the sense of Webb's point. In the equal pay struggles of the early 1970s, for example, it was essential to document the extent of underpayment for women's work, then at sixty cents to the dollar for full-time employment. Only when it was convincingly shown that low wages and salaries were the common lot of women, and not unhappy exceptions, would legislators bring in equal pay for work of equal value, and later pay equity programs. I do not believe that personal stories alone, the preferred method for many contemporary feminists, would have had remotely the same impact. Nor would the problems of wife beating and child sexual abuse have begun to be taken seriously without the hard documentation of their extent. Quantification, admittedly, can become fetishism and there is no guarantee of validity or wisdom through the use of any particular quantitative technique. Yet we really cannot do without some judgments of scale. What "qualitative" work entirely excludes estimates of more or less, higher or lower proportions, stronger or weaker tendencies?

Institutions to promote women's studies remain crucial to prevent another slide into oblivion. The problem, after all, is not that the women founders of the social sciences failed to publish but that the scholarly world failed to recognize their work. All the women discussed in this book were published, some even in numerous editions. (The few instances of unpublished journals and letters were not of key works. There may be instances of good manuscripts not being published at all but, if so, they and their authors remain unknown.) Men of comparable achievements had schools formed after them, graduate students to continue their work, and societies to promote it. The women at best had a son, daughter, or other relative who, for some time, published some work. (Mary Wortley Montagu's daughter, alas, burned material, a fate shared by some male methodologists as well.)

Universities did little to preserve, still less to promote, the scholarly work of women, even after women gained access to them in the late nineteenth and early twentieth centuries. Until and unless universities demonstrate that they have changed in this respect we will have to rely on what niches women have created in women's studies programs, centres, chairs, and publishing series.

Grateful as one must be for any work of recovery and publication, it remains disturbing that the presentation of these women contributors has so often been negative. Some of the most offensive biographies have been excluded here for their lack of scholarly content. Other sources have been included because they had some good content, if juxtaposed with churlish remarks, innuendo, and gratuitous insults. For example:

- a biography of Mme Roland entitled *A Lady who Loved Herself,* the last chapter of which, on Roland's death by guillotine, is sarcastically entitled "The perfect ending";[2]
- an article on Mary Hays, in which she is referred to in places as "Mary," elsewhere as "the very plain Miss Hays;"[3]
- a tract on Catharine Macaulay which, although entitled "The Female Patriot," discusses her love life;
- a biography of Mary Wollstonecraft, entitled *This Shining Woman: Mary Wollstonecraft Godwin,* nonetheless describes her as "not a woman of very brilliant gifts";[4]
- a biography of Mme de Staël, which describes her as "spoiled," "a thorough exhibitionist," made "vain and dictatorial, intoxicated with an exaggerated confidence in her own importance" by the "constant flattery" of literary men;[5]

Nor is this prejudice from the past, corrected in our day. A biography of Mme de Staël as recent as 1985 dismisses her contribution with: "She was not strictly speaking an original thinker," but popularized ideas which were "in the air."[6]

Key sources on a writer are sometimes negative. The most thorough coverage of the Harriet Taylor/J.S. Mill collaboration, for example, is

[2] Catharine Young, *A Lady who Loved Herself. The Life of Madame Roland,* 301.
[3] Burton R. Pollin, "Mary Hays on Women," 276.
[4] George R. Preedy, *This Shining Woman,* 13.
[5] Richmond Laurier Hawkins, "Madame de Staël and the United States," 61-62.
[6] Renée Winegarten, *Mme de Staël,* 115.

Hayek's *John Stuart Mill and Harriet Taylor*. The discussion is never rude, but the author, in my judgment, seriously undervalued Taylor Mill's ability. The result of this tendency is that, simply to gain information on a woman scholar, the reader will also pick up assessments of her that are ungenerous at best, demeaning at worst.

A comparatively minor complaint is the recent trend in biographies and selections of letters to focus on the woman's inner conflicts or those with close family members. Psychological turmoil, passion, intimacy, unrequited love, and relationships with one's mother are all, undoubtedly, of interest and importance. Still one can regret that such glaring gaps remain on the mature, scholarly work and professional relationships of these women. Nightingale and Martineau, for example, collaborated both as activists/lobbyists on their causes and as social scientists. How they, and theorists like Webb, arrived at their methodology and practised their craft similarly deserves more comprehensive treatment.

The lack of bibliographies on the women founders, similarly, remains acute. Without adequate bibliographies the extent and diversity of the person's work is simply not obvious or has to be rediscovered by each new reader. With adequate bibliographies, of course, the lack of collected works will become even more evident. Mary Wollstonecraft is the only woman methodologist to be well served in this respect. For all the others, the dedicated reader will find important works effectively unavailable — still in manuscript archives, out-of-print works, or scarce, obscure journals. By contrast, the feminist critics of the social sciences are widely available in recent books and journals, often accessible by computer search. University presses surely have an obligation to act, as do scholarly granting agencies which have generously subsidized the collected works of outstanding men theorists.

Candle Power and Enlightenment

Activists in reform movements often refer to the choice open to all of us as citizens: either to curse the darkness or light a candle to show the way. The same holds with regard to women and the creation of knowledge. Some feminists, and accordingly some courses and texts on "women and knowledge," lament the exclusion of women and bewail the barriers they face. Feminist postmodernists have been so busy decrying the faults of empiricism that they have scarcely noticed the significant role women played in its creation. Is this contribution of women to be recovered only to be dismissed as mistaken?

Many women did in fact contribute to the creation and shaping of empiricist methodology in the social sciences. They did this in the name of reason and the principles of the Enlightenment, believing that knowledge could be applied to make a better world. Their universalistic principles made them genuinely universal in their concerns, embracing all humanity, women and men, all classes and races. Some even went the next step to consider all sensitive creation in their universe. Yet the critics of the Enlightenment persist in viewing this universalism as imperialistic, as a penchant for generalization against all respect for specificity and context.

Many of the women proponents of the Enlightenment proved their commitment in actions as well as words. They did not just talk about discourse, but argued, persuaded, documented, and demonstrated the need for concrete reforms. They raised the most urgent issues of their day, and some even accomplished real changes in the world in which they lived. These were the women who worked for the vote, education, legal rights, marriage law reform, divorce, birth control, and women's control over birthing. They denounced the masculine appropriation of medicine and argued instead for health promotion. They demonstrated the harmful effects of child labour and saw age limits legislated for factory work. They argued against capital punishment and called for prison reform. They were members of the peace movement when few others were.

There are even some examples of environmental consciousness, scarce as that was in the period under review. Early in the eighteenth century Mary Astell and Damaris Masham both questioned the extreme anthropocentrism that then prevailed. Astell, tellingly, dealt with human/animal relationships in the same work that she dealt with husbandly dominion over the wife, *Reflections upon Marriage*. Mary Wollstonecraft, at the end of the eighteenth century, used the sympathy principle and moral sentiments theory to argue for kind treatment of animals. She also recognized the worth of the "lower" members of creation. Catharine Macaulay went much further, to appy the sympathy principle to human/animal relations in a comprehensive way. Much of her *Letters on Education* dealt with what we would now call environmental ethics.

The nineteenth century contributors did not pursue the ethical debate but did take up a range of environmental issues in the course of addressing social problems. Martineau, notably in her journalism, dealt extensively with agriculture, food, and water quality. Nightingale's analysis was always well grounded in physical reality, as was that of the whole "sanitary" movement; the word, of course, comes from the Latin for health, as does the familiar French *santé*. Nightingale's interests ranged from drainage at field hospitals to deforestation in India. The ecological feminist position, that adoption of "malestream" scientific methodology precludes environmental consciousness, simply does not hold when we examine the historical record.

Criticized as they have been for their white, middle-class preoccupations, it was these women who early perceived the evils of slavery and racism. Some joined the abolition movement, condemned racism, and called for just treatment of native people. This positive side of the universalism of the Enlightenment must be recognized. Whatever the privileges of their class, these methodologists were among the first to advocate public education for all, at public expense.

It is too easy for the living to criticize the dead for their failures of foresight. But look at the accomplishments of the women founders of the social sciences! Are they not sufficient to win them a hearing by the contemporary women's movement? Would that the critics of empiricism — and the rest of us — had as much to show for their/our lives! Should not the current critics have to confront these examples, instead of issuing blanket disapproval of their methodology and all endeavours at objectivity and generalization? Should not the critics of today have to give credit to their predecessors for some subtlety of thought, some sophistication in understanding that knowledge is always situated in a complex reality, and objectivity never completely realized? Must we continue to hear that these problems were not even *recognized* until phenomenology, ethnomethodology, or postmodernism came along?

If empiricism is necessarily against the feminist project for an equal and valid place in society, as has so often been alleged, how is it that so many committed women chose it as their methodology? If an anti-empiricist idealism is so much better a methodology, why is it that for centuries some of the worst misogyny came from it? This is not, of course, to argue that all idealists were anti-women or that all empiricists have been dedicated to gender equality. The pattern is never so neat. Yet the idealist separation of body and mind was, in fact, routinely used against women. Proponents of women's rights in past ages recognized this and acted accordingly. The male scholars most favourable to women's equality also rejected idealism in favour of a materialist-based empiricism.

For centuries women chose empiricist methodology because they found it empowering. Those who worked for equal rights in their period needed objective methods and real-world knowledge to fight the customs and prejudice against them. Cartesian doubt was turned to challenge all the preconceptions of male supremacy. Baconian empiricism gave women a tool with which to pose facts against received authority. Generations of women then used data in making their case for equality. They claimed objectivity against the subjectivity of male authorities and their theories.

Impact and Influence of Women on the Social Sciences

The question remains of the impact of these women contributors to the social sciences. To what extent can they be called the founders of their disciplines when their work was not so recognized? The extent of their actual influence on the development of the social sciences is at least an empirical question, although not one that can be explored in detail here. The fact that these women were little cited is inconclusive. Citing practices were haphazard even for male sources. Given the lower status of women and their complete absence from positions of academic power, one can only presume that contemporary and later male scholars would feel even less need to cite them or otherwise give them credit.

Nonetheless, I suspect that these women were used as positive sources by other scholars. These were all women who got into print when that was even more difficult for women than it is now; in some cases numerous editions and translations of their work were produced. Some of these women were well known in their day, prominent in society, and accepted in the highest political and literary circles. Their books evidently sold; presumably they were also read. That these women were later effectively lost to the history of the subject tells us more about how universities operate and why schools are needed than how well their work was actually known and used. Whether Durkheim read de Staël on suicide or Martineau on research methods I do not know. Nor do I know whether Marx or Engels read Tristan or Martineau, or if Weber read Webb. To explore such questions would require examination of the journals, early drafts, and correspondence of these male scholars. All this is, of course, feasible for those with the inclination and adequate research funding.

We might also speculate as to how different the social sciences might have been if these women had been paid more heed. If their examples had been emulated and their advice taken, in what ways would the social sciences be different? Short of admitting a distinctive women's

methodology, it is clear that these women show some distinct preferences or inclinations. Patterns are evident even if there is no full-fledged
school. Deegan covers a later period in her "sourcebook" *Women in
Sociology*, and her criteria for inclusion were different from mine, yet
she found divergence from patriarchal paradigms and dichotomies
similar to those I discovered (23). As well she documented a greater
emphasis on applied work among women, to argue no less than that
"female sociologists have shaped and changed the world" (1).

In epistemology proper the early women were consistent in disdain-
ing mind/body dualism, a persistent theme in the ongoing methodological debate among men. Even the one idealist discussed in this
history, Anne of Conway, qualified her idealism. Elisabeth of Bohemia,
Descartes's correspondent, early found the proposition that mind moved
body to be unlikely. The hierarchy of superior mind over inferior body
was routinely rejected. Instead, the women methodologists saw mind
and body as complementary. The things of the mind were no more
pure than those of the body, and the body could be a source of good
as easily as the mind. The arguments women philosophers have had
to wage since the emergence of the contemporary women's movement
would have been unnecessary if these earlier women had been heeded.
The debate would simply have been over a long time ago.

By and large these women methodologists had a more positive view
of human nature than certain prominent men. None was as negative
as Hobbes. Macaulay, notably, attacked Hobbes for his portrayal of the
war of all against all. She and other women theorists insisted on the
presence of positive bonds between parent and child from the earliest
forms of human society. Châtelet used Mandeville on early social bonds
precisely for his more positive approach.

The theological corollary here is the women's decided lack of interest in sin. A number explicitly noted the absence of the doctrine from
the Bible and blamed the concept on later, male, writers. Other women
conceded some place to sin but felt that it was all too much over-empha-
sized in men's theology. Consistent with this is the absence of the wrath
of God. The women found less to be wrathful about, and God seemed
little inclined to loss of temper. Wollstonecraft, a Christian believer, is
typical in considering that God would punish only for purposes of
reformation, as pain served to indicate disease.[7]

---

[7] Mary Wollstonecraft, *Vindication of the Rights of Woman*, 385. The book most
cited in this *Vindication* is the Bible.

These women had considerable confidence in the powers of reason. They varied considerably in their scepticism, but all saw a considerable place for reason. However impossible it might be to make statements about ultimate reality and predictions of the distant future, they believed that much useful learning could be achieved. None went as far as Hume or Descartes in their periods of doubt. Curiously, the one, minor, person to appear in this study who is identified as a Marxist, Florence Kelley, did not share Marx's view on the impossibility of intervening in history. She translated Engels' *Condition of the Working Class in England* and was decidedly left-wing in her politics. Yet she continued to work on social reform causes, including child labour and other factory legislation.

In political theory these women tended to moderation and compromise. Not one was as extreme as Rousseau or Marx. A number worked on finding a middle ground for reconciliation and rebuilding. De Staël is a major example in her proposals for the reintegration of royalists and learning from their tactics. Others who discussed the French Revolution, like Macaulay and Wollstonecraft, were relatively balanced in their treatment. They supported the ideals of the revolution while being cautious of the dangers. Roland, notably, was painfully accurate in her warnings of the consequences of violent upheavals. If few of these women were socialists they yet leaned to the left in their politics. None was an extreme conservative. Even those who had grown up with a laissez-faire ideology, as had Martineau and Webb, came to modify that position. Webb in fact became a socialist. All of these women rejected the "possessive individualism" which developed with and after Hobbes. Astell was a staunch royalist Tory, but her politics included a solidarity ethic. Nightingale lived at the height of influence of the political economy school but she, too, had a strong sense of community obligation to the destitute. Like Astell she saw this as a matter of right, not charity. Her unpublished work reveals contempt for social Darwinism.

These women theorists were in the sociological mainstream in another sense. None retreated into a biological determinism that made social action futile. They accepted biological variables as causal factors, but none considered them to be so influential as to overwhelm social factors. Webb specifically worked through and refuted Herbert Spencer's organic theory of society, which was the justification for his opposition to government intervention. If these women had been more prominent, in other words, there would have been less theory at the extreme contesting the scope for social action, and more in the middle, be it mildly reformist or advocating fundamental change.

However desirous these women were of fundamental, systemic change, they had little confidence in violent measures. There is no glorification of war in their writings. Several explicitly downplayed military values and warned of the consequences of war. Macaulay was eloquent here, Châtelet and de Staël clear and to the point. Wollstonecraft condemned the despotism of rank in the military as she condemned hierarchies of all kinds. Florence Nightingale, for all her years of involvement with the British Army, was never given to glamorizing war. She had seen all too well the horrors of battle, the stupidity of generals, and the drudgery and disease of barracks life. The mood conveyed in her writing, as in Martineau's, is that of how, practically, to minimize the suffering. Addams was a committed pacifist.

If these women contributors to the social sciences had had more influence, the applied side of the discipline would have developed more rapidly. Men founders of the social sciences were also committed to applied work, or so they often said, but these women actually provided cogent examples on key problems. Health promotion, preventive medicine, and what we call medical sociology would all have advanced more quickly had the work of Wortley Montagu, Nightingale, and Martineau been emulated. More and better data would have been collected, and such data would have been more imaginatively used. A question on health would have been included in the British census as early as 1861 if Nightingale had had her way. Evaluative studies on the expenditure of public funds, especially on new programs, would have become routine. Quantitative and qualitative work would have been well integrated if the advice variously of Martineau, Nightingale, and Webb had been acted on.

Last, but by no means an after thought, if these women had been treated as positive models, the move to inclusive, non-sexist language would have been well under way in the eighteenth century. Macaulay, Hays, de Staël, and the Mills all showed sensitivity to this issue. J.S. Mill considered the generic "he" a flaw in the English language. De Staël often referred to the "individual" when "l'homme" would have been more usual. Several of these women found ways to refer to God without resorting to a masculine form. Wortley Montagu and Hays used "humankind" in the eighteenth century, a usage that has still not caught on. Nor would this be only a cosmetic change, for if these women had been accepted as serious sources their values, concerns, and language would have been more accepted and exerted more influence in the discipline.

Whether or not sociology or the social sciences more generally would have been better as a result of women's influence is a matter of value judgment. My own answer is an unequivocal *yes*. Nor would I apologize for the greater emphasis on application. The social sciences were born in crisis, whether one dates them from the emergence of the term in the French Revolution, or back to Thucydides's *History of the Peloponnesian Wars* in the fifth century B.C. The great classical theorists were dedicated to studying societies in order to improve human life. The women discussed here followed this ancient tradition. The predilection for theory abstracted from the problems of social life is a more recent trend.

Methodology for Today

As a sociologist/activist/feminist/environmentalist I would argue that the kind of empiricism these women developed, including a healthy dose of scepticism, is still needed. That is, we should aim at general laws to explain a real, external world which exists and acts to some extent regardless of the attention we pay to it. Yes, we act on it and shape it, but we do not, fundamentally, *create* it. The knowledge we acquire must be treated as tentative and hypothetical, probable not certain. We should not be shy of admitting the values that motivate us. We are, rather, obliged to make them clear. We should recognize that the social sciences were born and developed in the many struggles to design and build a better world. If, as a result of our commitments, we are accused of being bleeding-heart liberals or naive radicals, so be it. We join a long history of the founders of the social sciences in both cases.

Let us be candid in asserting the nature and sources of the changes we seek. We should neither claim objective sources for our values, nor give up on objectivity as the goal in our search for knowledge. Nor should we hide behind ambiguous goals like "empowerment for social change," as if everyone could agree on what social change is desirable. In other words, let us accept, with Beatrice Webb and Max Weber, the fact/value distinction, admitting the subjectivity of our values while seeking objectivity for our facts. We remain aware that we will never wholly succeed at the latter. Ethical neutrality does not mean that we should be neutral about ethics, but that we do not claim scientific status for them, that we concede their origin in religion or philosophy.

Let us, by all reasonable means, improve the techniques we employ to conduct our research. Let us be modest in our claims, conscious of the limitations of our methods and our powers while trying to extend them. We should be open to learning from any relevant source. We must consider what level and kind of quantification is appropriate in any particular study, avoiding the extremes of both over use (in effect veiling our ignorance with numbers) and under use (which may result from number phobia).

Social scientists today have urgent responsibilities. To the age-old question of how to live more justly there is now the challenge of living more peaceably with our physical environment, the whole creation. Some of the early contributors to empiricist methodology even had something to say on this vital matter. A humble, sceptical empiricism is needed to face these issues. For social scientists with a feminist consciousness there are, in addition, all the concerns of gender equity and violence against women. On the positive side, there is the prospect of a women's perspective making distinctive contributions for the benefit of all humankind. For this we need the best skills, imagination, dedication, and all the examples we can draw on from the past. We have much to lose if the work of the women related here should again be excluded from the literature.

The empiricist tradition, like democracy, is easy to criticize for all the faults of its imperfect practitioners. Like democracy, however, it beats all the known alternatives. Empiricism has not lacked critics since its earliest beginnings in ancient Greece. Merely to criticize, however, is not to demonstrate the validity of any alternative approach. It is right and proper that criticism continue, but short-sighted to think that by rejecting empiricist methodology we will necessarily do better. The women founders of the social sciences chose empiricism because they found it to be serviceable. They demonstrated its usefulness in both their scholarly work and reform activities. The contemptuous, simplistic rejection of empiricism denies today's women their history. The women founders of the social sciences must not again be relegated to the ranks of missing persons. Their achievements deserve to be celebrated and their examples emulated for the sake of all humankind.

Bibliography

THE WOMEN
FOUNDERS OF THE
SOCIAL SCIENCES

(Original dates of publication in square brackets)
Primary Sources—the Methodologists

Addams, Jane, ed. *Hull-House Maps and Papers.* New York: Arno reprint, 1970 [1895].

—— *Twenty Years at Hull House.* New York: Macmillan, 1910.

—— *The Second Twenty Years at Hull-House.* New York: Macmillan, 1930.

—— *Peace and Bread in Time of War.* New York: Macmillan, 1922.

—— *Philanthropy and Social Progress.* Montclair, NJ: Patterson Smith, 1970.

—— *A New Conscience and an Ancient Evil.* New York: Arno reprint, 1972 [1912].

—— "A Belated Industry." *American Journal of Sociology* 1 (1895/96): 536-50.

—— *The Social Thought of Jane Addams.* ed. Christopher Lasch. Indianapolis: Bobbs-Merrill, 1965.

—— Emily G. Balch, and Alice Hamilton, eds. *Women at the Hague.* New York: Garland reprint, 1972 [1915].

Arnauld, Antoine, and Pierre Nicole. *Logique de Port-Royal.* Paris: Hachette, 1861 [1662].

Astell, Mary. *A Serious Proposal to the Ladies.* Source Book reprint of London: J.R., 1701 [1694].

—— *Some Reflections upon Marriage.* London: Parker: 1730 [1700].

—— *The Christian Religion.* London: Wilkins, 1705.

—— *Moderation truly stated.* London: Rich, Wilkin, 1704.

—— *An Enquiry after Wit*. London: Bateman, 1723 [1709].

—— *The Plain Dealer* no. 30 (July 1724): 239-48.

Blackwell, Antoinette Brown. *The Sexes throughout Nature*. New York: Putnam's Sons, 1875.

Booth, Charles, ed. *Life and Labour of the People in London*. 17 vols. London: Macmillan, 1902.

Butler, Josephine E. *Personal Reminiscences of a Great Crusade*. Westport, CT: Hyperion reprint, 1976 [1911].

Châtelet, Emilie du. Trans. Isaac Newton, *Principes mathématiques de la philosophie naturelle*. 2 vols. Paris: Desaint & Saillant, 1759.

—— *Institutions de physique*. Paris: Prault, 1740.

—— *Discours sur le bonheur*. ed. Robert Mauzi. Paris: Belles Lettres, 1961.

—— *Les lettres de la Marquise du Châtelet*. ed. Theodore Bestermann. 2 vols. Geneva: Institut et Musée Voltaire, 1958.

Condorcet, Jean Antoine Nicolas Caritat de. *Oeuvres*. ed. O'Connor and Arago. Paris: Didot, 1847- .

—— *Sketch for a Historical Picture of the Progress of the Human Mind*. trans. June Barraclough. London: Weidenfeld & Nicolson, 1955 [1795].

—— *Elémens du calcul des probabilités*. Paris: Royez, 1805.

—— "Report on the General Organization of Public Instruction." In *French Liberalism and Education in the Eighteenth Century*. ed. F. de la Fontainerie. New York: McGraw-Hill, 1932 [1792].

Condorcet, Sophie Grouchy de. Trans. *Théorie des sentimens moraux et huit lettres sur la sympathie*. 2 vols. 1798.

Conway, Anne. *The Principles of the Most Ancient and Modern Philosophy*. ed. Peter Lopston. The Hague: Nijhoff, 1982 [1690].

Defoe, Daniel. *An Essay upon Projects*. London: Cockerill, 1697.

Descartes, René. *The Philosophical Works of Descartes*. ed. Elizabeth Haldane and G.R.T. Ross. 2 vols. Cambridge: Cambridge University Press, 1973.

—— *Lettres sur la morale*. ed. Jacques Chevalier. Paris: Boivin, 1935.

—— *Oeuvres*. ed. Charles Adam and Paul Tannery. Paris: Vrin.

—— *Correspondance avec Elisabeth*. ed. Jean-Marie Beysrade and Michelle Beysrade. Paris: Flammarion, 1989.

Drake, Judith. (?) *An Essay in defence of the Female Sex*. New York: Source Book reprint, 1970 [1696].

Durkheim, Emile. *Les règles de la méthode sociologique*. Paris: Presses universitaires de France, 1947 [1895].

Eckenstein, Lina. *Woman Under Monasticism*. New York: Russell & Russell, 1963 [1896].

Engels, Friedrich. *The Condition of the Working Class in England in 1844*. Trans. Florence Kelley Wischnewetzky. New York: Lovell, 1887 [1845].

Evelyn, John. *Numismata*. London: Tooke, 1697.

Gage, Matilda Joslyn. *Woman, Church and State*. Watertown, MA: Persephone, 1980 [1893].

Gilman, Charlotte Perkins. *Women and Economics*. ed. Carl N. Degler. New York: Harper & Row, 1966 reprint [1898].

—— *The Yellow Wallpaper*. Old Westbury, NY: Feminist Press, 1973 [1892].

—— *Herland*. New York: Pantheon, 1979 [1915].

—— *His Religion and Hers*. Westport, CT: Hyperion, 1976 [1923].

—— *The Living of Charlotte Perkins Gilman*. New York: Arno reprint, 1972 [1935].

Gournay, Marie le Jars de. "Epistre de Mademoiselle de Gournay." In *Les essais de Michel de Montaigne*. Paris: Bechet & Lovis Baillaine, 1657 [1635].

—— *Fragments d'un discours féminin*. Jose Corti, 1988.

Harrison, Jane Ellen. *Prolegomena to the Study of Greek Religion*. 3d ed. Cambridge: Cambridge University Press, 1922 [1903].

Hays, Mary. *Letters and Essays, Moral and Miscellaneous*. New York: Garland reprint, 1974 [1793].

—— *Female Biography*. 6 vols. London: Phillips, 1803.

—— *Appeal to the Men of Great Britain in Behalf of Women*. New York: Garland reprint, 1974 [1798].

—— "The Talents of Women." *Monthly Magazine* (November 1796): 784-87.

—— "Essay on Insanity." *Monthly Magazine* (July 1800): 523-24.

—— "Mrs. Godwin." *Monthly Magazine* (September 1797): 232-33.

—— *The Victim of Prejudice*. Delmar, NY: Scholars' Facsimiles, 1990 [1799].

—— *Memoirs of Emma Courtney*. New York: Garland reprint, 1974 [1796].

Hutcheson, Francis. *A System of Moral Philosophy*. Hildesheim: Olms reprint, 1969 [1755].

—— *Collected Works*. 7 vols. Hildesheim: Olms reprint, 1971.

Locke, John. *An Essay concerning Human Understanding*. 2 vols. New York: Dover, 1959 [1690].

Macaulay, Catharine. *Letters on Education*. New York: Garland reprint, 1974 [1790].

—— *The History of England from the Accession of James I to that of the Brunswick Line*. 8 vols. London: Nourse, 1763-83.

—— *The History of England from the Revolution to the Present Time*. London: Cruttwell, 1778.

—— *Loose Remarks on Hobbes's Philosophical Rudiments*. London: Davies, 1767.

—— *Observations on the Reflections of the Rt. Hon. Edmund Burke on the Revolution in France*. London: Dilly, 1790.

—— *A Treatise on the Immutability of Moral Truth*. London: Hamilton, 1783.

—— *Observations on a Pamphlet entitled Thoughts on the Cause of the Present Discontents*. 5th ed. London: Dilly, 1770.

—— *An Address to the People of England, Scotland, and Ireland*. Bath: Cruttwell, 1775.

—— *A Modest Plea for the Property of Copy Right*. London: Dilly, 1774.

Malebranche, Nicolas. *La recherche de la vérité*. In *Oeuvres*, Paris: Vrin, 1962 [1674], vols. 1-3.

Martineau, Harriet. *How to Observe Morals and Manners*. London: Knight, 1838.

—— *Society in America*. ed. S.M. Lipset. Garden City, NY: Anchor, 1962 [1837].

—— *Illustrations of Political Economy.* 9 vols. London: Charles Fox, 1834.

—— *Miscellanies.* 2 vols. Boston: Hilliard, Gray, 1836.

—— ed. and trans. *The Positive Philosophy of Auguste Comte.* 2 vols. London: Kegan Paul, 1895.

—— *Autobiography.* 3 vols. London: Smith, Elder, 1877.

—— *History of the Thirty Years' Peace.* rev. ed. 4 vols. London: Bell, 1877.

—— *The Martyr Age of the United States of America.* Newcastle upon Tyne: Emancipation and Aborigines Protection Society, 1840 [1838].

—— *England and her Soldiers.* London: Smith, Elder, 1859.

—— "Results of the Census of 1851." *Westminster Review* no. 120 (April 1854): 171-89.

—— *Selected Letters.* ed. Valerie Sanders. Oxford: Clarendon, 1990.

Marx, Karl, and Friedrich Engels. *The German Ideology.* London: Lawrence & Wishart, 1938.

Masham, Damaris Cudworth. *A Discourse concerning the Love of God.* London: Awnsham & John Churchill, 1696.

—— *Occasional Thoughts in reference to a vertuous or Christian Life.* London: A. & J. Churchill, 1705.

Mill, John Stuart. *Collected Works of John Stuart Mill.* 33 vols. Toronto: University of Toronto Press, 1981-91.

Millar, John. *The Origin of the Distinction of Ranks.* In *John Millar of Glasgow.* ed. William C. Lehmann. Cambridge: University Press, 1960.

Montaigne, Michel de. *The Essays of Michel de Montaigne.* trans. Jacob Zeitlin. New York: Knopf, 1935 [1580].

More, Thomas. *Utopia.* trans. Robert N. Adams. New York: Norton, 1975 [1510].

Nightingale, Florence. Manuscripts: Florence Nightingale Papers, British Library Manuscripts; Wellcome Institute; and the Archives, British Library of Political and Economic Science.

—— *Introductory Notes on Lying-in Institutions.* London: Longmans, Green, 1871.

—— "A Note on Pauperism." *Fraser's Magazine* 79 (March 1869): 281-90.

—— "A Sub-'Note of Interrogation' I—What will be our religion in 1999?" *Fraser's Magazine* 8 (1873): 25-36.

—— "Answers to Written Questions." In *Report on the Sanitary Condition of the Army*. London: HMSO, 1858, 361-94.

—— *A Contribution to the Sanitary History of the British Army during the late war with Russia*. London: John Parker, 1859.

—— *Notes on Matters affecting the Health, Efficiency, and Hospital Administration of the British Army*. London: Harrison, 1858.

—— "Army Sanitation Administration, and its Reform under the late Lord Herbert." London: McCorqudale, 1862.

—— "Hospital Statistics" and "Letter from Miss Nightingale." Papers sent to the Second Section of the International Statistical Congress, London, 1860.

—— "A Missionary Health Officer in India." *Good Words* (August 1879): 565-73 and Part 2 "Nightingale Tracts," 635-40.

—— *Suggestions for Thought to Searchers after Religious Truth*. 3 vols. London: Eyre & Spottiswoode, 1860.

—— *Ever Yours, Florence Nightingale*. ed. Martha Vicinus and Bea Nergaard. Cambridge, MA: Harvard University Press, 1990.

—— *Cassandra*. Old Westbury, CT: Feminist Press, 1979.

Norris, John. *Letters concerning the Love of God*. London: 1695.

Pearson, Karl, ed. *The Life, Letters and Labours of Francis Galton*. 3 vols. Cambridge: Cambridge University Press, 1924.

Poullain de la Barre, François. *The Equality of the Two Sexes*. trans. A. Daniel Frankforter and Paul J. Morman. Lewiston: Mellen, 1989 [1673].

Quetelet, Lambert Adolphe Jacques. *Physique sociale*. 2 vols. Brussels: Muquardt, 1869 [1835].

Roland de la Platière, Marie-Jeanne Phlipon de. *Oeuvres de M.J. Ph Roland*. 2 vols. Paris: Bidault, an 8 (1799).

—— *The Works*. London: J. Johnson, 1800.

—— "Lettre de M. Roland." In *Histoire parlementaire de la révolution française*, ed. P.-J.-B.Buchez and P. C. Roux. Paris: Paulin, 1835 (for 1792), 15: 39-45.

—— *Mémoires de Madame Roland.* Mercure de France, 1966.

—— *Lettres de Madame Roland.* ed. Claude Pérroud. 2 vols. Paris: Imprimerie nationale, 1813.

—— *An Appeal to Impartial Posterity.* 2 vols. London: J. Johnson, 1796.

Saint-Simon, Henri de. *Mémoire sur la science de l'homme.* In *Oeuvres.* ed. Enfantin. vol. 11, 1875.

Schreiner, Olive. *Woman and Labor.* New York: Stokes, 1911.

Schurman, Anna Maria van. "The Learned Maid." London: Redmayne, 1659 [1638].

Scott, Sarah. *A Description of Millennium Hall.* London: Newbery, 1762.

Sinclair, John, ed. *The Statistical Account of Scotland.* 21 vols. 1976 reprint [1791-99].

Sophia. *Woman not Inferior to Man.* London: Hawkins, 1970 reprint [1739].

—— (?) *Woman's superior Excellence over Man.* London: J. Robinson, 1743.

Staël, Germaine Necker de. *Oeuvres complètes.* 17 vols. Paris: Treuttel & Würtz, 1820-21.

—— *Oeuvres complètes.* Paris: Firmin Didot, 1871.

—— *Considerations on the Principal Events of the French Revolution.* 3 vols. London: Baldwin, Craddock, 1818.

—— *Des circonstances actuelles.* ed. Lucia Omacini. Geneva: Droz, 1979.

—— *The Unpublished Correspondence of Madame de Staël and the Duke of Wellington.* London: Cassell, 1965.

—— *Madame de Staël on Politics, Literature, and National Character.* ed. and trans. Morroe Berger. London: Sidgwick & Jackson, 1964.

—— "Unpublished Correspondence of Mme de Staël with Thomas Jefferson." ed. and trans. Marie G. Kimball. *North American Review* 208, no. 752 (1918): 63-71.

—— *Réflexions sur le suicide.* Paris: Opale, 1984 [1813].

Stanton, Elizabeth Cady. *The Woman's Bible*. New York: Arno reprint, 1977 [1895].

Tocqueville, Alexis de. *Democracy in America*. 2 vols. trans. Henry Reeve. New York: Knopf, 1945 [1835].

Tristan, Flora. *The London Journal of Flora Tristan*. trans. Jean Hawkes. London: Virago, 1982.

—— *L'émancipation de la femme*. Paris: Vérité, 1846.

—— *Union ouvrière*. Paris, 1967 reprint [1844].

—— *Le tour de France*. ed. Jules-L. Puech. 2 vols. Paris: Maspero, 1980.

—— *Méphis ou le Prolétaire*. 2 vols. Paris: Ladvocat, 1838.

—— *Lettres*. ed. Stéphane Michaud. Paris: Seuil, 1980.

Trotter Cockburn, Catharine. *A Defence of the Essay of Human Understanding*. London: Will Turner, 1702.

—— *The Works of Mrs. Catharine Cockburn*. 2 vols. London: J. & P. Knapton, 1751.

Voltaire. *Letters concerning the English Nation*. New York: Franklin reprint, 1974 [1734].

—— *Elémens de la philosophie de Newton*. London, 1741.

Ward, Lester. *Pure Sociology*. New York: Macmillan, 1907 [1903].

Webb, Beatrice. Manuscripts: Passfield Papers, Archives, British Library of Political and Economic Science.

—— *My Apprenticeship*. 2 vols. London: Pelican, 1938 [1926].

—— *Our Partnership*. ed. Barbara Drake and Margaret Cole. New York: Longmans, 1948.

—— "Methods of Investigation." London: Sociological Society, 1906.

—— "Women and the Factory Acts." Fabian Tract no. 67 (February 1896). In *Women's Fabian Tracts*, ed. Sally Alexander, 17-32. London: Routledge, 1988.

—— "The Abolition of the Poor Law." Fabian Tract no. 185 (March 1918). In *Women's Fabian Tracts*, ed. Sally Alexander, 313-23. London: Routledge, 1988.

—— "Public Health Administration as a Means of Reducing Destitution." *The Christian Commonwealth* (April 1910): 515.

—— *The Diary of Beatrice Webb*. ed. Norman and Jeanne Mackenzie. 4 vols. London: Virago & LSE, 1982-85.

—— and Sidney Webb. *Methods of Social Study*. LSE/Cambridge University Press, 1975 [1932].

—— and Sidney Webb. *The History of Trade Unionism*. rev. ed. London: Longmans, Green, 1902 [1894].

—— and Sidney Webb. *Industrial Democracy*. London: Longmans, Green, 1902 [1897].

Weber, Marianne. *Ehefrau und Mutter in der Rechtsentwicklung*. Tübingen: Mohr, 1907.

—— *Frauenfragen und Frauengedanken*. Tübingen: Mohr, 1919.

—— *Max Weber: A Biography*. trans. Harry Zohn. New York: Wiley, 1975 [1926].

—— *Fichte's Sozialismus und sein Verhältnis zur Marx'schen Doktrin*. Tübingen: Mohr, 1900.

Weber, Max. *General Economic History*. trans. Frank H. Knight. Glencoe, IL: Free Press, 1950 [1927].

—— *Economy and Society*. ed. Guenther Roth and Claus Wittich. 3 vols. New York: Bedminster, 1968.

Wollstonecraft, Mary. *A Critical Edition of Mary Wollstonecraft's Vindication of the Rights of Woman*. ed. Ulrich H. Hardt. Troy, NY: Whiston, 1982 [1792].

—— *A Vindication of the Rights of Men*. Gainesville, FL: Scholars' Reprints, 1960 [1790].

—— *An Historical and Moral View of the Origin and Progress of the French Revolution*. London: J. Johnson, 1795 [1794].

—— *The Works of Mary Wollstonecraft*. ed. Janet Todd and Marilyn Butler. 4 vols. London: Pickering, 1989.

—— Review of *Letters on Education*, by Catharine Macaulay, *The Analytical Review* (November 1790): 241-54.

—— Trans. Jacques Necker, *Of the Importance of Religious Opinions*. London: J. Johnson, 1788.

—— *Letters written during a short residence in Sweden, Norway, and Denmark*. Lincoln: University of Nebraska Press, 1976.

—— *Collected Letters of Mary Wollstonecraft*. ed. Ralph M. Wardle. Ithaca: Cornell University Press, 1979.

—— *Political Writings*. ed. Janet Todd. Toronto: University of Toronto Press, 1993.

Wortley Montagu, Mary. *The Complete Letters of Lady Mary Wortley Montagu*. ed. Robert Halsband. 3 vols. Oxford: Clarendon Press, 1965-67.

—— *The Nonsense of Common-Sense*. Evanston: Northwestern University Press, 1947 [1737-8].

—— *Essays and Poems*. ed. Robert Halsband and Isobel Grundy. Oxford: Clarendon Press, 1977.

Wright, Frances. *Views of Society and Manners in America*. Cambridge, MA: Belknap, 1963 [1821].

—— *Life, Letters and Lectures*. New York: Arno reprints, 1972.

—— "Plan of National Education." In *Tracts on Republican Government and National Education*. London: Watson, 1840.

—— Trans. *Few Days in Athens*. Boston: Mendum, 1850.

Secondary Sources on the Methodologists

Abensour, Léon. *La femme et le féminisme avant la révolution*. Paris: Ernest Leroux, 1923.

Abrams, Philip. *The Origins of British Sociology*. Chicago: University of Chicago Press, 1968.

Adam, Charles. *Descartes. Ses amitiés féminines*. Paris: Boivin, 1937.

Alic, Margaret. *Hypatia's Heritage*. London: Women's Press, 1986.

Anderson, Bonnie S., and Judith P. Zinsser. *A History of their Own*. 2 vols. New York: Harper & Row, 1988.

Andrews, Wayne. *Germaine: A Portrait of Madame de Staël*. London: Gollancz, 1964.

Badinter, Elisabeth and Robert Badinter. *Condorcet*. Fayard, 1988.

Baelen, Jean. *La vie de Flora Tristan*. Paris: Seuil, 1972.

Baker, Keith Michael. *Condorcet: From Natural Philosophy to Social Mathematics*. Chicago: University of Chicago, 1975.

Balayé, Simone. *Madame de Staël. Lumière et liberté*. Paris: Klincksieck, 1979.

Ballard, George. *Memoirs of Several Ladies of Great Britain*. Oxford: W. Jackson, 1752.

—— Ballard Manuscripts, Oxford University.

Bell, Susan Groag, ed. *Women from the Greeks to the French Revolution*. Belmont, CA: Wadsworth, 1973.

Besterman, Theodore. "Emilie du Châtelet: Portrait of an Unknown Woman." In *Voltaire Essays*, 61-73. London: Oxford University Press, 1962.

Bishop, W.J., and Sue Goldie, eds. *A Bio-Bibliography of Florence Nightingale*. London: Dawson, 1962.

Brink, J.R., ed. *Female Scholars: A Tradition of Learned Women Before 1800*. Montreal: Eden, 1980.

Britton, Karl. *John Stuart Mill*. Harmondsworth: Penguin, 1953.

Browne, Alice. *The Eighteenth Century Feminist Mind*. Detroit: Wayne State University Press, 1987.

Brumfitt, J.H. *The French Enlightenment*. London: Macmillan 1972.

Clark, Alice. *Working Life of Women in the Seventeenth Century*. London: Cass, 1968 [1917].

Cohen, I. Bernard. "Florence Nightingale." *Scientific American* 246 (March 1984): 128-33, 136-37.

Cole, G.D.H. *History of Socialist Thought*. 5 vols. London: Macmillan, 1953-60.

Cole, Margaret, ed. *The Webbs and their Work*. London: Muller, 1949.

Columbine, W.B., ed. *On Liberty*. London: Watt, 1948.

Converse, Jean M. *Survey Research in the United States*. Berkeley: University of California Press, 1987.

Cook, Edward. *The Life of Florence Nightingale*. 2 vols. London: Macmillan, 1913.

Cullen, M.J. *The Statistical Movement in Early Victorian Britain*. New York: Harvester 1975.

David, Deirdre. *Intellectual Women and Victorian Patriarchy*. London: Macmillan, 1987.

Davis, Allen F. *American Heroine: The Life and Legend of Jane Addams*. New York: Oxford University Press, 1973.

Deegan, Mary Jo. *Jane Addams and the Men of the Chicago School*. New Brunswick, NJ: Transaction, 1988.

—— ed. *Women in Sociology. A Bio-Bibliographical Sourcebook.* New York: Greenwood, 1991.

Desanti, Dominique. *A Woman in Revolt. A Biography of Flora Tristan.* trans. Elizabeth Zelvin. New York: Crown, 1976 [1972].

Diamond, Marion, and Mervyn Stone. "Nightingale on Quetelet." *Journal of the Royal Statistical Society* (series A). 144, (1981): 66-79; Pt. 2: 176-213; Pt. 3: 332-351.

Diesbach, Ghislain de. *Madame de Staël.* Paris: Perrin, 1983.

Donnelly, Lucy Martin. "The Celebrated Mrs. Macaulay." *William and Mary Quarterly* 6 (1949): 173-207.

Duran, Jane. "Anne Viscountess Conway: A Seventeenth Century Rationalist." *Hypatia* 4 no. 1 (1989): 64-79.

Eckhardt, Celia Morris. *Fanny Wright.* Cambridge, MA: Harvard University Press, 1984.

Ehrman, Esther. *Mme du Châtelet.* Leamington Spa: Berg, 1986.

Farrell, John C. *Beloved Lady: A History of Jane Addams' Ideas on Reform and Peace.* Baltimore, MD: Johns Hopkins Press, 1967.

Ferguson, Moira, ed. *First Feminists.* Bloomington: Indiana University Press, 1985.

—— and Janet Todd. *Mary Wollstonecraft.* Boston: Twayne, 1984.

Flexner, Eleanor. *Mary Wollstonecraft.* New York: Coward, McCann & Geoghegan, 1972.

Forsberg, Roberta J. and H. C. Nixon. *Madame de Staël and Freedom Today.* London: Vision, 1963.

Frankel, Lois. "Damaris Cudworth Masham: A Seventeenth Century Philosopher." *Hypatia* 12 no. 1 (1989): 80-90.

Fritz, Paul, and Richard Morton, eds. *Woman in the 18th Century and Other Essays.* Toronto: Hakkert, 1976.

Gallagher, Catherine. "Embracing the Absolute: The Politics of the Female Subject in Seventeenth-Century England." *Genders.* 1 (1988): 24-39.

Gardiner Janik, Linda. "Searching for the Metaphysics of Science: the Structure and Composition of Madame Du Châtelet's *Institutions de physique.*" *Studies on Voltaire and the Eighteenth Century.* 201 (1982): 85-113.

Goldsmith, Margaret. *Seven Women Against the World.* London: Methuen, 1976 [1935].

Golemba, Beverly E. *Lesser-Known Women.* Boulder: Rienner, 1992.

Goncourt, Edmond de, and Jules de Goncourt. *The Woman of the Eighteenth Century.* trans. Jacques LeClerq and Ralph Roeder. Freeport, NY: Books for Libraries, 1972 [1928].

Gosse, Edmund. "Catharine Trotter, the Precursor of the Bluestockings." *Transactions RSL* vol. 34.

Granger, Gilles-Gaston. *La mathématique sociale du Marquis de Condorcet.* Paris: Presses universitaires de France, 1956.

Gréard, Oct. "Mme Roland." In *L'éducation des femmes*, 311-60. Paris: Hachette, 1886.

Green, F. C. *The Ancien Regime.* Edinburgh: University Press, 1958.

Guillois, Antoine. *La Marquise de Condorcet.* Paris: Ollendorff, 1897.

Gwynne, G. E. *Madame de Staël et la révolution française.* Paris: Nizet, 1969.

Halsband, Robert. *The Life of Lady Mary Wortley Montagu.* Oxford: Clarendon Press, 1956.

—— "New Light on Lady Mary Wortley Montagu's Contribution to Inoculation." *Journal of the History of Medicine and Allied Sciences* 8 (1953): 391-405.

Harrison, Royden. "Sidney & Beatrice Webb." In *Socialism and the Intelligentsia*, ed. Carl Levy, 35-89. London: Routledge & Kegan Paul, 1987.

Harth, Erica. *Cartesian Women.* Ithaca: Cornell University Press, 1992.

Hawkins, Richmond Laurin. "Madame de Staël and the United States. Cambridge, MA: Harvard University Press, 1930.

Hayek, F. A. *John Stuart Mill and Harriet Taylor.* London: Routledge & Kegan Paul, 1951.

Herbert, Raymond G., ed. *Florence Nightingale: Saint, Reformer or Rebel?* Malabar, FL: Krieger, 1981.

Herold, J. Christopher. *Mistress to an Age. A Life of Madame de Staël.* London: Hamilton, 1959.

Hill, Bridget, ed. *The First English Feminist.* Aldershot: Gower, 1986.

—— ed. *Eighteenth-Century Women: An Anthology*. London: Allen & Unwin, 1984.

—— *The Republican Virago: The Life and Times of Catharine Macaulay, Historian*. Oxford: Clarendon Press, 1992.

Hill, Christopher. *Intellectual Origins of the English Revolution*. Oxford: Clarendon Press, 1965.

—— *The World Turned Upside Down*. London: Temple-Smith, 1972.

Hill, Michael R., "Empiricism and Reason in Harriet Martineau's Sociology," Harriet Martineau, *How to Observe Morals and Manners*. New Brunswick, NJ: Transaction, 1989, pp. xv-lx.

Himmelfarb, Gertrude. *On Liberty and Liberalism*. London: Warburg & Secker, 1974.

Hoecker-Drysdale, Susan. *Harriet Martineau: First Woman Sociologist*. Oxford: Berg, 1992.

Hollis, Patricia. *Women in Public 1850-1900*. London: Allen & Unwin, 1979.

Hunt, Margaret et al., eds. *Women and the Enlightenment*. Institute for Research in History/Haworth, 1984.

Hunter, Michael. *Science and Society in Restoration England*. Cambridge: Cambridge University Press, 1981.

Ilsley, Marjorie Henry. *A Daughter of the Renaissance: Marie le Jars de Gournay*. The Hague: Mouton, 1963.

Irwin, Joyce L. "Anna Maria van Schurman." In *Female Scholars*, ed. J.R. Brink, 68-85. Montreal: Eden, 1980.

Jacob, Margaret C. *The Radical Enlightenment*. London: Allen & Unwin, 1981.

Jones, R.F. *Ancients and Moderns*. St. Louis: Washington University Press, 1962 [1961].

Kamm, Josephine. *John Stuart Mill in Love*. London: Gordon and Gremondesi, 1977.

Kandal, Terry R. *The Woman Question in Classical Sociological Theory*. Miami: Florida International University Press, 1988.

Kanner, Barbara, ed. *The Women of England*. Hamden, CT: Archon, 1979.

Keohane, Nannerl O. *Philosophy and the State in France*. Princeton: Princeton University Press, 1980.

Kinnaird, Joan K. "Mary Astell and the Conservative Contribution to English Feminism." *Journal of British Studies* 19 (1979): 53-75.

Lane, Margaret. *Frances Wright and the "Great Experiment."* Manchester: Manchester University Press, 1972.

Lane, Peter. *The Industrial Revolution*. London: Weidenfeld & Nicolson 1978.

Larg, David Glass. *Madame de Staël*. Paris: Champion, 1924.

Levine, Daniel. *Jane Addams and the Liberal Tradition*. Madison: State Historical Society of Wisconsin, 1971.

Lindsay, J. O., ed. *The Old Regime*. Cambridge: Cambridge University Press, 1957.

Linzey, Andrew, and Tom Regan, eds. *Animals and Christianity*. New York: Crossroad, 1988.

Lipset, Seymour Martin. "Harriet Martineau: A Pioneer Comparative Sociologist." In *Revolution and Counterrevolution*, 335-62. New York: Basic, 1968.

Lougee, Carolyn C. *Le paradis des femmes: Women, Salons, and Social Stratification in 17th Century France*. Princeton: Princeton University Press, 1976.

Lough, John. *An Introduction to Eighteenth Century France*. London: Longmans, 1960.

Mack, Phyllis. "Women and the Enlightenment: Introduction." In *Women and the Enlightenment*, eds. Margaret Hunt et al., 1-11. Institute for Research in History/Haworth, 1984.

MacKenzie, Donald A. *Statistics in Britain*. Edinburgh: Edinburgh University Press, 1981.

Macpherson, C.B. *The Political Theory of Possessive Individualism*. Oxford: Clarendon Press, 1962.

Manuel, Frank E. *The Prophets of Paris*. Cambridge, MA: Harvard University Press, 1962.

Mathias, Peter. *The First Industrial Nation*. London: Methuen, 1969.

Maurel, André. *La Marquise du Châtelet*. Paris: Hachette, 1930.

May, Gita. *Madame Roland and the Age of Revolution*. New York: Columbia University Press, 1970.

—— *De Jean-Jacques Rousseau à Madame Roland*. Geneva: Droz, 1914.

McDonald, Lynn. *The Early Origins of the Social Sciences*. Montreal: McGill-Queen's University Press, 1994.

Mead, Margaret, ed. *An Anthropologist at Work: Writings of Ruth Benedict*. Atherton, 1973 [1959].

Mineka, Francis E. *The Dissidence of Dissent*. Chapel Hill: University of North Carolina Press, 1944.

Mitchell, G. Duncan. *A Hundred Years of Sociology*. London: Duckworth, 1968.

Mitford, Nancy. *Voltaire in Love*. London: Hamish Hamilton, 1957.

Mönch, Walter. "Mme de Staël à la recherche d'un avenir de la société moderne." *Cahiers Staeliens* 9 (1969): 1-16.

Moses, Claire Goldberg. *French Feminism in the 19th Century*. Albany: SUNY Press, 1984.

Munteaud, *Les idées politiques de Madame de Staël et la Constitution de l'an III*. Paris: Belles Lettres, 1931.

Murray, Janet Horowitz, ed. *Strong-Minded Women*. New York: Pantheon, 1982.

Nevill, John Cranstoun. *Harriet Martineau*. London: Muller, 1943.

Nixon, Edna. *Mary Wollstonecraft*. London: Dent, 1971.

Nolan, Barbara E. *The Political Theory of Beatrice Webb*. New York: AMS, 1988.

Nord, Deborah Epstein. *The Apprenticeship of Beatrice Webb*. London: Macmillan, 1985.

Oberschall, Anthony, ed. *The Establishment of Empirical Sociology*. New York: Harper & Row, 1972.

Okin, Susan Moller. *Women in Western Political Thought*. Princeton: Princeton University Press, 1979.

Packe, Michael St. John. *The Life of John Stuart Mill*. London: Secker and Warburg, 1954.

Pappe, H.O. *John Stuart Mill and the Harriet Taylor Myth*. Melbourne: Melbourne University Press, 1960.

Paston, George. *Lady Mary Wortley Montagu and her Times*. London: Methuen, 1907.

Paul, C. Kegan. *William Godwin. His Friends and Contemporaries*. 2 vols. London: Henry King, 1876.

Penigault-Duhet, Paule. *Mary Wollstonecraft-Godwin*. Lille: Reproduction des thèses, 1984 [1975].

Pennington, Donald, and Keith Thomas. *Puritans and Revolutionaries*. Oxford: Clarendon Press, 1982 [1978].

Perkins, A.J.G., and Theresa Wolfson. *Frances Wright, Free Enquirer*. New York: Harper, 1939.

Perrot, Jean-Claude, and Stuart J. Woolf. *State and Statistics in France 1789-1818*. Chur: Harwood, 1984.

Perry, Ruth. *The Celebrated Mary Astell*. Chicago: University of Chicago Press, 1986.

Pichanick, Valerie Kossew. *Harriet Martineau*. Ann Arbor: University of Michigan Press, 1980.

Pinchbeck, Ivy. *Women Workers and the Industrial Revolution 1750-1850*. London: Routledge & Kegan Paul, 1930.

Pollin, Burton R. "Mary Hays on Women's Rights in the *Monthly Magazine*." *Etudes anglaises* 24 (1971): 271-8.

Popkin, Richard H. *The History of Scepticism from Erasmus to Descartes*. rev. ed. Assen: Van Gorcum, 1964 [1960].

Porter, Theodore M. *The Rise of Statistical Thinking*. Princeton: Princeton University Press, 1986.

Postlethwaite, Diana, "Mothering and Mesmerism in the Life of Harriet Martineau." *Signs* 14 (1989): 583-609.

—— *Making It Whole*. Columbus: Ohio State University Press, 1984.

Preedy, George R. *This Shining Woman: Mary Wollstonecraft Godwin*. London: Collins, 1937.

Puech, Jules-L. *La vie et l'oeuvre de Flora Tristan*. Paris: Rivière, 1925.

Radice, Lisanne. *Beatrice & Sidney Webb*. London: Macmillan, 1984.

Raison, Timothy, ed. *The Founding Fathers of Social Science*. Harmondsworth: Penguin, 1969 and rev. ed. London: Scolar, 1979.

Rauschenbusch-Clough, Emma. *A Study of Mary Wollstonecraft.* London: Longmans, Green, 1898.

Rendall, Jane. *The Origins of Modern Feminism.* London: Macmillan, 1985.

Reynolds, Myra. *The Learned Lady in England.* Gloucester, MA: Peter Smith, 1964.

Robson, John M. *The Improvement of Mankind.* Toronto: University of Toronto Press, 1968.

Rogers, Katharine M. *Feminism in Eighteenth Century England.* Urbana: University of Illinois Press, 1982.

—— ed. *Before Their Time.* New York: Ungar, 1979.

Rosenberg, Rosalind. *Beyond Separate Spheres.* New Haven: Yale University Press, 1982.

Rossi, Alice S., ed. *Essays on Sex Equality.* Chicago: University of Chicago, 1970.

—— ed. *The Feminist Papers.* New York: Columbia University Press, 1973.

Rover, Constance. *Love, Morals and the Feminists.* London: Routledge & Kegan Paul, 1970.

Rowbotham, Sheila. *Hidden from History.* London: Pluto, 1974 [1973].

Schiff, Mario. *Marie de Gournay.* Paris: Champion, 1910.

Seymour-Jones, Carole. *Beatrice Webb. Woman of Conflict.* London: Allison & Busby, 1992.

Smith, Florence M. *Mary Astell.* New York: AMS reprint, 1966 [1916].

Smith, F.B. *Florence Nightingale.* London: Croom Helm, 1982.

Smith, Hilda L. *Reason's Disciples.* Urbana: University of Illinois Press, 1982.

Spencer, Samia I. *French Women and the Age of Enlightenment.* Bloomington: Indiana University Press, 1984.

Spender, Dale. *Women of Ideas.* London: Routledge & Kegan Paul, 1982.

—— ed. *Feminist Theorists.* London: Women's Press, 1983.

Stenton, Doris Mary. *The English Woman in History.* London: Allen & Unwin, 1957.

Stigler, Stephen M. *The History of Statistics.* Cambridge, MA: Belknap Press, 1986.

Stillinger, Jack. "Who Wrote J.S. Mill's *Autobiography?" Victorian Studies* 27 (Autumn 1983): 7-23.

Stock, Marie Louise. *Poullain de la Barre: a Seventeenth-Century Feminist.* Ph. D. thesis, Columbia University, 1951.

Stone, Lawrence. *The Family, Sex and Marriage in England 1500-1800.* New York: Harper & Row, 1977.

Strumingher, Laura S. *The Odyssey of Flora Tristan.* New York: Peter Lang, 1988.

Strachey, Lytton. *Eminent Victorians.* London: Folio Society, 1967 [1918].

Sunstein, Emily W. *A Different Face: The Life of Mary Wollstonecraft.* New York: Harper & Row, 1975.

Tawney, R.H. "Beatrice Webb." *Proceedings of the British Academy.* 29.

Taylor, Barbara. *Eve and the New Jerusalem.* London: Virago, 1984.

Taylor, I.A. *Life of Madame Roland.* London: Hutchinson, 1911.

Thomas, Gillian. *Harriet Martineau.* Boston: Twayne, 1985.

Thomas, Keith. *Religion and the Decline of Magic.* London: Weidenfeld & Nicolson, 1971.

Thompson, Roger. *Women in Stuart England and America.* London: Routledge & Kegan Paul, 1974.

Todd, Janet, ed. *Dictionary of British Women Writers.* London: Routledge, 1989.

Tomalin, Claire. *The Life and Death of Mary Wollstonecraft.* New York: Mentor, 1974.

Tooley, Sarah A. "The Growth of a Socialist: An Interview with Mrs. Sidney Webb." *The Young Woman* no. 19 (February 1895): 145-51.

Traer, James. F. *Marriage and the Family in Eighteenth Century France.* Ithaca: Cornell University Press, 1980.

Trevor-Roper, H.R. *Religion the Reformation and Social Change.* London: Macmillan, 1967.

Tulloch, Gail. *Mill and Sexual Equality.* Hemel Hempstead: Harvester/Wheatsheaf, 1989.

Turner, Stephen P. *The Search for a Methodology of Social Science.* Dordrecht: Reidel, 1986.

Vaillot, René. *Avec Mme du Châtelet.* Leamington Spa: Berg, 1981.

Venturi, Franco. *Utopia and Reform in the Enlightenment.* Cambridge: Cambridge University Press, 1971.

Vrooman, Jack Rochford. *René Descartes.* New York: Putnam's Sons, 1970.

Wade, Ira O. *Voltaire and Madame du Châtelet.* Princeton: Princeton University Press, 1941.

—— *Studies on Voltaire with some Unpublished Papers of Mme du Châtelet.* Princeton: Princeton University Press, 1947.

Walker, Helen M. *Studies in the History of Statistical Method.* Baltimore: Williams & Wilkins, 1929.

Wallas, Ada. *Before the Bluestockings.* London: Allen & Unwin, 1929.

Wardle, Ralph M. *Mary Wollstonecraft.* Lawrence: University of Kansas Press, 1951.

—— "Mary Wollstonecraft, Analytical Reviewer." *PMLA* 62 (1947): 1000-09.

Waterman, William Randall. *Frances Wright.* New York: Columbia University Press, 1924.

Webb, R.K. *Harriet Martineau: A Radical Victorian.* London: Heinemann, 1960.

Webster, Charles. *The Great Instauration.* New York: Holmes & Meier, 1975.

Westergaard, Harald. *Contributions to the History of Statistics.* New York: Agathon, 1968.

Wheatley, Vera. *The Life and Work of Harriet Martineau.* London: Secker & Warburg, 1957.

Wiley, Margaret. *The Subtle Knot.* London: Allen & Unwin, 1952.

—— *Creative Sceptics.* London: Allen & Unwin, 1966.

Willcocks, Mary Patricia. *Madame Roland.* trans. Joseph Thérol. Paris: Hachette.

Willey, Basil. *The Seventeenth Century Background.* Garden City, NY: Doubleday, 1953.

—— *The Eighteenth Century Background*. London: Chatto & Windus, 1953 [1940].

Williams, David. "The Politics of Feminism in the French Enlightenment." In *The Varied Pattern: Studies in the 18th Century* ed. Peter Hughes and David Williams. Toronto: Hakkert, 1971: 333-51.

Wilson, Charles. *England's Apprenticeship*. London: Longmans, Green, 1965.

Woodham-Smith, Cecil. *Florence Nightingale*. London: Constable, 1950.

Woolf, Virginia. *The Second Common Reader*. New York: Harcourt, Brace, 1932.

—— *Three Guineas*. New York: Harcourt Brace Jovanovich, 1966 [1938].

Woolhouse, R.S. *The Empiricists*. Oxford University Press, 1988.

Yates, Gayle Graham, ed. *Harriet Martineau on Women*. New Brunswick, NJ: Rutgers University Press, 1985.

The Methodological Debate/Critique of Empiricism

Abir-Am, Phina G., and Dorinda Outram, eds. *Uneasy Careers and Intimate Lives. Women in Science, 1789-1979*. New Brunswick, NJ: Rutgers University Press, 1987.

Abbott, Pamela, and Claire Wallace. *An Introduction to Sociology*. London: Routledge, 1990.

Allen, Prudence. *The Concept of Woman*. Montreal: Eden, 1985.

Bernard, Jessie. *The Female World*. New York: Free Press, 1981.

Biehl, Janet, *Finding Our Way*. Montreal: Black Rose, 1991.

Bleier, Ruth, ed. *Feminist Approaches to Science*. New York: Pergamon, 1986.

Bologh, Roslyn W. *Love or Greatness: Max Weber and Masculine Thinking*. London: Unwin Hyman, 1990.

Bowles, Gloria, and Renate Duelli Klein, eds. *Theories of Women's Studies*. London: Routledge & Kegan Paul, 1983.

Bridenthal, Renate, and Claudia Koonz, eds. *Becoming Visible*. Boston: Houghton-Mifflin, 1977.

Caldecott, Léonie, and Stephanie Leland, eds. *Reclaim the Earth.* London: Women's Press, 1983.

Campbell, Kate, ed. *Critical Feminism.* Buckingham: Open University Press, 1992.

Center for Twentieth Century Studies, University of Wisconsin. *Feminist Studies/Critical Studies.* 1986 special issue.

Code, Lorraine, Sheila Mullett, and Christine Overall, eds. *Feminist Perspectives.* Toronto: University of Toronto Press, 1988.

Collard, Andreé. *Rape of the Wild.* Bloomington: Indiana University Press, 1989.

Coole, Diana H. *Women in Political Theory.* Sussex: Wheatsheaf, 1988.

Daly, Mary. *Beyond God the Father.* Boston: Beacon, 1973.

Diamond, Irene, and Gloria Femon Orenstein, eds. *Reweaving the World.* San Francisco: Sierra Club, 1990.

Duran, Jane. *Toward a Feminist Epistemology.* Savage, MD: Rowman & Littlefield, 1991.

Eaubonne, Françoise d'. *Le féminisme ou la mort.* Paris: Femmes en mouvement, 1974.

Eichler, Margrit. "The Relationship between Sexist, Nonsexist, Woman-centred, and Feminist Research." *Studies in Communications* 3 (1986): 37-74.

Flax, Jane. *Thinking Fragments.* Berkeley: University of California Press, 1990.

—— "Postmodernism and Gender Relations in Feminist Theory." *Signs* 12 no. 4 (1987): 621-43.

Fonow, Mary Margaret, and Judith A. Cook, eds. *Beyond Methodology.* Bloomington: Indiana University Press, 1991.

Franklin, Ursula, Hanna Gay, and Angela Miles, eds. *Women in Science and Technology. Canadian Woman Studies* special issue, 13 no. 2 (1993).

Garry, Ann, and Marilyn Pearsall, eds. *Women, Knowledge, and Reality.* Boston: Unwin Hyman, 1989.

Gergen, Mary McCanney, ed. *Feminist Thought and the Structure of Knowledge.* New York: New York University Press, 1988.

Gilligan, Carol. *In a Different Voice.* Cambridge, MA: Harvard University Press, 1982.

Gorelick, Sherry. " 'Giving Voice,' Giving Vision: Theory, Process, and Standpoint in Feminist Marxist Methodology." American Sociological Association paper, Atlanta, GA. August 1988.

Grant, Judith. " 'I Feel Therefore I am': A Critique of Female Experience and the Basis for a Feminist Epistemology." *Women and Politics* 7 no. 3 (1987): 99-114.

Griffin, Susan. *Woman and Nature.* New York: Harper & Row, 1978.

Grimshaw, Jean. *Philosophy and Feminist Thinking.* Minneapolis: University of Minnesota Press, 1986.

Harding, Sandra. *The Science Question in Feminism.* Ithaca: Cornell University Press, 1986.

—— and Merrill B. Hintikka, eds. *Discovering Reality.* Dordrecht: Reidel, 1983.

—— ed. *Feminism and Methodology.* Bloomington: Indiana University Press, 1987.

Hawkesworth, Mary E. "Knowers, Knowing, Known: Feminist Theory and Claims of Truth." *Signs* 14 (1989): 533-57.

—— "Feminist Epistemology: A Survey of the Field." *Women and Politics.* 7 no. 3 (1987): 115-27.

Hekman, Susan, "The Feminization of Epistemology: Gender and the Social Sciences." *Women and Politics.* 7 no. 3 (1987): 65-83.

Herschberger, Ruth. *Adam's Rib.* New York: Harper & Row, 1970 [1948].

Hirschmann, Nancy J. *Rethinking Obligation.* Ithaca, NY: Cornell University Press, 1992.

Holland, Nancy J. *Is Women's Philosophy Possible?* Savage, MD: Rowman & Littlefield, 1990.

Keller, Evelyn Fox. *Reflections on Gender and Science.* New Haven, CT: Yale University Press, 1985.

Kelly, Rita Mae, et al. "Liberal Positivistic Epistemology and Research on Women and Politics." *Women and Politics.* 7 no. 3 (1987): 11-27.

Kennedy, Ellen, and Susan Mendus, eds. *Women in Western Political Philosophy*. New York: St. Martin's Press, 1987.

Langland, Elizabeth, and Walter Gove, eds. *A Feminist Perspective in the Academy*. Chicago: University of Chicago Press, 1981.

Levesque-Lopman, Louise. "Phenomenological Sociology Reconsidered from a Feminist Perspective." American Sociological Association paper, Atlanta, GA. August 1988.

—— *Claiming Reality*. Totowa, NJ: Rowman & Littlefield, 1988.

Lloyd, Genevieve. *The Man of Reason*. London: Methuen, 1984.

McLaren, Arlene Tigar, ed. *Gender and Society*. Toronto: Copp Clark, 1988.

Merchant, Carolyn. *The Death of Nature*. San Francisco: Harper & Row, 1980.

Miles, Angela R., and Geraldine Finn, eds. *Feminism in Canada*. Montreal: Black Rose, 1982.

—— and Geraldine Finn, eds. *From Pressure to Politics*. 2d ed. rev. Montreal: Black Rose, 1989.

Nicholson, Linda J., ed. *Feminism/Postmodernism*. New York: Routledge, 1990.

Nielsen, Joyce McCarl. *Feminist Research Methods*. Boulder: Westview, 1990.

Nye, Andrea. *Feminist Theory and the Philosophies of Man*. New York: Routledge, 1988.

Osborne, Martha Lee, ed. *Woman in Western Thought*. New York: Random House, 1979.

Paludi, Michele A., and Gertrude L. Steuernagel, eds. *Foundations for a Feminist Restructuring of the Academic Disciplines*. New York: Haworth, 1990.

Pateman, Carole, and Elizabeth Gross, eds. *Feminist Challenges*. Boston: Northeastern University Press, 1986.

Plant, Judith, ed. *Healing the Wounds*. Philadelphia: New Society, 1989.

Reinharz, Shulamit. *Feminist Methods in Social Research*. Oxford: Oxford University Press, 1992.

Richards, Janet Radcliffe. *The Sceptical Feminist*. Boston: Kegan Paul, 1980.

Ritzer, George. *Sociological Theory*. 2d ed. New York: Knopf, 1988
[1983].

Roberts, Helen, ed. *Doing Feminist Research*. London: Routledge &
Kegan Paul, 1981.

Rossiter, Margaret W. *Women Scientists in America*. Baltimore: Johns
Hopkins University Press, 1982.

Rothschild, Joan, ed. *Machina ex Dea*. New York: Pergamon, 1983.

Schiebinger, Londa. *The Mind Has No Sex? Women in the Origins of
Modern Science*. Cambridge, MA: Harvard University Press,
1989.

Sherman, Julia A., and Evelyn Torton Beck, eds. *The Prism of Sex*.
Madison: University of Wisconsin Press, 1979.

Shiva, Vandana. *Staying Alive*. London: Zed, 1988.

Siltanen, Janet, and Michelle Stanworth, eds. *Women and the Public
Sphere*. London: Hutchinson, 1984.

Smith, Dorothy E. *The Everyday World as Problematic*. Toronto:
University of Toronto Press, 1987.

Snyder, Eloise C., ed. *The Study of Women*. New York: Harper & Row,
1979.

Stanley, Liz, and Sue Wise. *Breaking out: Feminist Consciousness and
Feminist Research*. London: Routledge & Kegan Paul, 1983.

—— ed. *Feminist Praxis*. London: Routledge, 1990.

Sydie, R.A. *Natural Women, Cultured Men*. Toronto: Methuen, 1987.

Terry, James L. "Bringing Women ... in." *Teaching Sociology* 10 no.
2 (1983): 251-61.

Tomm, Winnie, ed. *The Effects of Feminist Approaches on Research
Methodologies*. Calgary: Calgary Institute for the Humanities,
1989.

—— and Gordon Hamilton, eds. *Gender Bias in Scholarship*. Calgary:
Calgary Institute for the Humanities, 1988.

Unger, Rhoda Kesler. "Through the Looking Glass: No Wonderland
Yet! (The Reciprocal Relationship between Methodology and
Models of Reality)." *Affilia* 1 (1986): 9-32.

Vickers, Jill McCalla, ed. *Taking Sex Into Account*. Ottawa: Carleton
University Press, 1984.

Westby, David L. *The Growth of Sociological Theory*. Englewood Cliffs, NJ: Prentice Hall, 1991.

Zeitlin, Irving M. *Ideology and the Development of Sociological Theory*. Englewood Cliffs, NJ: Prentice-Hall, 4th ed., 1990 [1968].

$\mathcal{I}ndex$